LOOKING AT THE STARS

LOOKING AT THE STARS

Black Celebrity Journalism in Jim Crow America

Carrie Teresa

University of Nebraska Press | Lincoln

Library of Congress Cataloging-in-Publication Data
Names: Teresa, Carrie, author.
Title: Looking at the Stars: Black celebrity journalism in Jim Crow America / Carrie Teresa.
Description: Lincoln: University of Nebraska Press, 2019. | Includes bibliographical references and index.
Identifiers: LCCN 2018036128
ISBN 9780803299924 (cloth: alk. paper)
ISBN 9781496215451 (epub)
ISBN 9781496215468 (mobi)
ISBN 9781496215475 (pdf)
Subjects: LCSH: African American press—History—History—20th century. | African American celebrities—Press coverage. | African American newspapers—Political aspects—History—20th century.
Classification: LCC PN4882.5 .T47 2019 | DDC 071/.308996073—dc23 LC record available at https://lccn.loc.gov/2018036128

Set in ITC New Baskerville by E. Cuddy.

For Theresa "Bern" Teresa

Contents

Illustrations

Preface

Who cares about celebrities? It is a question that has nagged at me since I began this project nearly five years ago. It is a question that sometimes stopped me dead in my tracks—mid-thought, mid-sentence, in archives, and in front of my computer. Scholarship on black press newspapers and magazines had to date (and very rightly) dealt with weighty civil rights issues of the nineteenth and twentieth centuries, and by comparison my fascination with the beautiful, famous people featured in their pages felt unsatisfying, silly even. *I* felt silly.

Yet I have continued to develop this thing: from a proposal to a dissertation to now a book because there is one thing that I cannot let go. Celebrities have always been important to *me*. As I was growing up—in a Long Island suburb, diverse but not diverse enough, working to middle class with aspirations of bigger, better, newer houses, cars, dresses, a neighborhood filled with first- and second-generation college graduates—I found myself sitting in my small bedroom, headphones plugged into my Walkman permanently fixed over my ears, flipping through the pages of *Rolling Stone, Spin, Entertainment Weekly,* and *Sports Illustrated* looking, looking constantly for people like me. As a young woman, I never seemed to quite find anyone whose mold I could quite see myself fitting. I was hardly a thin, lithe little thing, and my hair never seemed to cooperate with the styles that I painstakingly emulated from the pages of the fashion magazines my older sisters left lying around the house, *Glamour* and *Vogue.* I rarely turned on my television or sat in a movie and saw anyone who looked like me, or talked like me, or dressed like me, or who I could someday see myself becoming.

I still don't, for the most part. Mainstream "media"—an imprecise term but fine for the point I am about to make—rarely depict anyone or anything who does not fulfill dominant, hegemonic discourses of gender, class, and, of course, race. Things are improving, as a glance at Annenberg's diversity reports have suggested over the years, but we are far from an American media environment that reflects who we are as a society.

And so I began to think about the readers of black press newspapers and magazines as folks not all that different from me, in at least one important way: they too likely opened the pages of newspapers and magazines, sat in movies, went to theater shows all looking for a version of themselves to be reflected back, maybe even a future, "better" self to which to aspire. They could not find any of that in the mainstream "media" of the time. The celebrities they might have found in the pages of *Photoplay* and other periodicals of the time were either white or they were a caricatured version of black and African American. They may as well have not been people at all. And that is *as* devastating, if not more so, than not seeing anyone who resembles you at all.

The beauty of black press periodicals is that many of them followed a networked journalism model, so that with few exceptions (the *Crisis* immediately comes to mind) the voices who were newsgathering, serving as sources, writing, and editing stories were Pullman porters, ANP correspondents, and citizen journalists, as well as leading politicians, intellectuals, and civic leaders. The stories that they told were stories about *people* and for *people*. Their motivations were not wholly economic, and their voices were not wholly institutionalized. The readers were often the writers and vice versa. And they all shared the same common goal: to present media representations of people like them, whom they could judge, emulate, celebrate, vilify, and venerate. These citizen-activist journalists shared this motivation with black filmmakers, radio producers, and literary authors.

Of course, the folks who wrote and read those papers *are* very different from who I am, and those differences matter and they helped to shape the (imperfect) book that I have written. Not only does one hundred years of history separate me from them but so do issues of identity—specifically race and, albeit to a lesser degree, gender. I did not seek to determine which celebrities constituted a "positive" or a "negative" representation of blackness. That is not my prerogative as a white scholar writing about black cultural experience. Rather, my main goal in constructing this book was to provide a platform whereby these journalists' voices could be heard within the context of the changing political and social conditions that influenced their writing as they together fought for a more equitable and just society.

Yet, in chapter 5, when I began to delve into discourses surrounding the dismissal of the brave, defiant "New Negro" women whose collective efforts to redefine womanhood still resonate today, I could feel my fingers type harder; I could hear the derisive words applied to women like Josephine Baker and Eslanda Robeson louder and more acutely than almost anything else I experienced writing the book. The forms of oppressive hierarchies change—over time, across privilege, and according to identity markers—but they are always deafening, and they are also always a call to action.

Scholars who have defended the inherent value of celebrity culture often point to the cultural implications of whom we as a society choose to worship. But I think that is only one-half of the story. There is also an emotional dimension to celebrity worship. Just ask my favorite student, Gabi Jackson, whose world was turned upside down when Beyoncé's *Lemonade* was released. At our small regional university in western New York, Gabi stood out: she was one of two students who spoke with an unmistakable Texas drawl, and she was a leader in a close-knit group of black student-activists who had revived both our Black Student Union and our campus newspaper during my first two years there. I know how much *Lemonade* affected her—she insisted on watching it during my class (I could not refuse—I was desperate to watch it too). When Beyoncé sang the line, "You mix that negro with that Creole, make a Texas bama," she may as well have sung it *to* Gabi, if the look on Gab's face was any indication. Hearing Gabi's reflections on *Lemonade* and, later, *Black Panther,* reminded me of myself at that age, and now. When I asked her what she liked so much about these things, she replied, "It's like all my worries go away while watching [*Black Panther*]. For two hours, I get to watch my people do shit that's amazing before I have to leave the theater into a world that doesn't view us the same way." Those emotional evocations matter, and they shape who we are and what we will become.

And I think that is a human need that cuts across historical lines, and it is the thing that has kept me plugging away at this project: we all deserve to have someone who, in public, can validate our human experience, speak truth to power, and give us something to dream of becoming. That's what celebrities, at their best, can do.

Acknowledgments

I share this work with a network of supportive mentors, colleagues, family members, and friends without whom this project would not have been possible.

I am indebted to Carolyn Kitch, Andrew Mendelson, Susan Jacobson, and Linn Washington. Your support and insight throughout the early stages of this journey was indispensable.

I am grateful to Aslaku Berhanu at Temple University's Blockson Collection, the staff of the Manuscripts, Archives, and Rare Book Division of the Schomburg Center for Research in Black Culture, and Joellen El Bashir at the Moorland-Spingarn Research Center for their assistance. I would also like to acknowledge Tim Ireland, David Schoen, Samantha Gust, and the members of the Niagara University Research Council who made sure I had what I needed (and for as long as I needed it—thanks, Sam!) along the way. Thank you to my NU colleagues Mark Barner, Doug Tewksbury, Joseph Sirianni, Jamie Carr, Dana Radatz, and Paula Kot for your encouragement and advice, and to Gabi Jackson, for reminding me why I wrote this book in the first place.

I am indebted to my editor, Bridget Barry, for her enthusiasm, guidance, and support. I would like to acknowledge the anonymous reviewers of this manuscript for their insightful critiques and comments on previous versions of it, and I thank everyone at the University of Nebraska Press who worked toward its publication.

Thank you to my family-friends (purposely combined because they are nearly impossible to distinguish), Carl Teresa, Annmarie

Teresa, January Magyar, Rudolph Magyar, Isabelle Magyar, Charlie Magyar, the Isard family, the Emrich family, and the Johnson family, for their love and support. Thank you to Paddington Gary Bear, who was by my side every day while I wrote this manuscript. I dedicate this book to the memory of my mother, Bern, and I thank her for teaching me by example how to be brave in everything that I do.

Most of all, I thank my husband, Brendan Isard, who first introduced me to Jack Johnson's story one rainy date night, which served as the catalyst for this project. Thank you for over a decade's worth of love, patience, good humor, and even better cooking. You are beyond category.

1

Untangling Discourses of Representation in Black Press Celebrity Reporting

"What does an artist owe to his race?" Ralph Matthews had become a fixture in the pages of the *Afro-American* by the time he posed that question, in 1931, in his Looking at the Stars weekly gossip column. Matthews asked his readers the question in response to the news that two of the nation's most famous black celebrities, actor Paul Robeson and tenor Roland Hayes, had both defected to Europe, "denouncing America and incidentally the American racial group to which they belong." Racial strife in the United States, the author posited, "makes some demands of the Negro artist, who has caught the ear of the dominant classes, and he should lend his efforts to break down as much as possible, those barriers which are raised against those less fortunate than himself."[1] In Matthews's view any race performer who achieved "celebrity" status had an obligation to advocate on behalf of the communities he represented—a duty previously reserved only for "uplifters": politicians, clergymen, educators, and civic leaders. Participation in entertainment culture represented a new opportunity to put the cause of civil rights on the nation's agenda.

Matthews's critique was part of a larger discussion unfolding in the pages of the newspapers and magazines of the black press that coincided with the development of an entertainment-based leisure market spurred on by technological innovations in photography, film, and radio.[2] By 1922 the *New York Amsterdam News* had established an entertainment section. Three years later both the *Chicago Defender* and the *Pittsburgh Courier* followed suit. In

1929 and 1930, respectively, the *Philadelphia Tribune* and the *Baltimore Afro-American* also began to dedicate a section to coverage of celebrities and popular culture. By the early 1930s, entertainment sections were commonplace in black press newspapers. Analysis of newspapers from this period revealed that by the mid-1920s discussions of celebrity culture had become more prevalent and had shifted from discussions about race representation to more-sensational coverage of celebrities' personal lives. For instance by the end of 1926, laudatory articles about tenor singer Roland Hayes's contribution to the race were replaced with discussions about his complicated love life.[3] Louis Armstrong's failed diet plans and Hayes's affair with an Italian countess were both well documented. One journalist went so far as to dismiss Josephine Baker's Italian fiancé as a "gigolo." Journalists shared with their readers the likely unpleasant long-distance phone call Jesse Owens received from his childhood sweetheart—a phone call that encouraged him quickly thereafter to put a ring on it. Actors, athletes, and musicians became popular, widely recognizable symbols. As such they played a decisive role in shaping how black and African Americans defined themselves as free citizens.

Though it might be tempting to disregard the influence of celebrity culture given our contemporary personality-saturated media system, in which it seems anyone can achieve "star" status, it is imperative to note that during the early twentieth century, celebrities were an exclusive sector of the population who performed an essential proscriptive function. They presented to audiences "an idealized concept of how people are expected to be or expected to act."[4] Orrin Klapp has connected the notion of exemplarity (or, to use his term, heroism) with celebrity performance and social dynamism. Klapp defines a "hero" as "a person, real or imaginary, who evokes the appropriate attitudes and behavior."[5] He writes of the mediated nature of heroism, noting that heroes are often constructed as symbols through discourses of news and public relations. Journalists construct heroes through discursive strategies that include venerating them, positioning them within familiar metaphors and myths, and commemorating their achievements on landmark dates.[6] Stars are particularly useful exemplary figures because they reflect changing social attitudes and mores. "An age of mass hero worship," observes Klapp, "is an age of instability."[7] Accordingly, the tenets of exemplarity evolve with changing social and cultural conditions.

In conjunction with the development of early film, the idea of public recognition, or "celebrity," was established as actors, singers, and musicians were increasingly present and visible entertainers.[8] The status of "celebrity" was not confined to artists. Filmed versions of boxing matches were popular with urban audiences, making stars out of the athletes featured. With the development of sound technology in the late 1920s, musical performance became an important part of the film industry. Film studios relied on journalists to promote entertainers. The concept of "celebrity" emerged during this period as a journalistic invention that was mutually beneficial for the newspapers that enjoyed elevated circulation figures due to their coverage of beloved celebrities and the film studios that promoted new projects based on the actors and entertainers who starred in their productions.

In the pages of mainstream urban dailies, black celebrities were subjected to the same snubs and prejudices as ordinary black citizens were. In contrast black entertainers in theater, film, music, and sports came to life in the front pages, gossip columns, and sports and feature pages of black press newspapers. Black journalists almost immediately understood the symbolic power of celebrities and quickly began to pursue news stories about them, which often appeared on the front page of popular metropolitan newspapers such as the *Chicago Defender*, the *Baltimore Afro-American*, and the *Philadelphia Tribune*.

Exploring the Representational, the "Real," and the Real

Black celebrities operated on three discursive planes: the representational, the "real," and the *real*. Journalists analyzed the performative dimensions of black celebrities. As Stuart Hall has noted, representation is both "a concept and a practice—the key first 'moment' in the cultural circuit." In the "Spectacle of the 'Other,'" Hall asserts that "the body itself and its differences were visible for all to see, and thus provided the 'incontrovertible evidence' for a naturalization of racial difference. The representation of 'difference' through the body became the discursive site through which most 'racialized knowledge' was produced and circulated."[9] "Racialized knowledge" was produced and circulated through depictions of black corporeality presented in mass culture, which of course included the burgeoning entertainment industry. Nineteenth-century public amusements, such as P. T. Barnum's American Museum, became "evidence" of white supremacy that could be bought and sold by audiences. Later films such as D. W. Griffith's *Birth of a Nation* stretched the economic possibilities of this model even further, though they were tempered by aggressive grassroots campaigns against damning racial imagery and by the tenacity of a handful of black creators who fought to attain equal footing in the structurally unequal theater and filmmaking industries. Race performers defined black American identity within the context of transnational imperial politics that relied on pseudoscientific theories from both the United States and Europe that sought to define racial power relations based on biology and reduce them to nonsensical minstrel characters. Scholar Daphne Brooks has argued that performance during this period was a way in which black Americans could "rewrite the ubiquitous master narrative of minstrelsy."[10] Therefore, the roles race performers chose or the songs they played and how they played them were ways of defining a collective and mediated enactment of blackness that was then presented to the masses as a rhetorical device designed to persuade blacks to feel proud of and empowered by their racial identity and whites to experience feelings of racial tolerance.[11]

Yet these celebrities were not just performers; they were people, and Americans quickly grew hungry for glimpses into their personal lives. These glimpses, though, could not be spontaneous—that would have been far too risky in the context of building a celebrity's "image." Instead, the "real," personal, behind-the-scenes information that audiences received were highly contrived productions orchestrated by journalists and public relations professionals. Discourses about celebrity culture that circulated more generally in sensational news reporting were the product of a symbiotic relationship between newspapermen and women and a celebrity's entourage. Audiences sought to find out relatable information about the private lives of their favorite celebrities, though these portraits were no less mediated than the public performances themselves. This constituted the "real" dimension of celebrity—the highly orchestrated peeks into private lives and private selves.

But then there was the reality (the *real*) experience of celebrities working to gain a foothold in the Jim Crow entertainment industry—the limited roles, the awards snubs, the separate accommodations, and the hostile racist audiences—which hung like an albatross around the necks of many race performers.

Public performances by black entertainers—whether it was Bert Williams lamenting onstage that he "isn't never got nothin' from nobody, no time!" or Jack Johnson strutting across the mat to mock his suffering opponent—were one part of the "representational matrix" of black celebrity. The "representational matrix," according to Stephanie Leigh Batiste, consists of the performers themselves, the material conditions of their performance (plot, imagery, setting, enactments), and the spectators' critical responses.[12]

Celebrities, as scholars have understood them, are enacted through the process of spectacle. They are inventions of public discourse; they operate as symbols constructed in "gossip, public opinion, magazines, newspapers and the ephemeral images of movie and television screen[s]."[13] The development of visual spectacle—spurred on by advances in printing, photography, and cinematography—meant that the black body was particularly on display for consumption by white audiences desperately seeking evidence of their "superiority" and the darker races' "inferiority." Laura Mulvey has noted that in Hollywood film, the hegemonic nature of the filmic gaze creates an unequal power relationship between those who are looking (represented by the camera's incessant snooping eye) and those who are being spied upon.[14] Though Mulvey is writing about gendered power relationships, a similar dynamic persists along racial lines. White audiences at minstrel shows and in nickelodeon theaters and white readers perusing daily newspapers enacted power over black subjects who were often reduced to their corporeal forms. It was difficult for black-owned production companies to remain financially viable long enough to counter hegemonic racial tropes, and those that did, such as the Lincoln Motion Picture Company, which produced early "race films," suffered financially. Too, these films lacked what Thomas Cripps has called a "usable" black past. The mythic stories of heroes and villains from which early popular culture derived its structural elements "did not fit as cleanly" when transposed onto black experience. Narratives that focused on the lived experiences of blacks without the realities of Jim Crow oppression—enacted in real life by whites but neglected on screen simply because black filmmakers did not want to employ white actors—seemed absurd to the audiences who watched them. This was particularly acute in narratives that attempted to reflect the experiences of black Americans of direct African descent, who carried with them the vestiges of slavery.[15] Spaces in which blacks both controlled the material conditions of representation and constituted the dominant gaze enacted upon performers of their race were limited even though technological modes of representation had evolved at lightning speed.

The pages of black press newspapers were one of the few sites where blacks controlled the conditions of looking. Black journalists covering black performers represented a "resistant gaze"—as black spectators, they were uniquely positioned to view performances by black entertainers through the veil to "read alternative, subversive, and multiple meanings in *black* performance" that challenged dominant cultural ideologies about racial difference.[16]

At the same time, these papers were instrumental in creating the "real" image that attracted large swaths of readers. Journalists, in conjunction with production studios, were in control of the narrative development of individuals who attained "celebrity" status based on audiences' desire to form parasocial relationships with them. Sociologist P. David Marshall has charted the symbiotic relationship between the nascent film industry and sensational urban newspapers. Around 1915 celebrity profiles in newspapers and magazines "began to change from carefully choreographed studies of public moments involving these people to revelations about their private lives and how that intersected with their public lives." Journalists began to structure narratives that "confirm[ed] the real person behind the image" presented on the screen or the playing field. Celebrities themselves functioned to symbolically connect alienated urban audiences together. Sharing in the stories of their favorite stars helped to unite disparate strangers in large, sometimes intimidating urban spaces. According to Marshall coverage of these stars provided "a constellation of recognizable and familiar people who filled the gap and provided points of commonality for people to reconnect both with celebrities and with each other."[17]

Often journalists adhered to a standard story structure that provided readers a symbolic connection between themselves and their stars. The "success myth" became integral to the perpetuation of fame. Journalists employed the success myth to feed fans' appetites for inside information about their favorite star; Cab Calloway's favorite breakfast food was as much a part of his "mythic greatness" as were his energetic musical performances. Inherent in the success myth, according to Richard Dyer, is the belief that "the class system, the old-boy network, does not apply to America."[18] As Jackie Stacey notes, the success myth allowed audiences "into a world [in] which their desires could potentially be fulfilled" while simultaneously legitimizing the values and characteristics that they themselves possessed. "One the one hand, [audiences] value difference for taking them into [that] world. . . . On the other, they value similarity for enabling them to recognize qualities they already have."[19]

Erika Spohrer has argued convincingly that the "real" dimensions of a celebrity's persona as they are presented in the context of the success myth allot "extratextual space" for such figures to explore identities that are distinct from the characters that they play but are no less representational. Paul Robeson, she has theorized, used the "extratextual space" created through journalists' speculation of his extramarital affairs to create a version of himself that was overtly activist and increasingly militant. In those news stories, he was not Othello nor was he Paul—he was "Paul Robeson," the public figure who could enact a separate identity from his most famous character but who was making public proclamations about racism and socialism as a celebrity rather than a private figure.[20]

The mythologizing of American celebrities eschewed the realities of black life in Jim Crow America. It promoted a uniquely American model of self-determination that applied only to segments of society whereby upward social mobility was possible.[21] Yet, this model of "celebrity" could apply only to white entertainers as discursive constructions of the mainstream (white) press for the benefit of white, urban audiences. The kind of social mobility that celebrity culture promised to American audiences was in the early twentieth century all but closed off to blacks and African Americans. Under Jim Crow segregation and discrimination, the likelihood of "transcending" their station as second-class citizens deprived of basic rights was miniscule for most.[22] Rayford Logan has characterized Jim Crowism as the "nadir" of American race relations.[23] "Celebrity" was a social construction that belied ideologies not only about the workings of social class but also accordingly racial segregation and disenfranchisement, which were designed around stripping black Americans of economic mobility. As such black press gossip columnists, Hollywood correspondents, theater critics, and sportswriters often challenged traditional conceptions of celebrity by connecting their stories with larger issues related to racial activism to capture the *real*, true nature of the problem of the color line.

Representational politics, sensational journalism's quest for the "real," and black performers' own struggles with constructed, performative blackness (at its best, their truest vision of a liberated, authentic, multidimensional self) and the pervasive racism in the film, music, and sports entertainment industries presented black journalists the complicated task of untangling the representational from the real, the public from the private, and the liberated from the subjugated. Black journalists were acutely aware of the limitations placed on the celebrities that they covered as a result of the color of their skin. After all like many black performers, black journalists also were forced to concede opportunities, access, and resources as a result of institutional racism designed to prevent any black professional—no matter how dedicated, talented, or famous—from achieving economic prosperity. Celebrities, they knew, were more than just one-dimensional objects viewed on a screen or heard through a speaker—they were real people struggling to survive in Jim Crow America.

Jim Crow the Movie Star

The goal of celebrity journalism in the black press at the turn of the century was to empower readers and fans by promoting exemplary figures to whose achievements they themselves could aspire. Entertainment, they realized, could be more than just another repository for race hatred, if only black performers could harness their symbolic and economic power to the benefit of the race collectively. This was, of course, no simple task, as the increasing emphasis on the visual nature of entertainment through the development of first photography and later motion-picture technology at the turn of the century reified extant perceptions of blacks that circulated in legislative, judicial, and public health discourses under Jim Crow.

Stereotypes that circulated via journalistic narratives, novels, illustrations, household ephemera, public spectacles, and nickelodeon theaters reduced black citizens in the white imagination to "feeble-willed noble savages, comically musical minstrel figures, and dehumanized brutes."[24] "Mass-media technologies and industries," writes Kevin Gaines, "provided new, more powerful ways of telling the same old stories of black deviance and pathology, confounding claims for a rational basis for the tangled meanings attributed to race."[25] The reduction of the black community to exaggerated, ridiculous, and negative stereotypes and the perpetuation of those stereotypes in popular culture were a means to entertain and comfort white Americans and psychologically oppress newly freed black citizens. Visual entertainment quickly became a reservoir for one-dimensional, offensive, and false depictions of black citizens that served only to feed into mainstream assumptions about a racial hierarchy in which whites were at the top and blacks were at the bottom. Some of the era's most celebrated films, including *Levinsky's Holiday* (1913) and *The Birth of a Nation* (1915), labeled the black race as subhuman, dangerous, wholly corporeal, and not at all cerebral. Wrote Kevern Verney of this period, "Images of African Americans in U.S. mass culture continued to reflect the needs and insecurities of white Americans rather than to represent the realities of black life."[26]

In the South the Ku Klux Klan was formally organized, emboldened in part by *The Birth of a Nation*. The film—a racist epic in which southern Night Riders (the early iteration of the Ku Klux Klan) are depicted as heroes and defenders of "white womanhood, white honor and white glory" against villainous black perpetrators in the Reconstruction-era South—was enthusiastically received by critics and audiences despite its inflammatory content. Considered the "most slanderous anti-Negro movie ever released," the film was an "advanced technical rendering of the traditional stereotypes of docile, loyal slaves, glad to be a part of the benign, paternal slave system" depicted in contrast to nonsubservient black men, who were portrayed as "brute and vicious rapists of white women," observes film historian Donald Bogle.[27] The power of Griffith's epic was almost entirely visual; Griffith made a spectacle out of "a vast reservoir of racial fear within his audience."[28] For blacks, according to John Hope Franklin, "the film did more than any other single thing to nurture and promote the myth of black domination and debauchery during reconstruction."[29] *Birth* capitalized on stereotypes of rapacious black men threatening the virtue of white women, overlooking the fundamental reason for racial anxiety during this period.

The Birth of a Nation justified lynching practices by recasting blacks' participation in the labor market as a somehow violent threat to southern white communities, thereby reflecting the nation's worst racial anxieties. Racist stereotypes in film, especially the kind depicted in *Birth* and promulgated in a number of films of that period, were especially problematic because they were often the only exposure that sheltered whites had to black "culture."[30] While black citizens were being unfairly portrayed in entertainment culture, they were also being segregated from it. Black spectators were denied access to all arenas of public amusements, from parks, circuses, and tent shows to sporting events, both as spectators and participants. Almost as soon as their doors opened in the second decade of the twentieth century, movie theaters became a site of contestation of Jim Crow segregation practices. Unlike the theaters that lined Broadway, movie theaters did not have assigned seating; therefore, the relegation of black spectators to balcony seats was not an institutional but rather a de facto social practice.[31] Theater owners and managers just assumed that blacks, when ordered to do so, would give up their prime seats. In 1914 moviegoer Madeline Davis took her little brother to see a film at the Ideal Motion Picture Company in Philadelphia. After they took a seat in the middle of the theater, the usher and the manager approached Davis and told her to move closer to the screen. She refused, and the two men, along with another theater employee, assaulted her. The three men—Joe Purzell, Richard Hughes, and William Buckman—were put on trial for the assault and were found guilty. The magistrate argued, "Moving picture managers have no right to usher their patrons to seats they do not wish to occupy. . . . Where tickets do not specify a particular seat the patron is entitled to occupy any vacant seat."[32] Two similar cases emerged in Philadelphia, one in 1915 and one in 1917.[33] In coverage of the 1917 case, in which again a movie-theater manager, William Goldenburg of the Victoria Theatre, attempted to remove a black patron from prime seating, the *Philadelphia Tribune* observed, "Not genuine Americans but men of foreign birth seem to be the most persistent in efforts to deny equal accommodations to all who desire to enter such places," which suggested growing tension in urban areas between black residents and European immigrants.[34]

The reductive and often negative images of African Americans that proliferated in early film were the only representations of the black community available to white Americans, who made certain that the "buffoons" and "brutes" be denied the opportunity even to join them during an evening at the movies. In such an environment, racist symbols proliferated freely.

Visual imagery continued to play an increasingly vital role in the struggle for civil rights as the age of spectatorship began in the United States thanks in large part to the development of the film industry and the popularity of urban neighborhood nickelodeons in the second decade of the century. By 1900 fifteen-second "films" were regularly shown in vaudeville theaters and penny arcades. By

1912 feature films were being shown in nickelodeons to nearly five million moviegoers per day. The development of the film industry accelerated through the 1920s. Film production companies moved from New York to Hollywood, California, at the beginning of the decade, and moviegoers steadily bought tickets, theaters became larger and more luxurious, and film stars became bigger and brighter. The development of the film industry opened up new but limited professional opportunities for black performers. Film production companies relegated black film actors to two primary roles: they were cast either as "scenery" extras for films that took place in, say, the African jungle or the antebellum South (indeed, *The Birth of a Nation* cast black extras to inhabit its fictional plantation) or as minstrel-inspired stereotypes, which slowly developed beyond the "coon" type to encompass an array of dissimilar but equally problematic archetypal characters. In addition to the "coon," or comedic buffoon, these filmic stereotypes included the "Tom," based on Harriett Beecher Stowe's protagonist in *Uncle Tom's Cabin*, a "submissive, stoic, generous, selfless, and oh-so-very kind" type that is seemingly content with his inferior position; a "tragic mulatto," who is often female and falls victim to "a divided racial inheritance" and is thus emblematic of the "problem" of miscegenation; a "mammy," a robust older woman who often acts as a comedic counterpoint to the coon character; and a "buck" or "brute," "a barbaric black out to raise havoc."[35]

Opportunities in film for blacks reflected the residue of the minstrel tradition, with which blacks had a conflicted relationship. Performed by the likes of Ernest Hogan, the comedy duo Bert Williams and George Walker, and M. Sisserietta Jones's (known by her stage name "Black Patti"), "coon" songs and their accompanying cake walk dance did little to challenge prevailing impressions of the race but instead commercialized negative images of black citizens. Also black actors such as Clarence Muse, Stepin Fetchit, Bill "Bojangles" Robinson, Louis Beavers, and Hattie McDaniel fell into the stereotyping trap early in their careers, as the only roles available to black actors were often those as bumbling servants and matronly maids. Of Fetchit, who changed his name from Lincoln Perry in order to sound more in step with the servant character he often played, one black journalist noted, "He went to Hollywood to get a job doing nothing and had been working ever since as the world's laziest man."[36]

The year 1927 marked a critical juncture for the film industry when *The Jazz Singer* debuted in theaters as the first successfully marketed sound motion picture. The advent of sound was a double-edged sword for many black performers. On the one hand, sound allowed for dynamic, multidimensional performances by blacks. A persistent myth about the better quality of the recorded black voice over the quality of the recorded white voice opened up opportunities for race actors, but those opportunities were once again based on simplistic stereotypes. The nature of aural performance was representational; critical discourses of the period celebrated sound's cinematic realism. The naturalness of sound in motion picture reified extant perceptions of blacks as unself-conscious and spontaneous. Racist ideologies mapped nicely onto blacks' aural performances in talkies as civic leaders tried in vain to find a balance between embracing new economic opportunities for blacks in the entertainment industry and countering persistent claims that black performers were somehow inherently musical and rhythmic.[37]

Some Depression-era films sought to rectify the overtly racist images that pervaded early major motion pictures. *Imitation of Life*, a popular film that depicted the doomed condition of a woman who tries to "pass" as white, inhabited a liminal space between being a truly transformative work that reflected actual African American experience and being simply an example of what Daphne Brooks has called the "spectacle of suffering" inherent in early mainstream depictions of African Americans.[38] The "spectacle" to which Brooks refers was the product of the lingering popularity of the controversial abolitionist bestseller *Uncle Tom's Cabin*. Couched very much in the realist tradition, Uncle Tom's tragic story, though originally published in 1852, was adapted and performed in different iterations through the beginning of the twentieth century. Between 1903 and 1927, for instance, at least nine film productions of the book were made. Many traveling theater productions were performed as well. The tragic end of *Imitation*, particularly in Peola's intense self-hatred and painful rejection of her race, could be read as such a spectacle, designed to exploit the suffering of Peola as a "tragic mulatto" for the benefit of white audiences who—consciously or not—ascribed to her suffering.

Mainstream newspapers capitalized on racial stereotypes, legitimizing as "fact" racist ideology propagated in film. David Mindich, in his comparative reading of lynching reports in the mainstream and black press of the 1890s, demonstrated how mainstream newspapers excused lynching as an unfortunate but necessary strategy for "civilized" whites to regulate the "savagery" of blacks.[39] When Jack Johnson fought the "Great White Hope" Jim Jeffries in 1910 for the heavyweight title, mainstream newspapers partnered with fight promoters to market the event as the "hope of the white race" versus "Negroes' deliverer."[40] Mainstream newspapers unabashedly drew on narratives that aggravated race tensions, demonized blacks, and authenticated judicial and pseudo-scientific discourses of white supremacy. "Normally, when a Negro does something commendable," wrote one contributor to A. Philip Randolph's *Messenger* magazine, "one needs a microscope to discover it in the corners of the white newspaper, if indeed it gets in at all. Should a Negro snatch a white woman's pocketbook, however, that will be published on the front page, most likely with big headlines."[41] Coverage of black citizens in mainstream newspapers of the period reflects the myriad ways in which pernicious forms of racism reinforced filmic stereotypes of the race that undermined the efforts of blacks to integrate.

Culture Wars in the Black Press

During a period of disenfranchisement, segregation, and violence, black press newspapers advocated for black communities by publishing stories that emphasized race pride, self-help, and community cohesiveness. These newspapers were among the very few news sources that chronicled issues affecting black communities nationally. "The editors and readers of the Negro press have an unusual unity of purpose: all Negros, in varying degrees, object to racial discrimination," wrote the *Defender*'s long-time contributor Metz Lochard in his unpublished work on black press newspapers.

"The editors are sure to hit a responsive chord of common interest in all their news and editorials, because all the items are angled to the subject of the race."[42] They published stories that challenged prevailing Jim Crow legislative and judicial practices, endorsed political candidates for office, investigated lynching, charted the migration of blacks from south to north, and supported black-owned business and social institutions.[43]

Black newspapers were particularly pivotal in the process of community building during urbanization in the Northeast, and they served an increasingly diverse local readership hoping to build familial and community bonds as southern blacks migrated to the North in search of greater job opportunities and less discrimination. Most black press papers reported frequently on news of local interest; this "indirectly created ethnic bonds and gave blacks a sense of cohesion in the face of the multiplicity of a large city," posits Andrew Bunie of the social function that the *Pittsburgh Courier* played at the turn of the twentieth century.[44] Church news, Howard-Lincoln football matches, and stories highlighting prominent community members graced the front pages of these newspapers alongside news stories about local and national politics. Black press newspapers provided both national and local news coverage to their readers through the use of a networked journalism model. This model of newsgathering relied on disparate sources, including the mainstream press, other black press newspapers, Pullman porters, the Associated Negro Press, guest correspondents and columnists, and readers themselves.[45]

Reading black press newspapers was an important act of citizenship. As Evelyn Higginbotham notes, after the Civil War ended, "African Americans were quick to identify literacy with personal fulfilment and upward mobility."[46] Armistead Pride estimates that by 1890, 575 black press newspapers had been established.[47] Emancipation, northern migration, the establishment of (albeit segregated) systems of primary and secondary education, and the influence of the church in many black communities led to skyrocketing literacy rates at the turn of the century. By 1930 many of the cities with the largest black populations also had the lowest rates of illiteracy compared with other urban centers. Because of the importance of reading black press newspapers as an introduction to city life, illiteracy rates were systematically lower in northern cities than in southern ones.[48] The very act of reading a black press newspaper was a communal activity. Newspapers were passed around communities (often to the chagrin of editors trying to make ends meet through subscription fees) and read aloud to citizens unable to read for themselves. This oral component allowed for the sharing of ideas and the participation of all segments of black society.[49]

Despite their popularity in black communities, many newspapers faced issues of low circulation and had trouble securing advertisers, which meant constant financial insecurity. It was not unusual for newspapers to make specific appeals to readers to either pay their subscription fees (which the *Baltimore Afro-American* did regularly on its front page) or to patronize certain businesses that advertised in their pages. For instance the *Philadelphia Tribune* asked of its readers: "When you are about to make purchases of any kind, first look in the advertising columns of your Negro newspaper and select from the business houses listed there the places where you will spend your money. And—in making your purchases, merely mention to the clerk or manager that you saw his advertisement in your Negro newspaper."[50] Those most likely to fund the newspapers through subscription—black working-class readers—had little cash to spend on "an inessential item like a newspaper," while middle-class black readers sometimes snubbed black press newspapers, which at the time were typically short (four to eight pages in length) and reprinted (often without permission) news from other sources.[51] One journalist of the time charged that middle-class blacks "thought such newspapers were beneath them, that they were too intelligent and classy to be caught with such a publication around their house."[52] Though some members of the black elite bristled at the sometimes haphazard reporting and design of black press newspapers, middle- and working-class blacks treated these newspapers as their main source of information on their communities, and reading them was an act of personal fulfillment.

Black press weeklies vacillated between publishing anything that would ensure their economic survival and selectively choosing content that faithfully served their readers' needs. On the one hand, black press newspapers struggled against everyday structural racism that prevented them from garnering the resources, leverage, or readership of mainstream newspapers. As such the most successful among them, such as the *Chicago Defender*, the *New York Amsterdam News*, the *Philadelphia Tribune*, and the *Baltimore Afro-American* (and later the *Pittsburgh Courier*) adopted the sensational reporting practices of their mainstream counterparts and made questionable advertising decisions in order to remain economically viable. On the other hand, these newspapers operated as symbolic sites for community building, racial uplift, and civil rights activism. These newspapers were "advocacy publications" that operated within the conventions of mainstream American journalism but existed apart from them because the needs and interests of their wholly black readership meant that what was considered "newsworthy" must also align with expediently securing basic rights for black citizens, whether it was a "sexy" story or not. The black newspaper industry, as any commercial enterprise might, precariously balanced its perceived civic duty with its need to survive in an increasingly competitive economic market.

Thanks to technological advances in printing and the simplified process of reproducing photographs in newspapers—as well as steadily increasing literacy rates in large urban centers—the black press as a whole enjoyed as-yet-unheard-of circulation figures and financial stability later in the second decade of the century. This impressive boost in circulation figures, however, came at a price, as the most successful black papers had adopted the sensational tactics of the mainstream "yellow" press in order to sell newspapers.

The black press very much aligned with the mainstream sensational press in establishing coverage of entertainment culture as particularly newsworthy. Black press editors borrowed some of the conventions they saw working well for the mainstream press of the time—big headlines boasting circulation figures, gossip, scandal, and the occasional showgirl. The *Philadelphia Tribune*, a conservative newspaper that rarely devoted front-page column space to anything other than stories devoted to politics and education, began to cover celebrities more aggressively to compete with other black newspapers in the Northeast. It even began to run a column called the Tribune Theatrical Night Life Page, which featured society news and "theatrical chit chat."

The newspapers that emerged during this period were among the most successful: the *Chicago Defender* and the *Pittsburgh Courier*. The *Baltimore Afro-American* also enjoyed increased success during this period under new leadership. Robert Sengstacke Abbott, an attorney-turned-journalist, began publishing the *Defender* in 1905 out of his landlady's Chicago dining room. The paper was most notorious for regularly adopting the attention-grabbing tactics of the mainstream "yellow" press, publishing stories on sex and crime. By 1919 the *Defender* had an international readership of 230,000.[53]

The *Defender* was no more scandalous than its main competitor, the revamped *Afro-American*. In 1922 Carl Murphy took over the paper and implemented a sensationalized formatting overhaul, along with an aggressive distribution and marketing plan. As a result its circulation had grown by 600 percent by 1919, to 19,200, making it the best-selling black newspaper on the East Coast. This growth was spurred on by the contribution of Ralph Matthews, who joined the staff in the early 1920s and acted as the "*Afro-American*'s answer to H. L. Mencken," serving as theatrical critic, city editor, and managing editor. By 1932 it was a bona fide competitor with the *Defender*, reaching circulations of over 45,000. At its height the *Afro-American* boasted a circulation of nearly 200,000.[54]

Robert L. Vann's *Courier* began to rival the influence of the *Defender* and the *Afro-American* in the 1930s, employing many of the same tactics those newspapers did. According to Roland Wolseley, the *Pittsburgh Courier* set itself apart from the familiar pattern of the black newspaper industry (in his words, "printing sensational news for the sake of sales, running campaigns in the news columns, printing editorials on behalf of readers, and struggling for advertising") by attracting and retaining on its staff some of the most notable and groundbreaking black journalists of the first half of the twentieth century, including George S. Schuyler, P. L. Prattis, William G. Nunn, and later Wendell Smith, whose coverage of Jackie Robinson for the *Courier* set the stage for the campaign for desegregation of Major League Baseball in the black and alternative presses. By 1926 the *Courier*'s circulation under Vann had risen to close to fifty thousand; by 1935 it had overtaken the *Defender*, selling one hundred thousand copies on the strength of its extensive coverage of up-and-coming boxer Joe Louis.[55]

The Great Depression nearly crippled the black newspaper industry, as its main subscribers—working-class, urban blacks—were among the most adversely affected by the stock market crash. For example the *Defender*'s circulation dipped to less than seventy-five thousand—nearly a third of what it had been at its highest. Some newspapers, like the *Courier*, actually thrived during this period, in large part because they shifted their focus almost exclusively to coverage of Louis's high-profile victories over James "Cinderella Man" Braddock and German Max Schmeling.

Sensational reporting, greater attention to visual content (photographs, comics, and illustrations), the use of local and national correspondents, and strides by race performers in film and on the radio made it possible (and attractive) for black press newspapers to begin to turn their attention to entertainment content. They not only covered film premieres and interviewed celebrities; they also critiqued popular culture representations of the race, organized collective action, pressured advertising sponsors, and lobbied for industry professionals.

Black press newspapers and magazines engaged in culture wars over racial entertainment content. Black newspapers refuted the filmic depictions of black culture by picking apart stereotypes and holding accountable race actors who sought to authenticate them. The misrepresentation of black culture on film, in these writers' view, negatively affected opportunities for blacks elsewhere. Writing about Hollywood during the 1930s, Associated Negro Press correspondent Fay Jackson argued that "[stereo]typing" meant that "a villain may never be a hero and a hero never a villain. And since every villain hopes some day to [attain] heroism and each hero dreams of the day he may [have] a villainous role, 'typing' is an awful thing."[56]

It was not unusual for black press newspapers to publish editorials by race leaders who at times sounded more like culture gadflies than political powerhouses. Booker T. Washington, for example, inveighed against Jack Johnson, complimented Bert Williams, and tried to adopt British classical composer Samuel Coleridge-Taylor as his own American brethren.[57] Washington understood the power of celebrity and courted it at times himself; when his influence began to wane in the face of more radical leaders, he would sometimes try to leverage his financial influence on black press newspapers to build public associations with celebrities to attest to his own cultural relevance.[58]

Consumption practices became an important mode of representation to black journalists. Black journalists took to task fans themselves; an emergent politics of "fan culture" characterized many early articles in the black press that addressed racism in film. When the "Hit the n——r" plot point in *Levinsky's Holiday* came on-screen, a black journalist lamented, "As usual the house was crowded with Afro-Americans evidently insult-proof for they laughed and applauded. Not a word of protest was uttered."[59] Later, when *Amos 'n' Andy* hit the airwaves, the *Pittsburgh Courier* reprinted remarks from Reverend William J. Walls condemning those who listened to the program as "laughing themselves into semi-slavery."[60] One reader, a Howard University student, lamented in a letter to the editor of the *Baltimore Afro-American* that black audiences "enjoy hearing Amos 'n' Andy tell us how ignorant we are, we are not only as 'patient as a jackass,' but just about as sensible."[61]

Black newspapers were staging grounds for collective action. Contributors wrote editorials, mounted boycotts, and put pressure on advertising sponsors. When *The Birth of a Nation* was released, William Monroe Trotter's *Boston Guardian* and W. E. B. Du Bois's *Crisis* mounted formal campaigns against the film, while the *Defender*, the *Philadelphia Tribune,* and the *Baltimore Afro-American* all dedicated column space to galvanizing readers to boycott theaters where it was shown. The protest proved moderately successful. The October 2, 1915, edition of the *Chicago Defender* announced in a large banner headline, "Birth of a Nation Kicked out of Ohio." The NAACP mounted successful boycotts and demonstrations against the film and managed to get different scenes cut in different cities, with five states and nineteen cities banning the film altogether for fear of riots. The *Crisis* monitored these censorship efforts in its pages, in one issue even offering its readers a rundown of which specific scenes were cut.[62] In the same issue, a *Crisis* contributor noted, "It is impossible to overestimate the importance of such alertness on the part of Massachusetts, and we cannot too seriously impress upon other states the need of continued and determined action. Our fight is not over."[63] When film star Will Rogers made cracks about African Americans on a radio broadcast, the *Crisis* led boycotts against the program's sponsor, Gulf Refining Company, and put public pressure on NBC until Rogers reluctantly apologized. The *Tribune* noted, "Will Rogers has a poor sense of humor. Negroes know what Rogers thinks about them."[64]

Black journalists also lamented the lack of opportunities available to black actors, filmmakers, and engineers. Writing in 1929 Floyd C. Covington offered an assessment of African Americans in Hollywood in three areas of employment: as extras, as principal stars, and as directors and producers. As he noted, "There have been many outstanding Negroes in pictures, but none rated as stars. . . . With the introduction and improvement of talking pictures comes perhaps the Negro's real opportunity to produce stars in his own right."[65] Covington stated, "The Negro's place in the motion picture industry in California depends largely upon himself"—implying, of course, that success would come with hard work and self-sufficiency.[66]

To that end editorial content supported labor organizations that fought for equal opportunities and increased compensation for blacks in the film industry. Beginning in the second decade of the century, film operators as well as actors and producers began to organize into labor unions. As Steven Ross has pointed out, though operator unions existed as early as 1910, unionization campaigns for actors and producers "remained sporadic and largely unsuccessful until the creation of Actors' Equity and the more radical Photoplayers' Union of 1916."[67] As labor issues intensified in the late 1920s to 1930s, black theater employees who worked as projector operators began to unionize and demand better pay and working conditions. The International Alliance of Theatrical

Fig. 1. May 22, 1915, edition of the *Chicago Defender* heralding the defeat of the film *The Birth of a Nation*. *Chicago Defender*, May 22, 1915, front page. *Black Studies Center*, Chadwyck-Healey, ProQuest.

Stage Employees and Moving Picture Machine Operators of the United States supported their efforts, and walkouts in Philadelphia, Washington DC, and Baltimore took place in the mid-1930s. Theater managers were described by one journalist as the "exploiter of Negro labor of the vilest type."[68] Black actors also sought to unionize; the *Messenger* encouraged them: "Remember, you are a wage earner, and as such you want the highest wages possible and the best possible conditions under which to work."[69] The Negro Actors Guild of America was formally organized in 1937, spearheaded by actress Fredi Washington.

Simply put, the black press was one of the few forums in which black communities could obtain and share news about themselves, debate local and national issues, and organize. Through news stories, columns, editorials, and letters to the editor, journalists, community leaders, and citizens actively engaged in discourse that helped to define African American identity at the turn of the century in the wake of Reconstruction and through a period of large-scale northern migration. Generally, the black press was a gatekeeper for black political, cultural, and social expression; the black press "offered its readers a definition of the black community," observes Hayward Farrar.[70] However, financial constraints and changing social philosophies meant that the cultural politics of celebrity reporting were complex and dynamic across newspapers and over time—meaning that the modes of representation that were defined and enacted in their pages hardly conferred a single, uniform version of African American identity or sense of community. Metropolitan weeklies' coverage of blacks' participation in the entertainment industry illustrated their geographical reach, influence on public opinion, large networks of readers and contributors, and ability to transform popular culture into terrain on which the battle for civil rights could be fought.

The Politics of Celebrity in Black Press Reporting

This book is an attempt to illuminate the dark, hidden spaces between the representational, the "real," and the *real* of black celebrity culture as it was charted by black journalists and editors who covered important race stars. What distinguishes celebrity reportage from discussions of entertainment culture generally, though, is that celebrities as news subjects enacted for black press journalists an extratextual space in which they could freely negotiate the relationship between public performance and private conduct. The extratextual space between the representational, the "real," and the *real* became a battleground for black press journalists struggling to sell both newspapers and a unified vision of liberation under Jim Crow.

The analytical perspective that threads a ribbon through the chapters that follow concerns the political nature of mediated representation that comes in the form of artistic performance and journalistic commentaries about it. Public performance as it was enacted on the stage and then later through radio and film beginning at the turn of the twentieth century morphed actors, singers, and athletes into celebrities. The "star phenomenon" relied on the symbiotic relationship between a performer's public persona and his or her "real" private personality, which was a journalistic construct. The gulf between those two representations offered an opportunity to critique the impact of stars in the community through the performances they gave, the public comments that they made in interviews, and the way they conducted themselves in private. The discourse of stardom was in fact defined not by an artist's public performance but by how much could be revealed about who he or she was as a person. Of course both the representational realm and the real realm are mediated through the eyes of journalists constructing narratives that resonate with the larger cultural values of the communities that constitute their readership. Thus the real was actually the "real"—a mediated discourse that tried to sell audiences a private glimpse into their favorite star's life but that was ultimately only a performance itself. Yet celebrities are not mediations; they are real people, who through hard work, talent, luck, or some combination of the three attain publicly recognizable status. In the Jim Crow era, the structural barriers that deprived black Americans of opportunities no matter how hard they worked or how talented they were were very *real*, and luck can do very little under those kinds of circumstances. Therefore, as W. Fitzhugh Brundage has noted, every public performance by a black American was potentially a political act, a transgression and subversion of prevailing racist ideology designed to economically, psychologically, and physically oppress anyone who was not white.[71] By simply pursuing fame, these noteworthy individuals were engaging in a subversive act, challenging the American racial ideology that determined who could rise and who could not.

This book uncovers discourses of the politics of celebrity that drew on shifting racial philosophies that alternatively emphasized racial progress, economic mobility, respectability, and later, collective action. The retention of most printed material from these black press publications in publicly held and digital archives has made them accessible to a new crop of researchers, who over the past fifteen years have increasingly studied them and expanded the interpretive approaches previous scholars have taken. Patrick Washburn's 2005 book, *The African American Newspaper: Voice of Freedom*, is the most recent and comprehensive cultural history of black urban weeklies. In it he traces the evolution and demise of the black press from the antebellum period through the consolidation of its two largest newspapers, the *Pittsburgh Courier* and the *Chicago Defender*, in 1966. Washburn's comprehensive framework has provided important institutional context for this work's critical approach to black press entertainment content.

Other contemporary examples of critical/cultural studies of black press content have illuminated how popular culture played an influential role in the everyday lives of black and African Americans. Amoaba Gooden has critiqued hair care and skin cream advertisements to uncover the hegemonic (whitewashed) beauty standards put forth by black press newspapers and magazines, Chris Lamb and Brian Carroll have investigated the role black journalists played in the desegregation of Major League Baseball, and Matthew Bernstein and Dana White have compared critical responses to *Imitation of Life* to gauge differences in the North and the South to interracial relationships.[72] In each example researchers have charted the negotiation of the black community's shared values and goals by examining the stuff of everyday culture, which includes popular culture. Brian Carroll, Sarah Jackson, and Charlene Regester have turned their attention to the black press's treatment of celebrities in particular, revealing—as this book hopefully does—some of the ways in which journalists treated celebrities as collective representations of racial experience and identity.[73]

Celebrity journalism, the following chapters argue, is essential to understanding the reality and aspirations of ordinary people who—just as fans do today—derive pleasure, satisfaction, a sense of self-worth, and inspiration from their favorite stars. Brian Carroll's work on the stars of the Negro Leagues sums up the mission of this project nicely: "By examining the values, goals, and actions held up by the black press as those to model and mirror, it is perhaps possible to better understand what the black community of the period sought in its hero figures and important people, and therefore how its members saw themselves and who they hoped to become."[74]

This book aims to critically engage with two common threads of black press research. First, it hopes to encourage researchers to move away from the "color line" trope. All too often scholarship that considers early black celebrities focuses on their role in the arduous process of desegregation. The persistence of the "color line trope" is essentially a methodological problem—journalism history scholars in particular have disproportionately analyzed representations of black Americans in mainstream newspapers, magazines, and films in lieu of focusing on black-centered media that catered exclusively to black communities across the country. By focusing only on black performers' participation in (and the related journalistic attention paid to) mainstream cultural events—in other words, the slow erasure of the color line on the stage, the playing fields, and in film—we forfeit an important piece of black cultural history. Namely, we risk losing forever the stories of those who tried, those who failed, and those who never had the chance to cross over to the mainstream and "make history." Whether it is Johnson's 1910 win over the Great White Hope Jim Jeffries, or Paul Robeson's dynamic performance as Othello, or Hattie McDaniel's historic Oscar win, we as a culture tend to revisit the same stories and venerate the same figures over and over again. Some of the "stars" of the following chapters—among them tenor Roland Hayes, theater actor Charles Gilpin, bandleader and war hero James Reese Europe, and prizefighter Harry "Black Panther" Wills—were deeply important to those who wrote about them and to those who read about them. Issues of representation and exemplarity have been overlooked in critical histories of the early civil rights struggle, as scholars have assumed that public notoriety came only to those black entertainers and athletes who successfully crossed the color line. This book shifts attention to black press publications to critically examine the discursive strategies that black journalists used in writing about black celebrities, and it explores the contemporary implications of the "color line trope" on public memory narratives that crystallize cultural myths about the civil rights struggle.

Second, it argues against the notion that the black press was unilaterally supportive of any successful black public figure. For instance in the case of controversial heavyweight champion Jack Johnson, Harvey Young insists that "evidence of the black community's support for the prize fighter appears in various black newspapers . . . which chronicled with great frequency and detail, the near-daily events in the boxer's life throughout his championship reign."[75] This assertion is true; Johnson's name appears in many "news in brief"-style pieces. These articles serve to highlight the interest that the black press had in Johnson but do not give a strong indication of what black journalists made of his tumultuous public life as expressed in feature articles, editorials, and letters to the editor. Shifts and tensions in whom black press journalists heralded, vilified, and venerated illuminate the ways in which black communities' perceptions of themselves changed and evolved over time. As the following chapters will show, those shifts often came at times of political upheaval, as liberation ideologies morphed and changed from accommodationism to respectability to militancy in the context of Jim Crowism, a national economic depression, and two world wars.

The following chapters place the emergence of celebrity journalism in the black press within the context of Jim Crowism from 1900 to 1940.[76] Each chapter discusses how celebrity reportage in black press newspapers and magazines employed discourse that resonated with their predominantly black readership, and like discussions about other sectors of black public life (politics, education, economics, and public health) drew on ideologies of liberation (uplift, respectability, and militarism) from the black intelligentsia of the period. The book then begins to explore the extratextuality of specific celebrities as journalists chose to disentangle them from discourses of performance or, alternatively, mythologize them as exemplary figures. Chapters 2 and 3 examine the development of celebrity journalism from 1900 through U.S. intervention in World War I, which signaled a shift in the political activism and social consciousness of many black and African Americans who had family members and friends "close ranks" to join the war effort and especially of those who fought themselves. Chapter 2 takes a close look at the nuances of "collective representation" of a disparate but united black community through the black press's treatment of two of its earliest and most controversial stars to enjoy mainstream attention: prizefighter Jack Johnson and stage star Bert Williams. Chapter 3 examines the concept of "racial uplift" as it related to celebrity personalities in coverage of classical musician Roland Hayes and the troubled yet venerated Broadway actor Charles Gilpin.

Chapters 4 through 6 examine the implications of black celebrities' increased visibility to both black and white audiences during the 1920s and 1930s in the context of the Harlem Renaissance. Chapter 4 charts the mythologizing of the "jazz mad generation," focusing on Cab Calloway, Louis Armstrong, and Duke Ellington. It also shows how black journalists constructed a sense of "imagined intimacy" between readers and their favorite celebrities by employing narrative strategies similar to mainstream celebrity journalism. Chapter 5 incorporates insights from feminist media studies to assess the visual and discursive representation of black female celebrities in black press newspapers. Though coverage of female celebrities was as voluminous as that of male celebrities, there was a deep disconnect between the women who received attention in the black press and the lives of the press's female readership. Chapter 6 assesses the crossover success of track star Jesse Owens and world champion Joe Louis as rhetorical inventions of American exceptionalism amid the backdrop of rising antagonisms from Hitler's Third Reich.

Chapters 7 and 8 explore the implications of the discursive strategies employed in black-centered celebrity journalism. Chapter 7 uses collective-memory scholarship to consider commemorative journalism published upon the deaths of Bert Williams and Joe Gans, arguing that black journalists realized their contributions to the race only *after* their deaths and in eulogizing these celebrities crafted a mediated "usable" black cultural past that had not existed in public discourse previously. The closing chapter provides a summary account of the major findings of the preceding chapters and offers some recommendations for a cultural studies approach to examining the historical black press.

2

Early Crossover Black Celebrities and the Onus of Collective Representation

Midafternoon of July 4, 1910, under the bright and cloying Reno sun, listening with disinterest to nervous shouts of "Don't let the n——r knock him out!" smiling and joking to the jeering crowd, Jack Johnson stalked into the center of the ring where an uncertain Jim Jeffries—the "great hope" of American white supremacy— tottered around, covered in blood, nose broken, tired, and mentally and physically defeated. Johnson pushed Jeffries back to the ropes, punched him four more times for good measure, and knocked him down. In the fifteenth round, Jeffries's handlers leaped between the two prizefighters to stop the fight, and promoter Tex Rickard laid his hand on Johnson's dark shoulder, declaring him the world champion while Jeffries lay prostrate before him. The Negro's Deliverer had summarily demolished the Great White Hope, thereby defending his 1908 World Championship title and, for the moment at least, silencing white critics who wanted desperately to see him destroyed in the name of Jim Crow racism.[1]

Somewhere in New York that same day, not far from Broadway, a reserved comedian was basking in the glow of a month's worth of positive reviews of his new gig as a part of the lauded *Follies of 1910*. Only a few months earlier, Bert Williams had accepted a position with Florenz Ziegfeld Jr.'s prestigious *Follies* after the revelation that his longtime partner, George Walker, had fallen ill with syphilis and would no longer be able to perform with the Williams and Walker Company. With Walker's health steadily declining, Williams was at a crossroads in his career when Ziegfeld, a man known both for his tantalizing showgirls and his transgressive attitudes about American racism, approached him with the offer to become the revue's first black performer. On June 10, 1910—barely a month before Johnson's victory—he shuffled on stage, burnt cork carefully applied to his brown skin, and to the chagrin of his white cast mates stole the show with his down-on-his-luck Jonah Man routine.

The growing demand for race performers by white audiences at the turn of the twentieth century was intimately tied to both American Jim Crow racist ideology and Western imperialism, which denigrated and fetishized black bodies as public spectacles. Black bodies were treated as commodities to be bought and sold, and onto them white audiences projected white colonialist discourses that disavowed African American identity and emphasized the superiority of whiteness over it.[2] Williams was a minstrel performer seemingly complicit in the perpetuation of racist stereotypes, a perception amplified by his choice "on a lark" to perform exclusively in blackface to audiences composed almost exclusively of whites. Williams's comedic Jonah Man character drew upon the "coon" minstrel stereotype, but instead of acting as a boisterous buffoon, Williams used character development and elements of drama to convey disillusionment and discontent through Jonah Man's signature songs, "Nobody" and "Constantly."[3] Johnson was the physical embodiment of racial transgression; his prowess in the ring symbolically undermined eugenic claims of white supremacy, though many white spectators of the time likely read his performance in the ring as just another example of the "inherently violent black buck." In the ring he would stalk around his opponents, laughing, chatting with spectators, and delivering one-liners. Outside the ring he appeared to many to be a "misguided minstrel who has forgotten his place"—a "dandy" strutting around town in expensive clothes with an entourage always in tow.[4]

Urban dailies in cities such as New York, Chicago, Philadelphia, and Baltimore were written by and for white readers, despite those cities' growing black populations at the turn of the century. The dailies covered Williams and Johnson extensively, but they presented to their readers narratives about race that fell in line with the ideologies of white supremacy—a slippage in understanding that overlooked the transgressiveness of both Williams's and Johnson's respective crafts. When Bert Williams debuted with the *Follies* in the summer of 1910, critics for white daily newspapers heralded his performance but found comfort in the idea that it "reified extant ideas about blacks as both chicken-thieves and pseudoreligious hypocrites," his biographer, Camille Forbes, has found.[5] Johnson represented the harbinger of "racial Armageddon" to mainstream journalists who inflamed racial tensions in coverage of both Burns-Johnson and Johnson-Jeffries.[6] The still image of Johnson looming over Jeffries, reproduced in newspapers and magazines all over the country at the time, represented in Harvey Young's view the "reclaiming and reappropriation" of the "disempowered black body."[7] Johnson, in that position of power over his white opponent, publicly became "the master of 'Mr. Jeffries'"—a horrific symbol to racists who were determined to devalue and disenfranchise black citizens.[8] In the immediate aftermath of the Johnson-Jeffries fight, race riots broke out all over the country; at least eleven and as many as twenty-six people killed and hundreds more injured. In recounting the postfight violence years later, the *Chicago Defender* charged that "much of the trouble following the fight grew out of the pre-fight ballyho [*sic*] in which the fight writers on the various newspapers stirred up the race question until it was about ready to burst like a bubble."[9] Black performers were either "in their place" (Williams) or they were not (Johnson); questions of artistic motivation, agency, and autonomy did not fall in line with white journalists' embedded assumptions about "simplistic" blacks.

Jack Johnson and Bert Williams could not have been more different had they tried—an extrovert and an introvert, a heel and a hero, a champion and a down-on-his-luck drifter, a black man who insisted race did not matter and one who darkened himself with paint in order to emphasize that he was the "real thing." Yet as contemporaries if not friends, they were subjected to the same judgmental forces in both the mainstream and the black presses. Where the mainstream press failed to see them as anything other than the stereotypes they seemed to superficially represent, the black press used them as ways to engage with larger political issues of accommodation, economic aspiration, and advocacy. Neither Johnson nor Williams set out to become exemplary figures, yet they both quickly became symbols of racial progress and pride to the black communities who marched together on a long journey toward civil rights. As this chapter will illustrate, both performers were heralded for their ability to rise economically in industries that were designed to prohibit the participation of blacks in any meaningful or lucrative way, delighting accommodationists who saw the path to liberation not through integration but through the economic advancement of black professionals. Yet judgment of their individual, private lives and their willingness (or not) to participate in collective action on behalf of their race led to mixed reception by black press journalists who themselves were trying to reconcile the best path to true liberation in the years before World War I. Coverage of Johnson and Williams that called them out for not acting on behalf of the race collectively foreshadowed the activist ethos that emerged at the end of the decade as soldiers returning home from battle demanded equality. Also, coverage that demonized Johnson's womanizing and celebrated Williams's conservatism reflected the widening gap between upwardly mobile blacks in northern communities and migrant blacks from the South, as conversations about "morality" quickly turned to rhetoric of "respectability." Both of these men were race performers navigating the disconnect between the reality of their private experiences as black citizens and their roles as race representatives against Jim Crow racism and black and African Americans' collective resistance to it. Whether Williams and Johnson liked it or not, courted it or not, or ascribed to it or not, they were transformed from private black citizens charting the realities of Jim Crowism to exemplary figures carrying on their shoulders the burden of collective representation.

Williams and Johnson Become Stars

Williams and Johnson were not the first black public performers, nor were they the first to be mentioned in the black press. Churches held concerts, fund-raisers, social galas, and dance parties, and many of their choir members, including M. Sisserietta Jones and E. Azalia Hackley, rose to first local and then national prominence. Howard University and Lincoln University sporting teams were widely popular with black spectators around the country. Indeed, Williams and Walker received comparatively less coverage before 1910 than either church or university sporting events did. However, Williams and Johnson were the first individuals to garner attention from both black and white audiences in the United States and internationally.

Black press newspapers were invested in subjects that reflected a spirit of "entrepreneurism and Booker T. Washington–style bootstrapping and self-help," as Brian Carroll's work on black press coverage of the Negro Leagues has suggested. Carroll argues that entrepreneurs were treated as "celebrities"; their work was representational but not performative. Black social conservatism was spearheaded by Washington, whose strategy of accommodation encouraged the pursuit of industrial job training over liberal arts education, social liberation through economic advancement, and racial separatism. At the Atlanta Exposition in 1895, he famously proclaimed, "In all things that are purely social we can be as separate as the five fingers, yet one as the hand in all things essential to mutual progress."[10] Following the 1895 Atlanta directive, black journalists focused their energies on covering subjects that reflected economic mobility. Business owners, as David Suisman has suggested of Harry Pace and his Black Swan Records, were seen as political agents who controlled "material resources that could cultivate and boost African Americans' creative spirits, support and encourage African American business development and economic self-sufficiency and, it was believed, help shape popular opinion to produce tangible social, political, and economic benefits for African Americans."[11] Working-class readers were encouraged to patronize only black-owned institutions, and ad campaigns by black entrepreneurs made explicit appeals to race pride. Racial progress, at least in part, was understood in terms of dollars and cents. Both Williams and Johnson enjoyed lucrative careers as performers, and much of the attention paid to their early successes framed them as economic, rather than cultural, exemplars.

Williams and Johnson were not only contemporaries, but they also had a great deal in common as performers. Both prizefighting and vaudeville theater were leisure activities that appealed to largely working-class white audiences, and Johnson and Williams were at the forefront of transforming each from racialized spectacles into "terrain of imperial power and resistance" on not only a national but also a global stage.[12] Williams was the first of the two performers to cross the color line. In 1903 his theatrical production *In Dahomey*, with partner George Walker, became the first black production to debut on Broadway at the New York Theatre. Five years later in Australia, Johnson beat Tommy Burns to become the first black heavyweight champion of the world.

Both performers became international sensations, and each of them spent time performing in Europe. Williams, as a part of the Williams and Walker Company, traveled to England to perform *In Dahomey* for King Edward VII at Buckingham Palace, much to the performer's delight, who was a Bahamian British subject, paid allegiance to the Crown, and would later exalt the performance as "the proudest moment of [his] life."[13] Johnson historian Theresa Runstedtler has characterized the troubled champion as a "rebel sojourner," traveling for seven years between England, France, Spain, and Mexico in an attempt to evade a human trafficking conviction in the United States. Despite the conditions under which he was forced out of the country, Johnson later mused that he had been "considerably broadened by the varied experiences and contacts" he made abroad.[14]

Both performers also harnessed the early influence of film with mixed results. Williams has been identified as the first black actor to appear in a narrative film; in 1914 he was cast in *Darktown Jubilee* and later in Biograph films *Natural Born Gambler* and *Fish*, though he reportedly failed to secure the financial backing to film, produce, and distribute his live vaudeville routines.[15] Of *Natural Born Gambler*, film critic Tony Langston wrote, "There are but few laughs throughout the bar room and gamblers den jamboree, with no moral, no theme, no nothing except Williams, who has underrated his standard."[16]

"Fight pictures" were a prominent part of the early film industry, and Johnson's bout with Burns was shown in theaters across

Australia, England, and the United States. Two years later, when the Johnson-Jeffries fight picture began to make the rounds, imperial nations across the globe mounted a censorship movement to prevent the film from being shown because "troubling questions of race and representation were galvanizing concerned white citizens across ethnic, regional, and national divides."[17] The footage of a black man beating a white champion into submission was so horrifying to American audiences that Congress placed a ban on the interstate shipment of *all* boxing films following the riots, effectively preventing the image of a triumphant Johnson looming over a prostrate Jeffries from garnering a national audience. According to then-congressman S. A. Roddenberry of Georgia, "No man descended from the old Saxon race can look upon that kind of contest without abhorrence and disgust." Roddenberry went on to call the Johnson-Jeffries fight "the grossest instance of base fraud and bogus effort at a fair fight between a Caucasian brute and an African biped beast that has ever taken place."[18]

Despite their similar experiences as black American entertainers, Williams and Johnson could not have been more different. Williams was born in 1874 in Nassau, Bahamas, to a multiracial family that relocated to Riverside, California, when Williams was two years old.[19] Throughout his career Williams was so intimidated by Jim Crow politics that he refused to perform south of the Mason-Dixon Line.[20] Johnson—four years Williams's junior—was a product of the South, born and raised in Galveston, Texas, and he was well attuned to southern racism though he spent his childhood regularly mingling with white children on the Galveston docks. He recalled fondly the "gang" of boys with whom he roamed: "So you see, as I grew up, the white boys were my friends and my pals. . . . No one ever taught me that white men were superior to me."[21]

Williams was an enigmatic figure with a closely guarded personal life. Very little is known about his personal affairs, including even those most central to his life: his relationship with his partner, George Walker, and that with his devoted wife, Lottie, with whom he adopted and raised her biological nieces. Though he made his name as a comedian, Williams was a quiet, unassuming man who was a voracious reader and historian and who struggled to assert himself professionally as he navigated the Great White Way. Sylvester Russell, one of Williams's staunchest critics, once charged that Williams "had no backbone."[22] Johnson, on the other hand, was a brash, arrogant self-promotion machine. He penned two memoirs, *My Life and Battles* (1914) and *In the Ring—and Out* (1927). Literary critics dismissed the latter as near-hagiography.[23] He courted attention and reveled in it so much that later in life he kept a scrapbook of flattering news clippings about himself.[24]

As performers in novel, internationally popular, and overwhelmingly white mass-culture activities, both Williams and Johnson became symbols of blackness, national identity, and racial progress, though both men refuted the idea that they were in any way attempting to act as representations of their race. In interviews Williams often disavowed his place within American racial politics, instead identifying himself as a Bahamian, and therefore British, citizen.[25] Johnson also dismissed the notion that he was acting on behalf of the black community collectively; rather, he claimed that his drive to punish his white opponents was not racially motivated but rather because he resented hecklers who claimed he was "yellow," or cowardly.

There is no evidence that Williams and Johnson knew each other personally, though as contemporaries and high-profile members of a small, exclusive cadre of black celebrities who often hobnobbed in the cabarets of Chicago, Harlem, and Paris, it is likely that the two men crossed paths. Williams even offered a public nod to Johnson's victory over Jeffries, working into the *Follies of 1910* a sketch called "A Street in Reno," in which the lanky Williams, made up in blackface, which intensified his physical similarity to the dark-skinned Johnson, strapped on boxing gloves and "fought" Billy Reeves among a crowd of white "spectators."[26] Whether they ever had a chance to get to know each other or not, both Williams and Johnson were struggling with the same antithetical forces at the same time.

Both performers were forced to operate on the axis of the *real* and the representational—one the one hand, as black men navigating structural and de facto racism in their everyday and professional lives and, on the other hand, as public performers through whom "ordinary," "invisible" (read: not famous) members of the black community could make sense of their own experiences with American racism. Their progress as "race representatives" was charted by urban black press newspapers, which were beginning to incorporate into their advocacy-based reporting practices content that reflected mainstream journalism's turn toward sensationalism. Black journalists applied their "resistant gaze" to Bert Williams and Jack Johnson and articulated in their news stories the ways in which each could collectively represent the entire race based on his individual advocacy practices and personal fortitude. Despite their protestations about race representation, it was impossible to separate Williams and Johnson from the representational milieu in which they resided as performers.

Williams's Sound Mind and Character

Bert Williams arrived in New York in 1896 with his comedy partner George Walker, with whom he had connected in San Francisco through his participation in Martin and Selig's Mastodon Minstrels. The duo quickly became popular on the vaudeville circuit with their act "Two Real Coons," an ironic nod to the fact that though they were surrounded by white performers in blackface, they were the "real thing," despite Williams's choice to also don dark makeup. The Williams and Walker Company, with the addition of a charismatic young comedienne, Ada Overton (later Aida Overton Walker), soon became the premier all-black theatrical company. In September 1900 the company brought its production *Sons of Ham* to the New York Star Theatre, and the show had a successful run all along the eastern seaboard in New York, Boston, and Philadelphia.[27] *Sons of Ham* was followed by the 1902 premiere of *In Dahomey*, a project that Williams and Walker had originally been inspired to undertake after attending San Francisco's 1894 Midwinter Exposition together, where they participated in a show with Dahomian natives. *In Dahomey*, a $15,000 venture, became so popular during the first year of its run that in 1903 it opened on Broadway in the prestigious New York Theatre, albeit to strictly segregated audiences.

Williams and Walker quickly settled into their respective roles— the former a "slow-moving, dim-witted oaf" and the latter "the grinning, strutting dandy."[28] Walker played the straight man to Williams's unique brand of comedy, which was predicated on "the impulse to laugh at other people's predicaments."[29] Offstage their personalities were just as distinct as their onstage personas: Walker was outspoken and aggressive, while Williams was quiet and accommodating. Walker would often foreground in interviews his desire to use the Williams and Walker Company as a platform with which to pursue racial equality in theater, while Williams often blanched at discussion of racial politics. After his death Walker was remembered in the *Chicago Defender* as "the one man who boldly stood up in his exalted position and made it possible for the Negro thespian of his time."[30]

Williams's Jonah Man act was very much the product of the minstrel tradition, which emphasized in its parody of American life the exaggeration of characters' personal traits through clothing, makeup, and speech along racial lines. White minstrel performers acted as the "ironic embodiment of blacks," who in their view lacked agency, independently defined identity, and a usable past from which to draw authentic experience. Minstrel performers treated their blackface personas as ciphers for racial anxiety and white supremacy. Minstrelsy "provided its urban white audiences a venue in which to release through laughter their uncomfortable feeling about blacks—who lived in cities among them," operating as "a space in which whites could reject the notion that blacks needed to be incorporated into society . . . by demonstrating blacks' immanent inferiority," argues Williams biographer Camille Forbes. Black minstrelsy became a "hyper-performance of blackness," as black minstrel performers, at least in the eyes of white audiences, did little but "ossify stereotypical images" of blacks.[31]

Historians Yuval Taylor and Jake Austen in their book, *Darkest America*, argue for a reinterpretation of the *black* minstrelsy tradition. Long dismissed as simply playing into whites' perceptions of them for fame, money, and notoriety, Austen and Taylor point out that black minstrels used ironic parodies of racial identities to highlight the absurdity of racism, not to feed the beast. Taylor and Austen call this transgressive performance style *signification*.[32] In particular black comedians, such as Bert Williams, have used minstrel stereotypes in a style of comedy dependent on the entertainer's ability to poke fun at himself. The notion of self-deprecation, they have pointed out, "doesn't necessarily include the point of view of the oppressor."[33] Rather, the evocation of racial stereotypes by race performers became a mode of authentic self-presentation.

In developing his comedic style, Williams began to "see himself as another person."[34] What separated Williams from the lineage of black minstrel performers who came before him was a sense of pathos. He used the mask to capture the verisimilitude of black Americans' experience as opposed to simply reifying false stereotypes of them. Years after Williams passed, comedian Eddie Cantor, who performed with Williams in the *Follies of 1917*, remarked, "There are only three emotions one can ordinarily express in black face. . . . They are joy, sorrow, and fright. Williams mastered these and more behind the cork."[35] Williams once told the *Defender*'s Eloise Bibb Thompson that he hoped someday to "paint a portrait of the Americanized Negro on the modern stage."[36] Late in his life, he expressed the desire to transition from comedy to drama in an effort to better capture the ordinary black American through harnessing such pathos: "Each of us who has Negro blood is one that never fails to stamp on the heart or the spirit its racial traits," he said. "The laughter I have done is only on the surface. Now I would like to strive deeper."[37] Despite these strong proclamations, however, Williams always seemed to be torn between professional ambitions and race consciousness; his desire to move to drama was in part compelled by his jealousy toward fellow race actor Charles Gilpin, who had secured the lead role in Eugene O'Neill's *The Emperor Jones*.[38]

Williams joined Florenz Ziegfeld's popular *Follies* revue in 1910 after George Walker had been diagnosed with syphilis and ceased performing in 1909. Williams was an instant sensation with the *Follies*, in which he performed until 1920, taking only a short hiatus in 1918. Williams as a solo performer often butted up against the White Rats, a white vaudevillian trade union that sought to exclude women and minority performers. Ziegfeld strongly disavowed racial prejudice, and he was one of the few whites in the industry to take a stand against racism. The White Rats routinely protested Williams's status as a headline performer, and even his longtime manager, F. Ray Comstock, buckled under pressure from the organization. Ziegfeld's choice to cast Williams was met with resistance from both the white members of the *Follies* and the show's producers, Klaw and Erlinger, who insisted that the audience be strictly segregated in northern theaters, where de facto, rather than de jure, segregation was commonplace. Ziegfeld balked at the objections to Williams, insisted that he was "indispensible," and threatened to fire the rest of the cast if they continued to complain.[39]

With Walker gone, Williams was left to contemplate his obligation as a race performer in his new, controversial role in the *Follies*. Though Walker had been the member of the pair most adept at articulating his frustrations as black performer operating in a structurally unequal entertainment industry, Williams quickly was thrust into a similar role. News stories about his turn as the revue's first black crossover star became imbued with issues of race representation. Lester Walton, the managing and theatrical editor of the *New York Age*, was one of Williams's most dedicated advocates.

Walton, whose reputation among black journalists was so revered that his Broadway columns would often be reprinted in race weeklies around the country, viewed Williams as a performer who was deftly working within the system to effect change, which he argued would eventually benefit other black performers. Walton wrote:

> Although Mr. Williams is traveling with a large white production and may not be so closely associated with members of his race, he reflects great credit on the race of which he is a member. No colored performer has ever reached the position now occupied by Bert Williams. As the real star of the large Broadway production he is certainly a bigger man individually today than when a member of the famous team of Williams and Walker. He is now playing in theatres in which it was never possible for Williams and Walker to secure booking.[40]

Williams's success "elevated" the rest of the race, he concluded.[41] It was no secret, however, that Williams had made concessions in order to peaceably participate in the *Follies* otherwise all-white cast. He had volunteered to add as a clause in his contract that he would not appear on the same stage with any of the female performers, and he admitted that he interacted with the cast only "by being polite and friendly, but keeping his distance."[42]

Black journalists often heralded Williams's equanimity when faced with racial discrimination, which he called "an American phase."[43] As a Bahamian native, Williams often attempted to divorce himself from the effects of American racism. He was of course only one of many black performers who preferred to identify along nationalist, rather than racial, lines. Lightweight champion Louis "Battling Siki" Phal, a black French free citizen, remarked to one *Defender* reporter in 1924, "You got that statue in New York—Liberty you call it—bah, it mean nothing. No freedom here—no, no, no—not for you—for me."[44] Identifying as a European rather than an American citizen, which Williams and Phal both did, begot a distinction that carried with it an implication of progressivism absent in American discourses about race though only superficial in European imperial discourses about it. Williams told *American Magazine*, "I have no grievances whatsoever against the world of the people in it. I am having a grand time."[45]

Williams was of "sound mind and character," and through his interpersonal relationships with white contemporaries, he seemingly embodied Booker T. Washington's accommodationist stance of social segregation.[46] Washington acknowledged a kinship with Williams, and he complimented him in the press often. Williams was "a tremendous asset to the Negro race," commented Washington in the *Defender*, "because he has succeeded in actually doing something and because he has succeeded the fact of his success helps the Negro many times more than he could help the Negro by merely contenting himself to whine and complain about racial difficulties and racial discriminations."[47]

Williams's lack of his old partner's racial sensitivity began to grate on Sylvester Russell, the *Chicago Defender*'s theater critic. While it was common for black journalists to bemoan Williams's lack of opportunity outside vaudeville, Russell argued that Williams's refusal to take on the race question would have dire consequences for other black performers.[48] "We look upon Williams as an example," he pointed out. "He is free from the commonplace of cheap other actors, a fact that makes him great, and if he had the bravery of his domiciled partner . . . he would assert these things in his interviews."[49] For Russell Williams was obligated to use his celebrity status to advocate for other performers of his race by reviving the Williams and Walker Company as the "race institution" that Walker had once envisioned.[50] "If Williams would only give up playing pool," he charged, "he could fill the idle time in writing a Negro play in which to star that would add to his usefulness in the greater establishment of his name in history."[51]

Despite both Russell's criticism and the amount of positive attention he received from the mainstream theater press, Williams carefully cultivated a congenial relationship with many black press journalists, including Walton, W. Calvin Chase (the *Washington Bee*'s editor in chief), and even Russell's colleagues at the *Defender*, managing editors J. Hockley Smiley and Eloise Bib Thompson. On tour stops in towns with large black weeklies, Williams would sometimes visit the newsroom to tell jokes to the staff.[52] Williams had timed his crossover success well, at least in terms of harnessing exposure in the black community. Increasingly over the second decade of the century, as Williams took on a greater role with the *Follies* and began to command a huge price tag on the vaudeville circuit, black weeklies were allocating resources to cover entertainment.[53]

Jack Johnson's Sporting Life

The *Defender* led the move toward more entertainment content under the direction of Smiley, who was both an experienced journalist and a gifted editor and designer. He joined the staff in 1910, as circulation figures for the paper steadily climbed. Robert S. Abbott, who was determined to make the *Defender* the premiere publication for black readers not only in Chicago but also all over the country, hired Smiley to begin to modernize the layout of the newspaper. Borrowing from Hearst- and Pulitzer-owned dailies, Smiley began to direct the *Defender* toward a more sensationalized look and feel—headlines became larger and bolder, content was divided into sections, and editorial focus shifted to crime and, of course, entertainment.[54] Urban black weeklies in other eastern cities began to follow suit.

Amid these changes the *Defender* formed a symbiotic relationship with popular but troubled heavyweight champion Jack Johnson, who had moved to Chicago after his victory over Burns in 1908. Johnson was both a gifted athlete and a natural entertainer. He was a skilled defensive fighter, which meant that despite his tall stature and ability to effect real damage with his punches, he was smart enough to anticipate his opponent's moves and quick enough to elude them. The most successful prizefighters, after all, spend their time in the ring *avoiding* punches. Twenty years after Johnson's championship reign ended, Bill Doherty of *The Ring* magazine reminisced that "[Johnson] was like a poker player who has a routine flush or four aces, and deliberately decides to sit on and watch the fun, just betting enough to stay and make sure of getting the stakes."[55] Johnson was particularly known for toying with his opponents for rounds before ultimately knocking them out. He boasted that he had delayed Jeffries's demise in the Fight of the Century by nearly eleven rounds only because he "wanted to show Mr. Corbett, Mr. Abe Attell and the other seconds that [he] could outbox, outfight, outpunch, and outsmart the 'white Hope' in every way."[56] As he boxed, he would often put on a "side show," bantering with his beleaguered opponent and his corner men, journalists in the ringside press box, and even spectators who heckled him. Although he claimed that his "jocular remarks" were "an old gag meant to shake the confidence of one's opponent," Johnson cultivated a flamboyant public persona that he extended far beyond ringside and into his private life, well after his championship reign ended.[57] Johnson's "audacious self-presentation" was a deliberate performance of resistance that Theresa Runstedtler convincingly argues "went against established racial and sexual norms but also mocked the Victorian values of industry, thrift, and restraint."[58] When not training or fighting, Johnson would often dress in expensive tailored suits, collect his entourage, which consisted largely of white prostitutes, and frequent Chicago's Stroll district.

Johnson was a "canny public relations operator" who harnessed his adopted hometown newspaper's advocacy mission to cultivate loyalty from his core fan base, which was predominantly black. Upon his arrival in Chicago, he visited Abbott's house to purchase a one-year subscription to the newspaper, and the two men became fast friends. The *Defender* was steadfast in its support of the champion, often framing his run-ins with law enforcement—which included traffic infractions and one bizarre incident where he was charged with allowing his dog to bite a pedestrian—as status quo Jim Crowism.[59]

In the lead-up to the "Fight of the Century," the *Defender* front page proclaimed in large, bold print, "Jack Johnson Is a Hero."[60] The *Defender* was not alone in heralding Johnson as an exemplary figure in the black community. The *Baltimore Afro-American* asserted, "Johnson as heavyweight champion of the world is a credit to the race, and every Negro should be proud of his achievement."[61] Johnson's bloody defense of the championship title only brought this public exaltation to a fever pitch. The *New York Amsterdam News* went so far as to align Johnson with the likes of Paul Lawrence Dunbar and Booker T. Washington.[62] Like Bert Williams, by virtue of being a visible member of the black community (read: famous), Johnson was rarely criticized by black journalists. He became an exemplar of upward economic mobility, often posing for photographs in expensive suits and top hats, canes, and other sartorial markers of class status.

The champion's perception in the black community began to change, however, after the Johnson-Jeffries bout, when Johnson's personal sexual indiscretions began to overshadow his ring successes. After the suicide of his first wife, Etta Duryea, in September 1912, Johnson began to appear in public with seventeen-year-old "sporting woman"-prostitute Lucille Cameron, whom he had met at his Chicago nightclub, Café du Champion, while he was still married to Duryea. Cameron's mother did not approve of her daughter's relationship with the black celebrity and contacted authorities to charge Johnson with taking her daughter over state lines for "immoral purposes." The Bureau of Investigation, one of the black community's foremost antagonists, formally charged Johnson under the White Slave Traffic Act, and in May 1913, he was convicted and sentenced to one year in prison and a $1,000 fine.

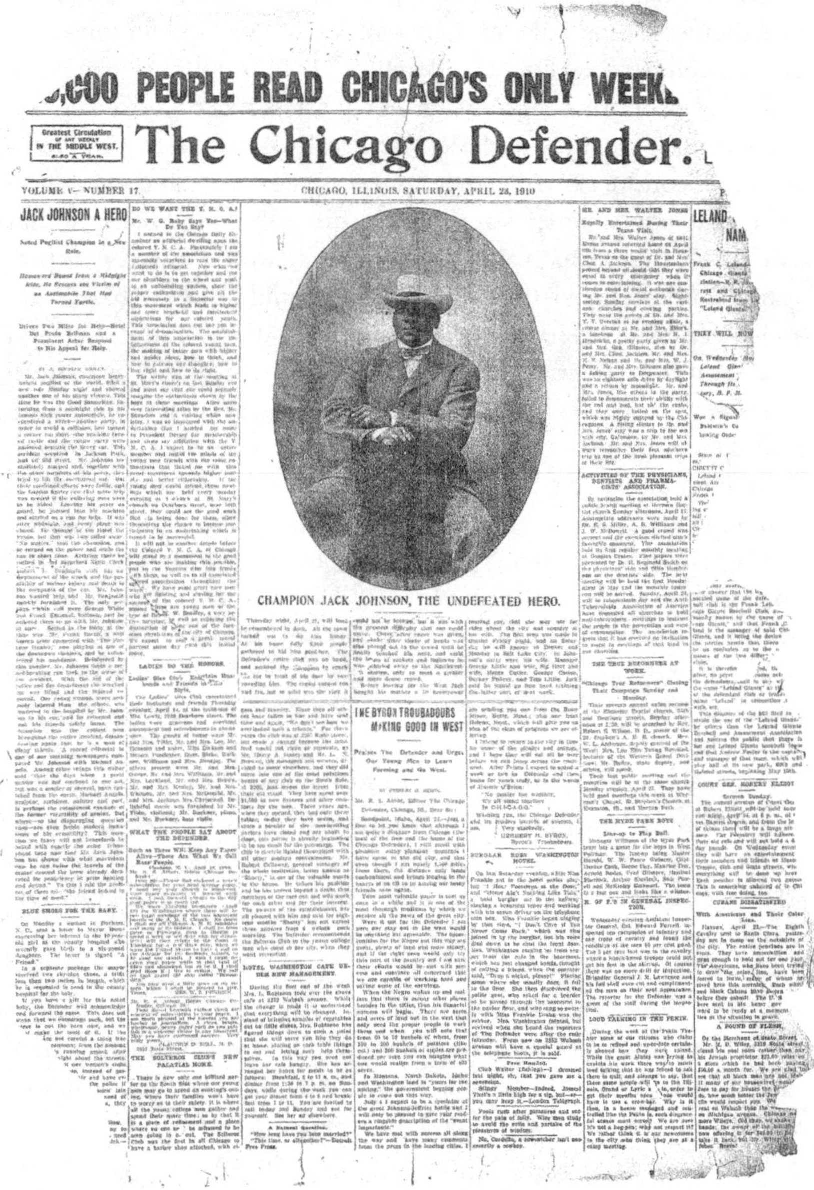

Fig. 2. An early edition of the *Defender*, celebrating heavyweight champion Jack Johnson. *Chicago Defender*, April 23, 1910, front page. *Black Studies Center*, Chadwyck-Healey, ProQuest.

Condemnations of Johnson's "sporting life" were commonplace, and they were especially resonant with black weeklies' middle-class, church-going, professional readership. Ida B. Wells-Barnett, a black celebrity in her own right given her fearless investigative reports on southern lynching practices, critically questioned Johnson's personal conduct in an article that was circulated and reprinted in several newspapers. "Some of the things that took place in that saloon [Café du Champion]," she wrote, "would have been prevented and perhaps Mrs. Jack Johnson would not have found life so intolerable as to be driven to suicide."[63] Wells-Barnett implied that Johnson, who was rumored to have been not only unfaithful but also abusive to Duryea, was responsible for his first wife's death. She disapproved of the stories of uncouth behavior—drinking, gambling, and illicit sex—that characterized Johnson's popular venue. A journalist for the *Baltimore Afro-American* balked at the concept of Johnson as a "race leader" and hoped the race would "not produce any more like him."[64] Discussions about morality as they related to entertainment began as early as the mid-1880s, when state, federal, and private forces banded together to form "a new regime of moral regulation in America," according to media historian Paul Starr. Native-born Protestants, who were at the forefront of moral regulation initiatives, were in many ways responding to the "obscenity, drunkenness, and other forms of immorality" associated with both immigrants and the black population.[65] Black intelligentsia, clergymen, civic leaders, and politicians internalized notions about morality and respectability as a key mode in the cultural representation wars, so they enacted upon newly migrated southern blacks (including Johnson) a strict code of prescribed public and private behaviors. Johnson's defiance of the sexual social mores of the period cost him valuable social capital and compromised his status as a race representative.

Just as their fates had seemed to symbolically converge in the monumental summer of 1910, Bert Williams's and Jack Johnson's paths sharply *diverged* three summers later in 1913. That summer Williams took part in the *Follies* triumphant London run, where he was guaranteed by the manager of the London Opera House, Clifford Fisher, that "he would be treated 'just like a white man' and absolutely no prejudice would be shown against him for his color."[66] Williams, as a British subject, had always enjoyed his sojourns to London. In 1903 he and George Walker had brought the cakewalk to Buckingham Palace. The queen was reportedly so taken with the duo that she "laughed and applauded, showing intense interest in the actual award of the cake."[67] Williams received top billing abroad, and during the 1913 tour even the White Rats could not prevent him from being listed as the show's top draw. His cast mates also began to warm to him; the clause in his contract preventing him from appearing onstage with female cast members was put aside, and he began to enjoy a more substantive role in the revue. The summer of 1913 solidified Williams as the true star of the *Follies*, and when he returned to the United States the Keith vaudeville circuit offered him a weekly salary of $2,000 to perform. Walton delighted in noting that this sum far exceeded what President Wilson or any of his cabinet members made per week.[68]

Johnson also traveled to Europe that summer, except hardly under the same triumphant circumstances. Rather, to avoid serving his prison sentence, Johnson and Cameron, whom he married in the winter of 1912 in order to deflect the Mann Act charges, fled for the U.S.-Canada border. From Canada he sailed to Europe, where he divided his time mostly between England, Spain, and France and eventually gained French citizenship. Johnson's time in France underscored to many black citizens at home the perceived racial tolerance of that country in comparison with the United States. He earned money to sustain his and Cameron's lifestyle by participating in exhibition matches; yet Theresa Runstedtler found in her analysis of French newspaper coverage of the star that, "although French sportsmen enjoyed gazing at African American pugilists on stage and in the ring, they ultimately viewed black men not only as different from white men but also as fundamentally removed from Western civilization."[69] Imperial politics made it impossible for Johnson to truly feel comfortable settling abroad, so he continued to roam, from the Continent back to North America via Cuba, where in April 1915 he lost the title to Kansan Jess Willard. He claimed to have thrown the fight in a bid to gain entry back into the United States as a free man, but instead he toiled for another five years in Mexico before surrendering himself to border authorities in July 1920.[70]

Johnson's and Williams's lives would not again converge. Just as Johnson was negotiating his reentry into the public world after seven years on the lam and one in prison, Williams was passing from this world to the next.

In early 1922 Williams contracted a case of pneumonia while on tour to support *Under the Bamboo Tree*, which received positive reviews but was struggling to sell tickets. Though sick Williams continued to tour, and on February 27, he passed out during a performance in Detroit. Few papers had time to report on the collapse though, because by the time the weekly editions were set to print, Williams was already gone. He passed away just before midnight on March 4, at the age of forty-seven. As Tony Langston of the *Chicago Defender* noted, "The report of Mr. Williams' death is a bound to be a shock. No reports regarding his illness had been published, and the fact that he worked up until a few days before his death makes it all the more a matter of surprise."[71] Three funerals were held for Williams: two private services for the family and one public service, during which an estimated five thousand to seven thousand mourners attended.[72] In the aftermath of Williams's death, black journalists used universalizing language to provide narrative closure to his legacy. One *Defender* reporter wrote, "His death is not only a national but an international calamity. It is not only a serious loss to the Race or group with which he was identified, but to the human race."[73] Fifty years later the same unifying language would be used to describe another black icon, Louis Armstrong, upon his death. In both cases, though, the realities of U.S. racial politics forbade true closure for either artist's legacy, as civil rights activism moved swiftly away from anything akin to the accommodationist stance that each performer had seemed to represent in his lifetime.

Upon his release from prison, Jack Johnson struggled to regain his former celebrity status, though he did manage to keep himself in the news. Johnson was released from prison in July 1921, and he returned briefly to Chicago before traveling to Harlem, New York,

Williams's old neighborhood. In 1922 he opened a Harlem cabaret, Café de Luxe, which became a favorite of gangster Owney Madden.[74] He spent the rest of his time fighting in exhibition matches, training up-and-coming fighters, performing in vaudeville, making workout records, and even reportedly securing a speaking role in the Broadway production of *Aida* in 1936.[75]

In the summer of 1934, Johnson returned to Chicago to appear in a sideshow exhibition match for Dave Barry's Garden of Champions, but he took a night off in early July to head to Bacon's casino to see Joe Louis make his debut. Johnson was taken with the young, talented fighter and later approached Louis's manager, John Roxborough, about training him. Roxborough not only rejected Johnson's offer but, according to witnesses, "cursed him out," charging that Johnson had "held up the progress of the Negro people for years with his attitude" calling him a "low-down, no-good n——r."[76] Roxborough did not elaborate, but he did not have to. He and the rest of Louis's management thereafter cultivated a public persona for Louis that was designed specifically to draw a sharp contrast between him and Johnson. Louis was not to talk about race publicly nor be caught by the press drinking or cavorting with white women. Instead, with the help of black newspapers such as the *Pittsburgh Courier*, Louis's public relations team cast Louis as a paragon of personal and moral fortitude—complete with a mythic heroic narrative.[77]

Johnson, in retaliation, launched a media campaign against Louis, claiming to sportswriters of both the mainstream and the black presses that Louis simply did not "possess the thinking and facilities of a 'great fighter.'"[78] When reigning champion James J. Braddock agreed to fight Louis, Johnson committed what many black journalists felt was the ultimate betrayal—he offered to train *Braddock*. "To us, you are a Benedict Arnold of the race," wrote one journalist in—of all places—Johnson's trusted ally, the *Defender*. "If you are interested in making a name for yourself, or if you feel that the people are forgetting you in favor of Louis, why don't you take some promising Race boy who is making good, and train him."[79] Johnson had relinquished his role as an advocate for the race—a mistake from which he would not recover in his lifetime.

Collective Representation and Jim Crow Realities

Race performers Bert Williams and Jack Johnson were among the first black crossover celebrities. Popular culture of the period emphasized the blurring of the *real* and the representational; it was impossible for performers such as Williams and Johnson to separate themselves as private citizens from the public personas they presented on stage and in the ring.

Black journalists, in covering these two men, returned again and again to three points. First, black celebrities, by virtue of their visibility to both black and white audiences, served as cyphers on which audiences could encode both the positive and the negative characteristics of the entire race. Celebrities were framed as collective representations of the race as a whole—whether they aspired to such a role or not. Second, journalists considered the personal fortitude that each performer showed in interpersonal relations and interviews as important as the skill and artistry that they displayed in their public performances. These celebrities operated as moral barometers for the largely middle-class, upwardly mobile black readership, who judged harshly activities thought to be uncouth, "low-class," or "sporting." Finally, individual success was nothing if it was not accompanied by a genuine attempt to advocate for other members of the race. Activism was not just about symbolic representation—it was also about making specific, strategic inroads into the structurally unequal entertainment industry. Black journalists covering Williams and Johnson as they became truly newsworthy beginning in that fateful summer of 1910 harnessed their "resistant gaze" to articulate a definition of celebrity that acknowledged the importance of their visibility across racial, geographical, and national borders and was based on shared ideals of advocacy and personal fortitude.

Just as celebrity culture seemed to be gathering some momentum in the black press, the United States' intervention in World War I shifted its attention sharply away from entertainment-driven news. When the United States entered World War I in the spring of 1917, the black press had little interest in discussing celebrities. Entertainment coverage dipped sharply during this period across all black press papers, but especially the *Baltimore Afro-American*, the *Chicago Defender*, and the *Cleveland Gazette*, which, more than their contemporaries, valued entertainment culture as particularly newsworthy. Instead, as black press historian Lee Finkle has pointed out, these journalists and editors turned their attention to covering the war effort and fighting for the right of African American men to enlist in the military.[80] World War I represented a rupture in the lives of many African American men and women who actively participated in the war effort. More than 360,000 black citizens enlisted in the military and were sent overseas.[81] The enlistment of thousands of white men in the armed forces created home-front economic opportunities never before enjoyed by black communities. Accordingly, coverage of entertainers sharply dropped during this period in favor of coverage not only of the war but also of the advances being made by black workers at home. For example in June 1918, the *Defender* declared new "Champions"—not Jack Johnson but rather a crew of black Bethlehem Steel Company riveters who broke the world record for number of rivets driven in nine hours.[82]

As a result of these developments, the metrics by which celebrities would be judged as race representatives changed, and changed drastically, over time as political movements toward first-class citizenship evolved, fragmented, and realigned after the Great War.

3

Black Celebrities Uplift the Race

Roland Hayes peered uncertainly at the audience from behind the curtain onstage. He tried to count the number of black faces he saw in the audience on the main floor of the Lyric Theater, but he did not see any. The Baltimore theater, just like those in which he had performed deeper in the South, had been segregated. His black fans were relegated to the balcony, while the main floor of the hall was reserved for white ticketholders only. He retired to his dressing room to inform the evening's promoter, Kate Wilson-Green, that he would not take the stage. He had endured protests leading up to the concert, he said, and he did not want to subject himself to more negative press.

This last-minute cancellation would cost the Lyric thousands of dollars, so tearfully Wilson-Green begged Hayes to perform. After about a half-hour of haggling, the two came to an agreement, and with his very nervous accompanist, Lawrence Brown, by his side, Hayes walked onstage and began to sing his well-known composition "Crucifixion."

Hayes's failed attempt at civil rights activism that January 1926 evening in Baltimore was met with harsh criticism from black press weeklies, which had hoped that the celebrated classical artist and "gentleman of culture and bearing" would advocate for his black fans against Jim Crow segregation.[1] His failure to do so was especially disappointing because he had promoted his records using specific appeals to racial uplift. "You wanted to bring to your home and to your family and to your friends the voice of the individual Negro singer or the playing of the individual Negro performer," read one such advertisement, "who would take high rank among the invisible makers of music and singers of song whom the phonograph has brought to cheer your spare moments after the grind of the day's work is done."[2] As the son of a former slave who would eventually make enough money to purchase the plantation on which his mother was held in bondage, Hayes was cautious to take on Jim Crow segregation—both because of his "regressive" stance on race relations shaped by his Jim Crow childhood and because as a classically trained singer who performed not only all across the country but extensively in Europe, he had a white fan base that he could not afford to alienate.[3]

"Highbrow" black artists such as classical singer Hayes operated on the same representational axis as other black mass-culture celebrities of the early twentieth century even though the entertainment that they provided was fundamentally different from (and according to some critics, more valuable than) the "silly" impressions of the vaudeville stage or the "brute" strength of the boxing ring— decidedly "lowbrow" entertainment. They were not performing for working-class audiences; these artists were representing the race on stages across the United States and Europe to (predominantly white) audiences who through education, travel, and the arts, set the benchmark for high cultural achievement. These were highbrow white audiences who wielded immense amounts of not only economic but also social and cultural capital.

Just a few months before the Lyric fiasco, Hayes was awarded the NAACP's prestigious Spingarn Medal. The *Pittsburgh Courier* proclaimed, "His singing, his fine impressions made up almost everywhere he appears help to lift us up higher."[4] The exaltation of the race based on communal achievement was a theme that black journalists revisited again and again in myriad forms as they documented the long journey toward civil rights. Classical race performers such as tenor singer Roland Hayes, classical composer Samuel Coleridge-Taylor, and Broadway actor Charles Gilpin not only represented blacks collectively; rather, as member of W. E. B. Du Bois's so-called Talented Tenth, they "uplifted" them.

If Jack Johnson and Bert Williams in the second decade of the twentieth century served as early indications of the ways in which social class mediated forms of collective representation for black journalists and fans, then the 1920s marked a schism in the ways in which black collective representation was informed by elitist notions of who in the black community was qualified to "uplift" the entire race. Uplifters were not simply those in the black community who were the most visible crossover stars. No one would have ever suggested that Johnson, for instance, uplifted anything but his own ego. Rather, uplifters were those public intellectuals, educators, professionals, and entertainers—nay, *artists*—who represented on a national and global stage the noblest and most laudable aspects of black identity. Artists such as British composer Samuel Coleridge-Taylor, tenor singer Roland Hayes, and stage actor Charles Gilpin entertained mixed (and sometimes exclusively white) audiences by employing in their respective crafts the influence of European artists who, according to leading intellectual of the time, W. E. B. Du Bois, were the purveyors of authentic culture. The artists covered in this chapter were masters of optics: they conveyed to fans and to readers a model (albeit unrealistic) version of black achievement. However, against the backdrop of disenfranchised veterans and widespread racialized violence, uplift had a short shelf life. Journalists quickly realized that "positive" representations of black citizenry did not prevent actual black citizens from employment discrimination, lack of adequate housing or healthcare, or lynching.

Celebrity coverage of uplifters revealed the erosion of respectability politics as black press journalists envisioned race representation as a means of promoting collective action instead of simply relying on the optics of what makes a "respectable" black citizen.

Racial Uplift and Classism

Kevin Gaines, in his analysis of turn-of-the-century "racial uplift" ideology, argues that the black intelligentsia's strategies for promoting racial progress against the backdrop of Jim Crow–era repression was to differentiate itself from and then lead the masses of southern agrarian and northern industrial blacks through an adherence to Victorian ideals: "Generally, black elites claimed class distinctions, indeed, the very existence of a 'better class' of blacks, as evidence of what they called race progress. Believing that the improvement of African Americans' material and moral condition through self-help would diminish white racism, they sought to rehabilitate the race's image by embodying respectability, enacted through an ethos of service to the masses."[5] In the antebellum period, racial uplift signified the liberation of all black slaves from bondage but became more narrowly defined as black communities became stratified along class lines. Uplift ideology "required that the race demonstrate its preparedness to exercise" the rights granted by Emancipation.[6] Uplift ideology was expressed not in terms of free will but rather in terms of strictly proscriptive behaviors. To "uplift" the race, citizens had to be economically self-reliant, act "respectably" (that is, quietly) in public spaces, and adhere to patriarchal familial structures. Uplift ideology embodied the intermingled, oppressive dimensions of *both* racism and classism, so that "the two fused together in a manner that grants neither one supremacy."[7]

The resettlement of southern blacks in northern cities that began around 1916 emphasized the different conceptions of propriety that existed between northern, urban, middle-class blacks and southern, rural, poor migrants. Black leaders, including editors and publishers, began to circumscribe for black citizens appropriate, or "respectable," ways to act in public and in private. As Felecia Jones Ross has demonstrated, the *Cleveland Gazette* framed southern migrants as unruly and uncouth, and the newspaper directed northerners to "reach out and teach the migrants high moral values."[8] The *Defender* also published directives aimed at newly arrived migrants to Chicago; at times, Davarian Baldwin has noted, the newspaper read as much like a "how-to" guide on public engagement and behavior as it did a legitimate news source.[9] "Unseemly" behaviors included gum chewing, loud talking, wearing bright colors, going to the nickelodeon theater, listening to jazz music, and a host of other activities.

Urban living proved to be challenging in the 1920s as families settled into postwar life. Poor living conditions in cramped slums led to the proliferation of tuberculosis, pneumonia, syphilis, and other diseases among black populations. Despite decreases in death rates in the black population overall (most notably in youth mortality rates), death rates in cities by 1930 were 19.8 per every 1,000 black residents as compared with 14.2 in rural districts. Death rates among blacks remained proportionally higher than among whites in all areas.[10] One Howard University physician, writing in 1935, states, "It has been definitely established . . . that tuberculosis is associated with poverty and unhygienic conditions. The high rate of tuberculosis among colored people in the United States . . . is due almost entirely to conditions under which they live rather than racial disposition."[11] Black leaders called on their citizens to "embody the virtues of hard work, good manners, hygiene, education, and circumscribed sexuality," writes Jonathan Coit, as an anecdote to toxic urban living conditions in Chicago.[12]

Evelyn Brooks Higginbotham has argued that middle-class black women in particular circumscribed the politics of respectability as both a form of political mobilization and a chasm between classes of black citizens. Higginbotham has suggested that "while adherence to respectability enabled black women to counter racist images and structures, their discursive contestation was not directed solely at white Americans; the black Baptist women condemned what they perceived to be negative practices and attitudes among their own people. Their assimilationist leanings led to their insistence upon blacks' conformity to the dominant society's norms of manners and morals. Thus the discourse of respectability disclosed class and status differentiation."[13] Dignified, constrained behavior in public and circumscribed sexual and romantic behaviors in private were believed to be the key to collective racial progress. Black elites used uplift ideology to counter public perceptions of blackness.

The rhetorical dimensions of racial uplift were developed as a response to Jim Crow antagonisms against black communities that pervaded all aspects of public life, including popular culture. "The exaltation of domestic virtue, symbolized by home, family, chastity, and respectability," writes Gaines, "all infused with an ethic of religious piety, provided the moral criteria for uplift's cultural aesthetic."[14] At the turn of the century, newspapers exalted entertainers such as Samuel Coleridge-Taylor, Roland Hayes, and Charles Gilpin who were considered highbrow entertainers who could counter racist stereotypes. Yet in so doing, they also reinforced classist ideologies by drawing a clear distinction between black migrants, who frittered their time away in darkened nickelodeon theaters, and the "better class" of established, northern black intelligentsia.

For black weeklies "racial uplift" came in the form of individuals, programs, movements, or institutions that promoted a progress narrative of black American history. Carter G. Woodson's "National Negro History Week," which began in 1926, was characterized by the *Philadelphia Tribune* as such a "racial uplift movement." During the second week of February, which marked the birthdays of both Abraham Lincoln and Frederick Douglass, schools, churches, and other black-centered "social agencies" celebrated "the story of these great characters and others who have worked for the benefit of humanity and for the Negro in particular." The hope was that "the brilliant record of the Negro may be so dramatized as to inspire the Negro youth to noble deeds."[15] Racial uplift, then, distinguished itself from simply proscribing moral behaviors—uplift was also about defining black American identity in the context of growing interest in antebellum history and liberal education.

The notion that individuals could serve as communal agents of racial uplift was proposed by education advocate W. E. B. Du Bois in 1903, when he suggested that a "Talented Tenth" would "elevate the mass" of black American citizens to "guide [them] away from the contamination and death of the Worst, in their own and other races."[16] In his essay Du Bois proclaimed, "The Negro, like all races, is going to be saved by exceptional men." These "exceptional men," whom Du Bois termed as the "Talented Tenth," were a conceptual group of elite, noteworthy men who "strove by word and deed to save the color line from becoming the line between bond and free," who "set the ideals of the community in which [they live], direct its thoughts and heads its social movements." These exemplary figures were meant to act as community leaders to fill the void of a usable past, customs, familial ties, and social structure—characteristics that bondage had robbed from black communities. Du Bois's Talented Tenth included teachers, preachers, politicians, and artists–"leaders of thought and missionaries of culture among their people." Du Bois's essay argued that 10 percent of the black community would be capable of attaining the level of academic and personal achievement necessary for the overall uplift of the race. The essay challenged Booker T. Washington's emphasis on vocational training, which Du Bois believed could be sustained only through a foundational liberal arts curriculum emphasizing "intelligence, broad sympathy, knowledge of the world that was and is, and of the relation of men to it."[17] The Tuskegee Institute, after all, needed talented and competent teachers to lead its vocational courses.

During a lecture at Baltimore's Sharp Street Memorial Church in support of *The Souls of Black Folk*, which was published on the heels of "The Talented Tenth," Du Bois expounded upon his Talented Tenth theory of racial uplift. He suggested that education for blacks "must strive towards three ideals: 1st, To give Negroes leadership and trained guidance in civilization and in the morals of sane and sanity living—to find the exceptional men. 2nd, To put the keys of knowledge into the hands of youth. 3rd, To give black boys an opportunity to learn the teachings of modern industry."[18] He did not indict industrial education; rather, he noted that in addition to learning a vocation, black students must also be trained in the liberal arts—history, literature, and philosophy—to achieve full and equal participation in American democracy. The Atlanta University professor's interest in liberal education stemmed from his own training, first at Fisk University, "the most famous college for the uplift of his people in the nation," and later the University of Berlin and Harvard.[19] Most concerning to Du Bois, of course, was black citizens' ability to harness the right to vote to drive social change, which could not be accomplished without a black citizenry versed in its antebellum history and in political philosophy.

The "Talented Tenth" rhetoric also reflected Du Bois's growing interest in Pan-Africanism, "the idea of the solidarity of the world's darker peoples, of the glories of the forgotten African past, [and] of the vanguard role destined to be played by Africans of the diaspora in the destruction of European imperialism."[20] In 1900 he attended the first Pan-African Conference in London, which was organized to confront British imperial tendencies in the West Indies and parts of the African continent. Though Du Bois's participation in this first conference was minimal, it was there that he first described "the problem of the color line" in global terms. In Baltimore's Sharp Street Memorial Church, he reminded his avid audience that the slave trade had affected "not only the ten millions [sic] in the United States but fully another ten million in the West Indies and South America." "Shall you measure good men by their manhood," he asked, "or by their race and color?"[21]

What was less clear was how Du Bois operationalized the term *culture*, which denoted to him the most valuable form of capital. The metrics by which "good men" should be measured had to do with their accumulation of culture, which Du Bois concluded filtered only "from the top downward."[22] It was clear that Du Bois's concept of culture was deeply influenced by the time he spent in Europe as a student. Du Bois had spent his midtwenties studying in Berlin and traveling the Continent, where he "was transplanted and startled into a realization of the real centers of modern civilization and into at least a momentary escape from [his] own social problems," which were, of course, born of American Jim Crow racism.[23] "Who, judged by any standard," he asked in "The Talented Tenth," "have reached the full measure of the best type of European culture?" Du Bois—who described his lineage as "a flood of Negro blood, a strain of French, a bit of Dutch, but, thank God! No 'Anglo-Saxon'"—had a clear affinity for Europe, despite the imperial tendencies that he had challenged directly in his participation in the Pan-African Conference just three years earlier.[24]

"The Talented Tenth" essay was first published in the 1903 compilation, *The Negro Problem: A Series of Articles by Representative American Negroes of To-day*, and it is an indication of early, collaborative discussions between Du Bois and Booker T. Washington (who was involved in compiling the work) on the best means to pursue political and social enfranchisement of black American citizens. Washington emphasized that blacks would secure full citizenship through economic means, as producers and consumers who would "bring recognition and respect to the community by accumulating wealth, occupation, and material acquisitions."[25] Du Bois, too, valued economic equality. Yet he did not believe that economic independence alone would win for black communities full and long-lasting equal citizenship. Rather in "The Talented Tenth," he emphasized the need for social and cultural, as well as economic, capital.

Du Bois and Washington got along well through about 1905, when their ideological differences and personal affiliations began to create a wedge between them. One of the greatest sources of strife between the two men was Du Bois's affiliation with staunch Washington critic William Monroe Trotter, whose newspaper, the *Boston Guardian*, was founded as an anti-Tuskegee publication. Trotter was hardly the only black journalist of the period to be weary of Washington's accommodationist politics; celebrated investigative journalist Ida B. Wells-Barnett and Harry C. Smith of the *Cleveland Gazette* regularly critiqued Washington's policies. Other urban weeklies, like the *Baltimore Afro-American* and *Chicago Defender*, showed editorial independence, alternately praising and criticizing *both* Washington and Du Bois in issue-specific stories.[26] In 1905 tensions between Du Bois and Washington came to a head when, in an essay for the Atlanta publication the *Voice of the Negro*, Du Bois implied that the Tuskegee machine had doled out bribes to black press newspapers to silence Washington's critics.

Of course, Washington *did* have some influence over the black newspaper industry. By placing or withholding advertisements, Tuskegee financially pressured editors in the black press to align with Washington's political views, which created a certain amount of de facto censorship in the press. Because black weeklies were often struggling financially, advertising sales could determine whether a given issue made it to press.[27] Du Bois's comments rankled his colleague, who believed that they implied that he had little support within the black community.[28] There is no doubt that Washington was stinging not only from the criticism he had received but also from the fact that Du Bois was beginning to gain traction in black intellectual circles—particularly with the winter 1903 release of the acclaimed *The Souls of Black Folk*.

Du Bois, despite his friendship with Trotter, had very little interest or investment in black weeklies. He sometimes appealed to these newspapers for assistance in gathering information on local matters, as he did in 1932 when he wrote to Robert Vann to ask after black students enrolled in the University of Pittsburgh.[29] When he took the editorial helm of the *Crisis*, the NAACP's official monthly magazine, in 1910, he reportedly designed the publication in contrast to what he considered to be the poor quality of black weekly publications. The *Crisis* sought to "set forth facts and arguments to show the dangers of race prejudice; serve as a newspaper to record important events and movements bearing on interracial relations; review books and press comments; and publish a few appropriate articles."[30] Du Bois, like many upwardly mobile blacks, was skeptical of black newspapers lack of institutional longevity, sometimes-haphazard reporting practices, sloppy writing style, and increasing investment in sensationalism.

As a journalist, an educator, and a philosopher, Du Bois was determined that racial uplift should be defined in terms of cultural expression and not simply economic prosperity and commercial consumption. Despite his equivocation on defining just what culture meant, it is clear from his writings of the period that two things were particularly important to him: first, that authentic articulations of black culture were central to the collective uplift of the race; and second, that figures who enjoyed public visibility should be only those who represented the best of the race.

Samuel Coleridge-Taylor and Roland Hayes Lift Us Up Higher

British composer Samuel Coleridge-Taylor was born in England in 1875 to an African father and an English mother, and by 1900 he was undoubtedly the most famous black artist in Britain. His father, a surgeon, returned to his native Freetown, Sierra Leone, where he could more easily find work, and so Coleridge-Taylor was raised by his mother and maternal grandparents in the London suburb of Croydon. At an early age, his grandfather instilled in him a love for music, reportedly purchasing for the young boy his first violin. Educated at the Royal College of Music in London, the young composer had drafted his first symphony by the time he was twenty-one.[31]

His groundbreaking work, *Scenes from the Song of Hiawatha*, comprising three cantatas, *Hiawatha's Wedding Feast* (1898), *Death of*

Minnehaha (1899), and *Hiawatha's Departure* (1900), was based on his interpretation of American poet Henry Wadsworth Longfellow's epic poem *Song of Hiawatha*. Longfellow inspired Coleridge-Taylor both artistically and personally: he made note of his friend Harry Burleigh's collaborations with Dvorak at the National Conservatory of Music in New York. Dvorak himself used passages of Longfellow's narrative in his own work, which offered Coleridge-Taylor the impetus to attempt his own interpretation of the poem. He was moved by Longfellow's keen portrayal of racism and xenophobia, expressed through the tragic love story of Hiawatha and Minnehaha, which seemed to mirror his own relationship with eventual wife, Jessie Walmisley.

Du Bois and Coleridge-Taylor first met in July 1900 at the first Pan-African Congress in London, and the two men—one an American-born activist determined to bring together blacks of African descent across the diaspora and the other a British-born citizen of African descent with a deep sympathy for African American culture—soon thereafter became close friends. In *Darkwater* (1920) Du Bois fondly recounted the time he spent at Coleridge-Taylor's small British cottage, heralding the by-then deceased composer as "sweet-tempered, sympathetic comrade, always willing to help, never knowing how to refuse, generous with every nerve and fiber of his being."[32] The young, "bohemian" composer delighted Du Bois, who saw him as the embodiment of his cherished Talented Tenth sitting before him: he was well-educated (and in Europe no less), he reflected the cultural competence and social sophistication of his white counterparts, yet his compositions were imbued with Pan-African motifs.

Young Du Bois had left Berlin with a deep love of classical music; the compositions of Mozart, Beethoven, and Wagner were especially important to him. What is more Du Bois came to believe that music could be an important tool for racial uplift, and his affinity for European composers was tempered by an equally deep appreciation of African spirituals. Indeed, *The Souls of Black Folk* was configured to employ well-known African spirituals as metonyms for American racism, and according to Lawrence Schenbeck in his study of racial uplift in American music, Du Bois used *Hiawatha's*

Wedding Feast at the climax of the 1915 *Star of Ethiopia* pageant to drive home to his largely black audience that "a man of African descent could create something equal to [Handel's] *Messiah* or [Mendelssohn's] *Elijah*."[33] His use of Coleridge-Taylor's work in this context seems to suggest that uplift for the entire race would come when it could establish an artistic tradition that rivaled that of Europe. Of course Du Bois did not discount the importance of African spirituals as genuine artistic creation, nor did Coleridge-Taylor, as his *Negro Melodies* (1905) attests. Nonetheless, Du Bois's use of *Hiawatha* in this context perhaps clarifies what he meant by his nebulous use of "culture" in his 1903 essay.

Orchestras both in the United States and abroad adopted Coleridge-Taylor's compositions, and he spent time stateside visiting high-profile friends, including Du Bois, fellow composer Harry Burleigh, and poet Paul Lawrence Dunbar. In a December 1906 review of *Hiawatha* that appeared in the *Baltimore Afro-American*, the author hailed Coleridge-Taylor's "peculiar, unostentatious" composition. Coleridge-Taylor "is bringing before the world a distinct school of music," he wrote. "What Chopin did in his Polonaise . . . or what Dvorak has done to depict the pastoral life of the Hungarian . . . so has this modern composer [Coleridge-Taylor] brought to us a new message of race—a message of pathos, of suffering, of sacrifice and hope—transforming the humble, mournful and lowly songs of this race of mankind to Mastoso movements of a greater day and a brighter future for those of us here and those of us in Africa."[34] *Hiawatha* signaled to many the perfect cultural marriage between Africa and the West, and to black journalists it reflected the possibilities of the race globally. Coleridge-Taylor was a leader poised to enlighten the black masses with his art.

Coleridge-Taylor's Afro-British heritage seemed to support the myth of the Continent's greater appreciation of members of the diaspora as full and equal citizens. One journalist argued that were Coleridge-Taylor to have been American-born, he likely would not have enjoyed the opportunity to achieve the artistic and commercial success that he had as a British citizen: "The wonderful fact shown by Great Britain in treating with the race question has made it possible for the young genius who is the son of the romance between the Sierra Leone Negro and an English girl to pursue the career his talents entitle him to without encountering the obstacle that would here overshadow him in America."[35] Yet the Victorian bourgeois mentality of turn-of-the-century Britain prevented Coleridge-Taylor from being truly accepted, as preconceived notions of the "Dark Continent" influenced the ways in which he navigated British middle-class life. In 1892 the composer met Jessie Walmisley, a fellow Croydon-area musician and student at the Royal College of Music. The two struck up first a musical collaboration, then a friendship, and finally a romance, despite the fact that she was eight years older than he and British socialites frowned on interracial relationships.

Indeed, Walmisley's family intensely disliked the "young half-caste" and forbade her to marry him. As Coleridge-Taylor's friend and biographer, Jeffrey Green, recalled, the Walmisleys "considered their would-be son-in-law as being only a generation removed from the status of an African savage, and they tearfully warned their Jessie that if she married him in all probability he would inflict upon her strange shifts—perhaps take her to the 'Dark Continent,' compel her to live amongst his naked relations and wear no clothes."[36] The pair married anyway, on December 30, 1899.

The Walmisleys' fears about Coleridge-Taylor reflected just how *little* they understood about him or his lineage and how *much* imperial anxieties about the "Dark Continent" in the context of Britain's ongoing conflicts in South Africa clouded their impression of British citizens of color. Indeed, it was not uncommon for Coleridge-Taylor to be subjected to racially charged reviews in the British music press. One such review remarked, "We are apt to connect the musical attainments of men of colour with the primitive minstrelsy which relies for its support on clattering bones and throbbing banjo," but Coleridge-Taylor "had proved his ability to scale the loftier heights of the musical Parnassus and to meet on equal terms the best of our white composers."[37] The rhetoric employed by British writers to describe Coleridge-Taylor reeked of what might today be called "racial exceptionalism." Yet like Du Bois, some black journalists of the period allowed their romantic notions about European tolerance to obscure the more troubling realities of its imperial mind-set.

Coleridge-Taylor passed away in September 1912, at just thirty-six years old, of pneumonia, and his death affected his friend Du Bois for years to come. The *Crisis* dedicated two issues to commemoration of the composer. Coleridge-Taylor was named one of October's "Men of the Month," a column designed by Du Bois to promote members of his Talented Tenth. The article described the composer's work as "true Negro music," capturing the "melancholy beauty, barbaric color, charm of musical rhythm and vehement passion" of the African American folk song tradition.[38] Eight years after Coleridge-Taylor's premature passing, in his 1920 memoir, *Darkwater: Voices from Within the Veil*, Du Bois honored him again: this time, he spoke at length of the composer's leadership at the Royal College of Music, Trinity College, and the Guildhall School of Music. He described the effect that Coleridge-Taylor's success had on black citizens all over the world who also lived "within the veil." And he emphasized Coleridge-Taylor's time at the Royal College of Music as an example of the potential influence of liberal education. "What is the real lesson of the life of Coleridge-Taylor?" he asked. The answer, of course, was that black children must be provided with the educational opportunities to "be trained and guided and out of it as out of a huge reservoir must be lifted all genius, talent, and intelligence to serve all the world."[39]

In January 1913 Du Bois served as the keynote speaker for Samuel Coleridge-Taylor Choral Society's memorial concert at Boston's Jordan Hall, which was designed to honor the late composer. Among the performers were Coleridge-Taylor's longtime friend, Harry Burleigh, and a young tenor singer by the name of Roland Hayes. Hayes had began the decade by being unceremoniously dismissed from Du Bois's alma mater, Fisk University, by his mentor and Fisk's musical director, Jennie Robinson, who had felt slighted by his increasing interest in the Fisk Jubilee Singers. Robinson, a staunch traditionalist who had very little interest in the more modern composition of the Jubilee Singers, had financed young Hayes's education at Fisk herself. Hayes took the dismissal as a sign of fate, and instead of fighting for reentry into the institution, he relocated to Boston, where he endeavored to continue his formal education under the direction of Arthur J. Hubbard.[40] By 1913 he had begun collaborating with Burleigh, who suggested that the Samuel Coleridge-Taylor tribute would be a good opportunity for exposure.

Within ten years, Hayes was an international star. Relentless touring, promotion, and recording had finally paid off. In spring of 1921, Hayes was invited to perform at Buckingham Palace, where he sang compositions by Handel, Schumann, and Dvorak in addition to his beloved African spirituals, which "he [had] introduced to the European public and with which he [had] so deeply impressed them."[41] The following year he signed a recording contract with England's Vocalion Records after unsuccessful attempts at signing with record labels stateside. Hayes and his accompanist, Lawrence Brown, recorded six spirituals with Vocalion, which sold well in both Europe and the United States.[42]

Capitalizing on his success touring Europe, Hayes returned to Boston in fall of 1923 to accept an invitation to perform with the Boston Symphony Orchestra. The concert had been the brainchild of the BSO's maestro Pierre Monteaux, who had attended Hayes's Paris concert in 1922. Boston's elite eagerly anticipated Hayes's performance. The *Boston Globe* looked forward to hearing the race performer who had "won the highest praise . . . everywhere, not just as a Negro singer, but as one of the few really fine tenors to be heard in this generation, regardless of racial and national considerations."[43] Together with the BSO's general manager and Hayes's mentor, Hubbard, the concert was set for November 17, 1923. That evening Hayes took the stage and performed a program that included an aria from Mozart's *Cosi fan tutte* juxtaposed with spirituals "Go Down Moses" and "Bye and Bye," each arranged by his collaborators Burleigh and Brown, respectively. Hayes became the first black soloist to perform stateside with a major symphony orchestra. He had effectively erased the color line, at least for one evening, of the American classical music stage.

Black weeklies all over the country quickly became enamored of the tenor, and in covering him they emulated the same "Talented Tenth" rhetoric that they had applied twenty years earlier to coverage of Coleridge-Taylor. The *Pittsburgh Courier* was particularly taken with Hayes, who in 1925 was awarded the NAACP's highest honor, the Spingarn Medal: "Mr. Hayes is known as an artist. . . . But Mr. Hayes is more than an artist. He is a benefactor. Everywhere he sings he makes two impressions: one as an artist and another as a gentleman of culture and bearing. . . . We are deeply grateful to Mr. Hayes for his contribution. We need him and that sorely. . . . His place, attained and held at great sacrifice, offers the world an illustration of our possibilities. We shall owe Mr. Hayes more than we appreciate for his contribution to our advancement."[44] The stamp of approval awarded to Hayes by European audiences signaled to American audiences the beauty of African artistry, and as a result the entire race was uplifted. The *Courier*'s J. A. Rogers was especially fond of Hayes, whom he described as "one of the most charming personalities" he had met in his life who acted as "an ambassador not only to a single European nation, but an ambassador to all of Europe."[45]

Hayes's notable accomplishments on the classical stage, punctuated by his BSO performance, caught Du Bois's attention, and the two men formed a friendship that was mutually beneficial: Du Bois agreed to promote Hayes's recordings in the *Crisis*, and in return Hayes would use his star power to draw attention to Du Bois's revived Pan-African Congress. Hayes also must have attracted Du Bois, a consummate classical music fan, with his command of German, Italian, and French arias and frequent performance of Coleridge-Taylor's *Hiawatha*. Like Coleridge-Taylor he represented a functional marriage between European culture and authentic African spirituality and exemplified Du Bois's Talented Tenth ethos. The popularity of entertainers who eschewed their obligation as race representatives threatened to derail the uplift scheme that Du Bois had previously outlined. After all Bert Williams and Jack Johnson were hardly agents of racial uplift in Du Bois's terms. So when Roland Hayes began to sell out music halls across the country, Du Bois could not have been more pleased by this clear evidence of race progress.

Uplifters versus New Negroes

The Talented Tenth Renaissance that Coleridge-Taylor and Hayes represented was tempered by the increasing urgency felt in black press newsrooms across the country to address the avalanche of racialized violence that spread through urban communities beginning in the summer of 1919. The black press's networked journalism model helped to spread the news of Jim Crow horrors beyond a local level to attain national reach. "The Negro press continually focuses nation-wide attention on the discriminations and injustices of the American caste system," pointed out Metz Lochard. "And these discriminations are factual, specific, and horrible. They happen every day. It is sensational news; and the Negro press treats it as such."[46] Sensationalism's key features—strong language, bold headlines, and the use of visuals—helped to convey to the public the horrors of lynching and other forms of racialized violence that plagued black communities throughout the country.

With northern migration, the racialized violence common in the South erupted in the North and the Midwest. Full-scale rioting in New Orleans (1900); Springfield, Ohio (1904); Greensburg, Indiana, and Atlanta, Georgia (1906); Springfield, Illinois (1908); and Philadelphia and Chester, Pennsylvania (1917) all prefigured the explosion of urban, racial violence that gripped the country after the war ended. Riots in Washington DC; Omaha, Nebraska; Longview, Texas; and Knoxville, Tennessee, during the summer of 1919 (the "Red Summer") signified to many blacks just how little they were welcome in the "Promised Land" of the North. Cities in the North became divided as economic competition for industrial jobs, political clout, and access to housing coupled with segregated religious, entertainment, and social life divided white and black working-class communities. As Felecia Jones Ross and Joseph McKerns have demonstrated, the *Chicago Defender*—the very newspaper that had launched the "Great Northern Drive" campaign—"started to reflect the breadth and depth of the nation's and the city's racial discrimination almost to a point where the paper began to be reconsidering the benefits of migration."[47]

Historian Jonathan Coit's work on the 1919 Chicago riot charts a shift in rhetoric from uplift to collective action espoused by black leaders in the city who viewed the spectacular violence enacted on black urban communities as a revised form of lynching. Coit argues that the Chicago race riot that took place during July 1919 was a turning point for many of the city's black leaders away from the politics of respectability, including the *Defender*'s influential editor, Robert S. Abbott. The riot began with the murder of a young black boy, Eugene Williams, at the Twenty-Ninth Street Beach on Lake Michigan by a white man, George Stauber, who resented the child's presence on the beach. During the race riot, blacks around the city took up arms to defend themselves against white aggressors; in many cases those who took up arms were returning veterans from the war who were disgusted by the Jim Crow treatment they received upon their return from battle. In 1925 the *New York Amsterdam News* pointed out that "the unfair attitude of the American white man towards his brother in black—that same brother who went to the front lines of France with a cheer and a hope that the very thing of which [the newspaper was] about to speak would be a thing of the past upon his return to the land for which he so readily and willingly gave of his blood and of his treasure."[48] "The warlike nature of American race relations in the aftermath of World War I," writes historian Chad Williams, "prompted many black veterans to question the meaning of their service and seek new strategies for achieving racial justice."[49]

This new consciousness led many African Americans to turn away from organizations such as the NAACP and the Urban League for support and instead to seek alternate perspectives that focused increasingly on the economic exploitation of black workers and the militarization of resistance to Jim Crow practices.[50] Veterans took on leadership positions in some of the most radical black movements of the period, including the League for Democracy, the African Blood Brotherhood, and Marcus Garvey's United Negro Improvement Association. "Black armed defense in the riot," observes Coit, "was not an unfortunate necessity but a trial by fire of a new anti-racist consciousness."[51]

According to black press historian Richard Digby-Junger, 1919 marked a "radical wave" for black publications.[52] In particular the *Messenger*, A. Philip Randolph and Chandler Owen's socialist publication, began to build a steady readership. The *Messenger* "fought American officialdom and the 'Old Crowd' among blacks that allied with them," paying especially critical attention to Du

Bois, whom Randolph and Owen saw as "reactionary, opportunistic, and insensitive to class struggles among blacks and workers who opposed the establishment."[53] World War I soldiers and returning veterans "appropriated the black press as their voice, and in the process jolted readers with accounts of their wartime experience."[54] With the additional voices of black veterans disenchanted with undignified service positions, lack of training, and antagonism by white soldiers abroad and racial violence and Jim Crow discrimination at home, black press publications began to reflect a new, more militant ethos that eventually replaced their emphasis on racial uplift and respectability. This shift is reflected in the evolution of the *Defender*'s response to the riots. At first black leaders, including Abbott, blamed lower-class members of *both* races for the city's unrest, but soon it became apparent that the narrative emerging in mainstream newspapers placed the blame for the bloodshed squarely on the shoulders of the black citizens who participated in it, despite the fact that blacks were disproportionately victimized during the riot. Black community members were the victims in two-thirds of the deaths and injuries recorded as a result of the violence. The majority of the property damage took place in the Black Belt, the city's largest black neighborhood. Accordingly, Abbott pivoted coverage of the riots to emphasize the role that whites played in enacting violence against innocent blacks, and in his editorials he began to argue "that black men in the Chicago riot were called to defend their status as citizens entitled to equal treatment."[55]

This "New Negro" mentality was spurred by migration, Irish and Russian revolutionary struggles, the growth of the black press, and the political mobilization of returning veterans. Abbott, Du Bois, and the editors of the *Messenger* all came to see the New Negro as any black citizen "willing to sacrifice anything to strike against the structures, institutions, and people who used white supremacy to oppress and exploit black people," Coit argues.[56] Political mobilization became married to other aspects of black culture, including literature and entertainment. Alain Locke's *New Negro* anthology highlighted the generational differences between black authors of the Reconstruction generation who focused only on narratives that portrayed the best, most uplifting qualities of the race and the new generation of writers who focused on the realist dimensions of black experience, many of whom either had their work reprinted in black magazines and weeklies *or* were regular contributors to the publications.

Accordingly, coverage of black celebrities shifted to reflect new modes of collective representation, and uplift no longer seemed like an adequate path to liberation.

The Practical Limitations of Uplift

The New Negro ethos was an awkward fit for Roland Hayes, whose childhood in the South influenced his adult attitudes toward American racism as "just the way it was" and who spent the majority of his career catering to white, rather than black, audiences. Nor did it fit fledgling stage actor Charles Gilpin, a working-class man from Richmond who stumbled into acting in the second decade of the century only to find himself center stage in one of the largest Renaissance-era Broadway productions of the 1920s: Eugene O'Neill's *Emperor Jones*.

Gilpin began his career on the vaudeville stage in 1896, and after performing a series of odd jobs that included being a printer and a reporter, he soon began to perform with the Fisk Jubilee Singers in 1903. He then toured with the Williams and Walker Company's *Abyssinia* production from 1905 to 1906 before his big break came with O'Neill's *Emperor Jones*.

In *Emperor Jones*, which debuted on Broadway in 1920, Eugene O'Neill crafted the "modern primitive" character Brutus Jones, a Pullman porter who escapes to an unnamed Caribbean Island to evade prosecution for a murder he committed in the United States. Once on the island, Jones convinces the naive natives that he is a "magician," and he becomes ruler. Corrupted by his newfound power, Jones abuses his subjects, who plan a coup d'état against him. He flees into the jungle only to confront demons of his own past; ultimately, he is hunted down by his subjects and shot to death. Jones was a complicated figure, and a far cry from the comedic portrayal of black men that Broadway had become accustomed to with Bert Williams's work. Upon its debut some black weeklies quickly became discouraged by O'Neill's anti-uplift antihero, Jones. "Nowhere in the entire play," complained the *Afro-American's* Edgar M. Gray, "is the Negro made to feel that he is capable of respectable behavior or high attainments. One might see the play all one's life and not gather anything sensible from seeing it."[57] Gray particularly resented O'Neill's discursive treatment of the race. Any actor who played Brutus Jones, he charged, "was made to speak the most ignorant, improper and ungrammatical English, and to use such degrading and humiliating phrases about his race."[58] According to historian David Levering Lewis, to O'Neill and his peers, the black subject represented "the only American supposedly still ruled by his id, a modern primitive wearing a loose-fitting super-ego."[59] Nonetheless, O'Neill's willingness to open the dramatic Broadway stage to black actors made the role of Brutus Jones a highly coveted opportunity for black theater actors. As Gwendolyn Bennett of the *Opportunity* noted, "I am willing to wager that for many a round year Negro actors will be spoken of in terms of their ability to do O'Neill's hectored character."[60] Indeed Bert Williams reportedly desired a chance at the role, which to his chagrin went to Gilpin.

Despite how high-profile his dramatic turn as Brutus Jones was, Gilpin hardly had the pedigree of the typical member of the Talented Tenth. Born in Richmond, Virginia, in 1878, he had a decidedly working-class upbringing. After the death of both of his parents, he was raised by his uncle Joseph Gilpin, and though he reportedly dropped out of high school to pursue a career in theater, it is likelier that the financial demands of his uncle's household forced the young Gilpin to leave school and enter the workforce.[61]

Black journalists framed his success in the controversial drama as "one of the greatest demonstrations of what perseverance, study, and education will do for a person."[62] The black press delighted at Gilpin's portrayal of Jones; the *Afro-American* called his performance "a masterpiece of histronism" and "the greatest currently on view in the metropolis," while the *Defender* lauded it as "a most remarkable dramatization of the psychology of fear." The *Tribune* proclaimed that the performance "marks an epoch in the progress of the colored people and should be an inspiration to the youth of the race."[63] G. Grant Williams of the *Tribune* called Gilpin "the man who [had] made history for the race, and enlightened the white people considerably."[64] Despite its displeasure with O'Neill's characterization of Jones, the *Afro-American* counted Gilpin's interpretation of the hectored character as a source of racial uplift: "George Jean Nathan—generally regarded as the foremost theatrical critic in America—having recently declared that he [Charles Gilpin] is 'the most important dramatist that the American theatre has produced': Therefore, it should be a source of soul-stirring pride to colored America, and written by the nation's greatest playwright has as its star, a man of their race."[65] Gilpin encapsulated the highbrow "best of the race" ethos espoused by Du Bois, who rewarded him with a "Men of the Month" profile in the February 1921 issue of the *Crisis*. Gilpin received the NAACP's highest honor, the Spingarn Medal, that June in a ceremony in Detroit. Previous award recipients had included biologist E. E. Just, Liberian diplomat Colonel Charles Young, composer Harry Burleigh, critic William Stanley Brathwaite, Archibald Grimke, and Du Bois. When Gilpin received the award, the *Defender* proclaimed, "The choice of Charles Gilpin as the recipient of the Spingarn Medal, awarded annually by Major Joel Spingarn through the National Association for the Advancement of Colored People, for the most distinguished contribution of the year by an outstanding member of the Race will be most heartily approved by the general public."[66] The award was a tangible acknowledgment of the positive influence its recipient had on his race, but it was also a marker of elitism; for instance, when it was awarded to Burleigh, the *Philadelphia Tribune* noted that Burleigh's composition of "Deep River" was "high class."[67] Gilpin's Spingarn Medal win was an important marker of distinction not only for him but also for the gradually increasing influence of entertainment on black leadership during this period. Hayes received the award in 1924, and *Green Pastures* star Richard Harrison in 1931.

The year 1921 was pivotal for Gilpin. In addition to the Spingarn Medal, he became the first black actor invited to the White House, where he received compliments from President Harding, though it was unclear if the commander in chief had actually seen Gilpin perform.[68] The Drama League of New York joined in raining praise on Gilpin, naming him one of the ten best artists who had made valuable contributions to American theater in 1921. However, instead of an invitation to their annual gala, the league decided to send Gilpin merely a letter of congratulations—as the only black actor to be honored, the league was concerned that his attendance at dinner might offend its white patrons. Members of the theater industry, including O'Neill, George Cram Cooke, and Gilda Varesi, were outraged by the league's snub of Gilpin and issued a statement refusing to attend the gala if he was not included. In it they argued, "If there is any place on earth where race ought not to be considered, it is in the church and in art. God is God and genius is genius, and race ought not to make any difference."[69]

Gilpin had been Jim Crowed by the very organization that sought to honor him.

As a compromise, Gilpin agreed to "drop in [and] pay his respects" at the event but declined to stay for dinner, lest he make any of the white attendees feel uncomfortable in his presence. He told the *New York World*, "As for the Drama League—well, I don't know its members very well, and I do not wish by any means to force an association."[70] A. Philip Randolph and Chandler Owen's socialist publication, the *Messenger*, condemned Gilpin for allowing himself to be Jim Crowed. "If [Gilpin] simply wants to confine this 'personal acquaintance' qualification test to Negroes," wrote the anonymous *Messenger* author, "then, he will receive nothing but bouquets and blessings from those philanthropic white people who stand for the Negro remaining in 'his place' and the time-serving, hat-in-hand, me-to-boss Negro who descants piously on the danger of 'rocking the boat.'" Later in the article, the author pegged Gilpin's attitude as a "slave psychology."[71]

The representation of black culture by white playwrights should have been a watershed moment for black performers, but Gilpin's experience with the Drama League was a harsh reminder of the *real* Jim Crow experience. Whites may have taken an interest in Brutus Jones, but they showed little respect for the man who played him. The controversy over Gilpin's nonresponse to the Drama

League snub was emblematic of the rift taking place between Du Bois, for whom racial uplift lay in representational politics, and the more radical leaders in Harlem, tired of these commonplace insults and slights.

Gilpin's insistence that his art not be overshadowed by Jim Crow racism was a difficult position to take. Rattled by the undue attention this event was drawing to him (Gilpin always claimed that it was his art, not his "person," that he most wanted to promote), the actor finally relented and attended the dinner, with actress Gilda Varesi in tow. The *Afro-American* deemed Gilpin the "hero" of the evening.[72]

It seems, however, that Gilpin simply could not win. In 1924 O'Neill dismissed him over a disagreement with the use of the word "n——r" in the screenplay. Gilpin wanted the word removed; O'Neill refused. The 1925 revival of *Emperor* starring Paul Robeson in Gilpin's place was met with rave reviews. Will Anthony Madden, special correspondent to the *Courier*, gushed, "Robeson's interpretation of the role left nothing to be desired. To begin with, Robeson has the physical build that makes him look the part of just what the character portrays and with that powerful, rich voice and the ease with which he acts, I must say the theatre has gained a great deal by the addition of this sterling and promising actor to its ranks."[73] Madden's review of Robeson's performance typified black theater critics' initial reaction to Robeson; the actor "left nothing to be desired," which included Gilpin, who was quickly discarded by black journalists. Robeson's interpretation of the character even silenced negative reactions to the script itself. He signified on Jones, rewriting the "brutish" character as a symbol of liberated black (masculine) identity.

Despite how the black press had feted him previously, Gilpin was quickly eclipsed by Robeson's shadow, and though he attempted to transition into film, his personal demons prevented him from attaining the level of success he had enjoyed as Brutus Jones. Reports of antics on the set of Universal's *Uncle Tom's Cabin* and *Hearts in Dixie* resulted in Gilpin's dismissal from both of those film projects.[74] Gilpin became "a star for the moment, a person whom the fickle public will worship for a while."[75]

Gilpin was not the only uplifter to find himself at odds with an increasingly activist group of black press journalists. In December 1927 the *Courier*'s J. A. Rogers traveled to Paris—a trip arranged by Lawrence Brown—to interview Roland Hayes. Rogers was a fan of Hayes, and he was thrilled with the prospect of finally meeting the celebrated tenor. "Hayes is as delightful a man to meet off the stage as on," Rogers wrote, "very thoughtful and cultured, with ideals apparently as vigorous and untarnished as when he started his marvelous career."[76] Despite Rogers's deference to Hayes, the tenor approached their conversation with great trepidation as Rogers cautiously turned to the topic of race activism. Hayes fretted that the journalist expected him to "make some pronouncement on the race question."[77] Hayes was particularly concerned about his image to both his white and black fans; he had kept his affair with a married Austrian countess and the child resulting from their relationship a closely guarded secret for fear of becoming "another Jack Johnson."[78] Just as he did not want to alienate his white fans, he had no interest in alienating his black ones either. A shrewd businessman and self-promoter, Hayes cared about his bottom line, not racial uplift.

In the prestigious southern American concert halls in which he often performed, black Americans were subjected to segregated seating practices, which frustrated classical music fans eager to see the tenor perform. The *Defender* took Hayes to task over an Atlanta performance in December 1925, in which he performed in front of a starkly segregated audience. The *Defender*, in a particularly scathing article, noted, "[In Atlanta] the seats were governed by the applicant! Yet, Roland Hayes was the same color in Atlanta that he was here [in Chicago]. . . . [In Atlanta] we had white people occupying the main floor seats and boxes and our people sitting in corners of the balcony and gallery."[79] In northern theaters de facto segregation often took the form of preferential ticket schemes that, in cities such as New York and Boston, favored symphony subscribers and donors—a luxury often out of reach for the average, middle-class black family.

Tensions came to a head in January 1926, when Hayes refused to take the stage at Baltimore's Lyric Theatre, caving to pressure from the *Baltimore Afro-American* and the local chapter of the NAACP to take a stand against segregation in one of the country's most diverse cities. Hayes, in the days before the concert, scrambled to contact Kate Wilson-Green of the Wilson Green Agency—who had arranged the concert—to demand that the evening's black ticketholders be accommodated on the main floor of the theater and refusing to perform otherwise. Upon his arrival in Baltimore's Penn Station, Hayes had been greeted by protesters carrying signs that said "Roland 'Uncle Tom' Hayes" and "Jim Crow Roland"; the protest had been organized by the NAACP and several prominent city ministers who resented the performer's acceptance of Jim Crow practices. Though Hayes claimed that he did not intend to perform, he and Lawrence Brown arrived at the theater that afternoon, where he was met with further protest.[80]

When Hayes arrived at the venue for the performance, he was apparently assured that the accommodations had been made, and after thirty minutes of uncertainty, he took the stage to perform. The arrangements that were actually made, however, were unacceptable; according to the *Afro-American*, black spectators were seated "in the balcony mainly and on the left side of the first floor. This [was] the same arrangement that [had] prevailed at the Atlanta, Ga., concert."[81] Hayes made himself unavailable for interviews in the days after the Lyric show. Whether he understood the seating arrangement before he took the stage is unclear from the surviving evidence.

Black weeklies were divided on whether Hayes should have performed that evening, and their editorial stances were augmented by a virulent response from readers. Some newspapers, like the *Defender*, praised Hayes for attempting to take a stand against Jim Crowism (and of course, the *Defender* credited itself with Hayes's heroic actions), while others, like the *Pittsburgh Courier*, charged that it was the job of Hayes's manager—not Hayes—to ensure that the seating arrangements were corrected. The *Afro-American* dedicated two columns' worth of space in its January 16 issue to readers' thoughts on the controversy, which ranged in sentiment from "Hayes should not have betrayed his race for gold" to "I am in sympathy with Roland Hayes' course at the theatre Thursday night."[82]

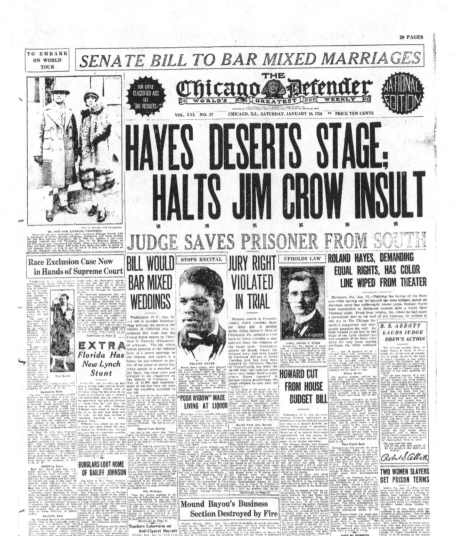

Fig. 3. The January 16, 1926, edition of the *Defender* illustrates its integrationist tendencies by celebrating as civil rights pioneers *both* Roland Hayes, who stood up against racist seating practices, and Judge James Drew, a white jurist who fought against southern lynch law. *Chicago Defender*, January 16, 1926, front page. *Black Studies Center*, Chadwyck-Healey, ProQuest.

The *Defender*, which had come down hard on Hayes's segregated Atlanta concert just months earlier, featured two civil rights heroes on its January 16 front page: Hayes, who, the headline proclaimed, "Deserts Stage; Halts Jim Crow Insult," and Pittsburgh judge James B. Drew, whom editor Robert Abbott personally praised in a front page editorial for refusing to extradite a black man, Sandy Huser, back to North Carolina for violating its liquor laws before fleeing to Pennsylvania.[83] Both men, in the *Defender*'s view, had dealt blows to southern Jim Crowism—Judge Drew, a white jurist who had prevented lynch law from doling out injustice to Huser, and Hayes, for "fighting battles of his race even while carving out for himself the most brilliant career an American tenor has achieved in recent years."[84] These lead stories about Jim Crow activism also represented the *Defender*'s integrationist tendencies.[85]

The *Pittsburgh Courier* absolved Hayes of any responsibility to take action against Jim Crowism that evening, arguing that because his art made such a significant contribution to the race, there was no need for him to also act as an activist on behalf of "the masses." The *Courier* asserted, "For further redress it is the duty of the masses to contend for their rights in public places and through the medium of the law." The article continued, "The work of a public artist is a great nerve strain. Mr. Hayes should not refuse to sing to an audience under any of these conditions."[86]

The *Baltimore Afro-American* and its syndicate paper, the *Washington Afro-American*, stood alone in their condemnation of Hayes's behavior at the Lyric. In a scathing article derisively titled "Rolling Hayes," the author criticized Hayes for disavowing his place "in the hall of fame by refusing to sing at all, but he passed it up and went away with a $2,000 check and the shreds of his self-respect." Hayes, a child of the Jim Crow South, "illustrated the old adage—it is easier to get a man out of the country than the country out of the man."[87] Though he had an ardent interest in Pan-Africanism, had spent time in more "racially enlightened" Europe, and dreamed of turning the plantation on which his mother was enslaved into a school for black children, Hayes routinely performed in front of segregated audiences all over the country. That was the reality of Hayes's experience as a race performer—he had been raised to understand Jim Crowism as "just the way things were" and to work within its broken system.[88] As a classical performer whose ticket-holding audience was largely white, not black, he had little choice but to voice his grievances and then capitulate. As one *Afro-American* reader pointed out, "It must be considered that Roland Hayes was started in his career by white people. That consideration probably influenced his decision to sing under the circumstance."[89]

So when a year later Rogers sat before him in Paris poised to ask about the material conditions of black citizens, Hayes was undoubtedly cautious. Rogers tried to put the singer at ease: "I assured him that in my opinion no sensible Negro expected [race activism] of him: that I thought it would spoil his role of artist; and that besides it was necessary to leave some fields to us writers and speakers and others of lesser brilliance. I assured him that at each appearance he was doing more to break down race prejudice than a large number of us together were able to do by writing and speaking."[90] Rogers's supportive words were enough to mollify Hayes, and the two spent the rest of their time together discussing Hayes's plans to trace the roots of the African spirituals he regularly performed and his plans to turn his mother's old plantation into Angelmo, a school for the arts. The Lyric controversy did little to infringe on Hayes's popularity; after all it was white audiences, not black ones, who had the economic resources to truly keep him in demand. Over time, though, Hayes fell victim to his unwillingness to harness modern technologies to market his art. He refused to perform on radio broadcasts, despite the fact that Paul Robeson had done so; Hayes felt that the sound quality of radio "cheapened his art."[91]

Charles Gilpin and Roland Hayes were not "entertainers"; they were "artists." This distinction was very clearly drawn first by Du Bois, who suggested that the accumulation of cultural capital would lead to the liberation of black communities, and was later echoed by black press journalists who subscribed to the same classist tendencies that formed the foundation of the uplifters generally. However, uplift could accomplish only so much, so when Gilpin and Hayes failed to act collectively on behalf of the black fans who supported them, they were quickly vilified in the pages of the black press.

Racial Solidarity as the One True Uplift

"What does an artist owe to his race?" The answer, at least for many black press journalists who witnessed the hostility and violence that greeted black veterans returning from the Great War, was clear: the courage to stand up when they were undermined, segregated, or disrespected for the color of their skin. The representational and the real began to quickly blur together during this period as optics became overshadowed by calls to action.

Language describing British composer Samuel Coleridge-Taylor, actor Charles Gilpin, and singer Roland Hayes as uplifters ties in directly with Du Bois's Talented Tenth—the notion that a select few noteworthy individuals would be responsible for the collective success of all blacks. These individuals seemed to most explicitly meet the criteria that Du Bois laid out for "leaders of thought and missionaries of culture among their people," and they traded in the most valuable type of cultural capital—that which encompassed both authentic Pan-African values and mastery of the European classical tradition. Despite their almost nonexistent relationship with him, black weeklies joined Du Bois in his celebration of racial uplift, adopting Talented Tenth rhetoric to frame these individuals as representations of the "possibilities" inherent for other members of the race. However, racial uplift mattered little if it was not accompanied by an activist's mind-set; it is clear in coverage of both the Drama League and the Lyric Theatre controversies that black journalists had begun to adopt the rhetoric of the New Negro, as migration, the end of the first World War, and an upturn in urban racial violence radically changed how black citizens organized collective action against Jim Crow.

4

The Mythologizing of Black Celebrities

"When Mr. Charles P. Buchanan told me about Cab Calloway, and said he was worth looking up," wrote Floyd Calvin in a January 1931 *Courier* article, "I was skeptical." Calloway, the young, energetic bandleader of the Missourians, was poised to take over Duke Ellington's residency at the Cotton Club, and his distinctive vocal style—soon known as simply "hi-de-ho'ing" in the press—set him apart from other big bandleaders of the time: Louis Armstrong, Fletcher Henderson, and Duke Ellington. "My feature articles are reserved for high-powered people," continued Calvin, "and I wasn't sure an orchestra leader could make the grade."[1] By 1933 Calloway was reportedly an even more recognizable figure in the black community than W. E. B. Du Bois, and Calloway's ascendance to fame mirrored that of several notable black jazz musicians who had gotten their starts playing dingy city clubs along the Mississippi northbound to Chicago, New York, and Philadelphia.

Migration and urbanization had encouraged black citizens to come together and publicly celebrate their cultural heritage, as evidenced by the popularity of Chicago's Stroll district and the clubs and cabarets of Harlem, New York. The "Harlem Renaissance" comprised a group of black intellectuals, artists, and activists who led a cultural movement that foregrounded the experiences of urban blacks. They encouraged a renewed interest in their own African roots, replacing questions of respectability with proclamations of race consciousness. The work of authors Langston Hughes, Zora Neale Hurston, Jessie Fauset, Wallace Thurman, Claude McKay, and James Weldon Johnson shaped the ethos of the movement. They emphasized the artistic value of their work, often seeking to capture the multiplicities of life in Harlem—whether they constituted "positive" representations of black citizens in the eyes of white America or not.

Jazz music provided the ideal accompaniment to this milieu. It married the modernity of urban life in the 1920s with the "primitivism" of early African American musical traditions, including Baptist gospel music, ragtime, and blues, originating in the black section of New Orleans in the late 1890s.[2] In an interview with the *Defender*'s Ollie Stewart, bandleader Noble Sissle described jazz music as a "jungle symphony": "There is a certain element of life in [jazz music]—religion, romance, tragedy, faith, hope and primitive abandon—brought together and paid for at a tremendous price."[3] The influence of Sissle's dear friend, bandleader and World War I hero James Reese Europe, whose ragtime compositions were wildly popular before his untimely death in 1919, was undeniable, but jazz also borrowed heavily from the blues tradition of singers like Ma Rainey, Mamie Smith, and Bessie Smith. The syncopated sounds that traveled north along the Mississippi River from the nightclubs of New Orleans and Memphis to Harlem, and Chicago appealed to a broader, more urban, and increasingly modern fan base. By 1924 both Duke Ellington and Louis Armstrong were active in Harlem's burgeoning music scene; in 1931 Ellington went on tour, and his gig at the Cotton Club was taken over by the young Cab Calloway. Harlem soon became the epicenter of black celebrity—a place where celebrity, publicity, and journalism collided in ways that mirrored the more institutionalized structures of mainstream celebrity journalism and, for the first time, sounded a lot like it, too.

The celebrities discussed in this chapter are "stars": performers with highly orchestrated public personas controlled by managers and public-relations professionals who help to develop a strategic "narrative of stardom" that appeals to their fans by making them seem both relatable and exemplary. Major changes took place for black performers in the 1920s. Jazz blew the doors open for performers hoping to attract mass audiences of both races, and the style and tone of the genre challenged black journalists who remained concerned about the optics of positive representation. Making stars "marketable" to mass audiences became more and more common as the decade wore on, and entertainment coverage grew exponentially during this period.

Coverage of celebrity gossip ranging from the mundane (Calloway's favorite foods) to the salacious (Hayes's affair with a married countess) is the kind most often maligned by critics who dismiss popular culture as dreck, yet as previous cultural histories of celebrity culture have shown, these reports served a critical purpose for black readers. By 1930 it was commonplace to read celebrity profiles that adhered to a carefully cultivated "success myth" that was designed to create both closeness and distance between star and audience. Creating an "imagined intimacy" between star and fan was critically important to the success of black press newspapers. Eager for an escape from the bleak reality of the Depression, fans hungered to know the most intimate details possible about their favorite celebrities. These details humanized the otherwise untouchable stars, lending hope to black fans around the country that they too might experience the "American dream." Yet the parasocial relationships promoted in the pages of the expanding entertainment sections of these newspapers were journalistic constructions, not authentic connections, and they obfuscated the *real* experiences of black celebrities—and black communities—under Jim Crow.

From "Lift Us Higher" to "Just One of Us"

As the realist aesthetic of the Harlem Renaissance threatened to overshadow the work of the uplifters, Du Bois began in his writings to directly address the work of race performers in their role as representatives of the race, transposing the ideals of the Talented Tenth into "propaganda" designed to promote the progress of the race at any cost. At first thrilled at the notion of a "Talented Tenth Renaissance," Du Bois soon began to resent Renaissance writers' investment in "ghetto realism," arguing that it would lead to the exacerbation of racial stereotyping and resentment. In his "Criteria of Negro Art" (1926), Du Bois argues that "all art is propaganda, and ever must be."[4] The idea of "art as propaganda" was shared by other black elites. "With propaganda plays I think wonders may be done for the cause of the Negro," wrote Willis Richardson in the June 1923 issue of the *Messenger*. "On the stage his desire and need for social equality (without which there is no other equality), for equality before the law, equality of opportunity and all his other desires may be shown."[5] However, not everyone agreed that racial propaganda belonged in entertainment. Writing for the *Opportunity*, Rowena Woodham Jelliffee argued, "The theatre [should not] be considered a medium of propaganda. Undue concern about putting the best racial foot foremost should be forgotten. I believe that the Negro artist achieves in the field of drama in about the proportion to which he is able to escape the bonds of race consciousness. Then is he able, having acquired the necessary perspective, to portray and interpret the life and mood of his race beautifully and truly."[6] Debates about the optics of blacks' participation in entertainment were mired in a liminal space between highbrow culture as espoused by Du Bois and the "ghetto realism" of the Renaissance writers. This disparity between the functions of black-centered art and performance led to discord within the *Crisis*. In 1926 Jessie Fauset, a regular contributor, a fixture in the Harlem literary scene, and Du Bois's longtime friend, ceased contributing to the publication altogether.

Despite these critiques Harlem in the 1920s was the locus of black-centered cultural production as writers and poets, editors and journalists, and singers, actors, and athletes congregated there at the exclusive parties thrown by Madam A'Leila Walker and in cabarets and nightclubs all over the neighborhood. Prestigious Harlemites hobnobbed together in speakeasies and cabarets, where literary giants such as James Weldon Johnson, Carl Van Vechten, Fannie Hurst, and even Du Bois crossed paths with entertainers on a nightly basis. "In Harlem," wrote author Rudolph Fisher in a 1925 *Atlantic Monthly* short story, "The City of Refuge," "black was white."[7]

The myth of Harlem was not perpetuated for—as Langston Hughes put it—"ordinary Negroes" but was rather perpetuated by middle-class blacks and interested whites who traveled to nightclubs in Harlem to experience "black bohemia." In hindsight it is reasonable to suggest that the emergence of black culture in white American consciousness that took place then was the product of the "repackaging of people of color" by white writers and playwrights such as Carl Van Vechten, e. e. cummings, Fannie Hurst, and Eugene O'Neill.[8] Fisher, again writing about Harlem in his 1928 novel *The Walls of Jericho*, described the three types of "fays" (whites) who frequented the district: those who came simply to enjoy themselves without considering too deeply the question of race; the "professional uplifters," allies and activists of black organizations; and "the newcomers, drawn by Harlem's legendary license, hence giggling and ogling with barely concealed racism."[9] In fact one of the most famous cabarets associated with the movement—the Cotton Club—did not allow black patrons; only black performers gained entry. The artistic output of the Harlem Renaissance—which manifested itself not only in literature but also in theater and music—"could be packaged and delivered to those less daring [whites], who were content to experience Harlem vicariously," wrote historian Cary Wintz.[10] The most popular novel set in Harlem to emerge at the time was even written by a white man, Carl Van Vechten, in 1926.

Meanwhile, ordinary black citizens dealt with slum-like living conditions and few real economic opportunities. Harlem led the rest of the city in vice, crime, juvenile delinquency, and drug addiction.[11] This latter portrait of Harlem—as slum-like, depressed, and oppressive—was all but absent from the pages of black newspapers and magazines, which chose instead to focus on the burgeoning nightlife and entertainment culture as their primary version of life there. It seemed as though black newspapers fed into the fantasy of glamorous Harlem.

The modest gains that the black community enjoyed during the period immediately following World War I in the form of increased education and economic opportunities, new political leadership, and a more prominent place in entertainment were replaced in the early years of the 1930s by hardship and hopelessness. In November 1932, when some 13 million Americans were unemployed, Franklin Delano Roosevelt was elected and immediately instituted a series of government programs, the New Deal, to bring recovery, relief, and reform to the American public. The Great Depression impacted nearly every American citizen, but none as virulently as those in the black community. Historians have suggested that the economic downturn for black communities began as early as 1926.[12] Manual-labor jobs, which had been particularly steady employment for black workers after World War I, were lost to whites who were forced to downgrade their employment. By 1932 unemployment among black and African Americans was 50 percent in the South and in the large urban areas of the North (Harlem, Chicago, and Philadelphia). More black citizens migrated to the North during this period in search of public assistance—which was almost impossible for blacks to obtain in the South—but found little reprieve.[13]

Though many black urban weeklies had endorsed Roosevelt for president, they resented his reticence to go all-in on racial justice initiatives. Like Woodrow Wilson before him, Roosevelt pandered to white southerners at the expense of blacks. Black press newspapers had pushed him to support the Costigan-Wagner Bill, an antilynching bill that was introduced to Congress in 1934 during what black press historian Leonard Teel called a "lynching epidemic."[14] However, Roosevelt was deeply influenced by his progressive wife, Eleanor, who, through her friendship with the NAACP's Walter White, became increasingly concerned with improving conditions in urban areas in the North and rural areas in the South inhabited largely by blacks. By 1934 the Roosevelts together began to publicly acknowledge the plight of black citizens, and the New Deal included provisions to assist them. Specific New Deal programs worked to increase the income and education level of black and African Americans. The Farm Security Administration guaranteed that black farmers could purchase land and taught new farm owners innovative methods of production and marketing. The Public Works Administration created playgrounds, hospitals, colleges, and community centers for black residents all over the country. The Works Progress Administration offered material relief and some employment, while the Federal Public Housing Authority created construction jobs and built new homes in black communities. Though the implementation of these programs on a local level—particularly in the South—at times proved challenging, overall they undermined traditional patterns of discrimination and afforded blacks opportunities they had not previously had.

Historian James Tuslow Adams has traced the emergence of the American dream mythology to this period, when the Depression began to cripple the aspirations of ordinary Americans. Entertainment media played a decisive role in shaping American dream mythology. Donald Bogle estimated that during the Depression, 70 percent of the population went to the movies at least once a week.[15] Hollywood studios navigated the murky economic waters by forming an oligarchy to monopolize the production, distribution, and exhibition of films.[16] A major reason for the film industry's survival during this period was the public's need to escape the harsh realities of everyday life, which movies could provide. The advent of sound in film added to an already intense sense of realism that attracted audiences to movie theaters, making them feel as if they were stepping into another, simpler world. As Richard Jewell notes, "In the romantic realm of 1930s Hollywood entertainment, heroes triumph, villains are punished, love conquers all, benevolent political leadership is assured and dreams come true. Even though surely confounded and disillusioned by the staying power of the Depression, movie patrons never stopped going to the movies and never stopped believing in these movie myths."[17] Celebrity stories that appeared in mainstream entertainment magazines and urban dailies, and increasingly in black press urban weeklies and elite monthly magazines, mythologized celebrities as natural, "real" extensions of the fantasies that appeared on screen. Celebrities "provide[d] continual examples that the American Dream of rising from the bottom of the economic ladder is real for those willing to work hard," Jewell argues.[18] The stars of Harlem and Hollywood provided black urban audiences a vision of the American dream that for the first time looked, sounded, and shone like them, even if it may as well have been a constellation light years away.

Abandoning Respectability Politics in the Jazz-Mad Generation

Nightclubs featuring jazz performers garnered large audiences, and jazz musicians were among the highest-paid black entertainers of the era, far outselling records by classical artists. In 1935 Duke Ellington received $2,500 for his singular composition, "Solitude," while William Dawson's full symphony earned him only $100, prompting the *Afro-American* to ask, "Does America pay its highest rewards for jazz while music of a more serious nature goes begging?"[19] Though the *Afro-American* declared that "by 1929 the world was becoming tired of hot-jazz" as a result of the stock market crash, jazz continued to enjoy steady popularity.[20]

Jazz stars embraced the modernity of the time by harnessing new radio technology to reach as many listeners as possible. By 1924 Duke Ellington's orchestra was being broadcast regularly on New York station WHN, while stations in Cincinnati and Ohio regularly played jazz music created by black artists as well. As Floyd Calvin of the *Courier* noted, "Cab Calloway is crazy about broadcasting, and likes to please people who he can't see. He also likes to hear from his radio fans and know they like his numbers."[21]

The jazz craze troubled some black journalists, especially those writing for the historically conservative *Tribune* and *Afro-American*, both of which were established well before industrial capitalism turned their cities into booming metropolises. Journalists for these publications feared that listeners would drink too much, sacrifice their morals, and cease going to church. According to an *Afro-American* article published in 1920, listeners were simply "not normal after jazz." The article quoted physicians who claimed that listening to the music resulted in "bad temper, bad health, and ruined homes."[22] It also "makes one drunk . . . [having] the same effect as whiskey or drugs."[23] Children were particularly susceptible to jazz's negative effects; journalist Betty Barclay wrote of the troubles of the "jazz-mad modern generation" in 1930.[24] Jazz was also viewed as an interruption in religious worship; one minister railed against the playing of jazz music at church services: "I think jazz music should be played where it belongs. . . . When people are worked up over jazz tones in religious service . . . these people are not religiously stirred, they are emotionally animated."[25] Jazz music was viewed as a threat to the most established social institutions of the black community. When Eleanor Roosevelt invited Roland Hayes to perform at the White House in 1935 with a jazz performer to demonstrate the versatility of black American music, he declined; he "found such an arrangement inappropriate."[26] Rather than treat the aging singer as a dinosaur of a bygone era, black journalists heralded his resistance to becoming completely commercialized as so many of his contemporaries had. "Hayes denounced again the commercialism of both the radio and the motion picture industries," wrote Ralph Matthews, "by which he has steadfastly refused to be exploited."[27]

Criticisms of jazz reflect "the ideal of Victorian gentility" of middle-class blacks invested in racial uplift. Many blacks considered jazz to be lowbrow entertainment, played by musicians whose status, wrote Louis Armstrong's biographer James Lincoln Collier, was "only a cut above a prostitute."[28] One journalist hoped that Duke Ellington would abandon "hot jazz" and would "soon realize that the public [was] getting him down wrong and [would] contribute something to the immense sum of culture, and upon some occasion let [people] know that real musicians [were] playing real music."[29] In fact there was little denying that Ellington's orchestra was "the finest orchestra of its kind in the world"; articles that compared Ellington with other musicians—including Calloway and Armstrong—repeatedly emphasized the distinction between Ellington, an "artist," and other musicians, who were merely "entertainers."[30] Ellington, the son of middle-class parents who were classically trained pianists, was one of the most critically acclaimed bandleaders of the period, and journalists sought to extract him from their critiques of jazz. Frank Marshall Davis of the *Afro-American* explained that Ellington didn't "consider his offerings as jazz but as African interpretations. And his interpretations ha[d] drawn praise of the highest and most serious critics."[31] Here Ellington's music is not termed "jazz"; rather it is described as "African interpretations"—and therefore is highbrow and worthy of black critics' high praises. "Duke Ellington says that he is not playing jazz," maintained the *Philadelphia Tribune*, "but that he is trying to play the natural feelings of the people."[32] Warren Scholl dismissively noted, "There are many colored orchestras in America, but none can compare favorably with this one. Louis Armstrong, Cab Calloway and Don Redmon are showmen. Ellington at his best is a refined interpreter of hot jazz."[33] Journalists writing about Ellington sought to resituate him as an "artist," drawing similar distinctions as those that were drawn between ordinary entertainers and uplifters Coleridge-Taylor, Hayes, and Gilpin.

Suspicion surrounding early jazz's cultural merit was no doubt amplified by the popularity of cornetist Louis Armstrong. Armstrong grew up with his mother and younger sister in Storyville, New Orleans's prostitution district. At only twelve years old, he was sent to a juvenile detention facility called the Colored Waif's Home for Boys, where he served an eighteen-month sentence for firing a gun in public on New Year's Eve 1912. His family was poor, and until Joe Oliver picked him up to be part of his band and brought him to Chicago in 1922, he worked a variety of odd jobs to support a household consisting of his mother, sister, and his mother's various boyfriends. Armstrong dominated the Chicago jazz scene until 1929, when he moved to New York to appear in *Hot Chocolates*.

Although Armstrong mounted a successful East Coast tour and recorded his iconic "When Its Sleepytime Down South" during the early 1930s, it was nonetheless a tumultuous period for him. He had trouble retaining managers; he was involved with the mob, who at times interfered with bookings and gigs; he separated from his wife, Lil Hardin; and he was busted for marijuana possession, for which he served a short jail term.[34] The *Courier* dedicated only two paragraphs to his drug arrest. An Associated Negro Press release detailing Armstrong's subsequent release from prison quickly shifted the focus to his weight loss while incarcerated.[35] Because of these personal struggles, Armstrong as a race representative came off as far less polished than Ellington or even the young Calloway; as the *Afro-American* noted, "Radio, as a matter of fact, is a little wary of his improvisations. Several times he has been switched off the air for getting profane or slipping in sly remarks about his friends' extra-marital escapades."[36]

As the *Courier*'s James Miller admitted, "The cultural value of jazz is low"; however, Miller and other writers for newer publications like the *Courier* and the *Defender* understood its value as *popular* entertainment, and these publications were far less concerned with moral grandstanding. "One of the greatest reasons for the success of jazz, it seems to me," wrote Miller, "is that it is on the level of the mentality of the majority of people. This gives the artist a large audience. This realization of appreciation of efforts contributes greatly to its success. Besides, there can be no real art without an audience."[37] Miller's concession to the mass popularity of jazz music implied a larger shift in black press reporting: a turn away from lecturing readers on what was respectable and instead simply capitulating to their desires as fans to learn more about their favorite stars.

The Celebrity Beat

For the first time, thanks to technological advances in printing and the simplified process of reproducing photographs in newspapers—as well as steadily increasing literacy rates—many black urban weeklies enjoyed unprecedented circulation figures and financial stability. Celebrity journalism became a regular addition to these newspapers—literally. The addition of entertainment sections in the major weeklies of the period lengthened the weekly page count of these papers by typically four pages, which meant the expenditure of additional resources and newsroom staff changes. The *New York Amsterdam News*, the *Chicago Defender*, the *Pittsburgh Courier*, the *Philadelphia Tribune*, and the *Baltimore Afro-American* all had added entertainment sections by the early 1930s. Economic growth allowed black weeklies to hire and retain regular columnists. Ralph Matthews, who joined the staff of the *Afro-American* in the early 1920s, was a theatrical critic, city editor, and managing editor. Matthews also wrote two popular entertainment columns: Looking at the Stars and Watching the Big Parade. The *Defender*'s Chappy Gardner and the *New York Amsterdam News*'s Romeo Dougherty received regular bylines as well. Most urban weeklies subscribed to and reprinted the Associated Negro Press's celebrity beat. The work of Associated Negro Press writers such as Fay Jackson and Harry Leavitt brought the stories of Hollywood to the readers of the *Courier, Tribune, Afro-American,* and other smaller newspapers that subscribed to the wire service. Jackson's Hollywood Stardust column was carried in large papers, including the *Afro-American* and the *Pittsburgh Courier.*

In adapting the changes to design, structure, and reporting practices of the mainstream press, black weeklies established coverage of celebrities as particularly newsworthy to their readership. Though early film was a repository for some of the most vicious attacks on the black community, the advent of the Jazz Age combined with the development of talkies made black actors particularly attractive film subjects. Some of the most popular films of the 1930s—including *Imitation of Life* (1934), the Shirley Temple–Bill Robinson film series (*The Little Colonel* and *The Littlest Rebel*, both released in 1935), and *Gone with the Wind* (1939)—all featured black actors in prominent roles. Calloway, Ellington, Armstrong, and the dance duo the Nichols Brothers all appeared as themselves in motion pictures for Paramount and Universal.

By the 1920s film studios were not only capitalizing on technological innovations to make feature-length productions but were also marketing to audiences actors themselves as commodities. Writing about the development of celebrity culture in the mainstream press, sociologist P. David Marshall has argued, "It is difficult to separate the histories of journalism and the emergence of the contemporary celebrity system."[38] Entertainment publications such as *Motion Picture Story Magazine, Photoplay, Picture Play,* and *Motion Picture Classic* all had formalized relationships with Hollywood studios that subsidized printing costs in exchange for favorable coverage of its stars, films, and the industry in general. Toward the end of the first decade of the century, entertainment magazines were "a central ancillary to the film industry."[39] By the 1930s Hollywood was the third largest news source in America, employing three hundred correspondents.[40]

Black journalists were all but cut out of the studio publicity machine. When Universal denied black press reporters press credentials for the premiere of *Imitation of Life*, one ANP writer complained, "With very few exceptions, the [black] performer never receives mention in the white press, and almost without exception he is portrayed [as a stereotype]. . . . Consequently, only plugging of any degree of dignity or self-respect is done by his own race reporters and published in his own race papers that are not in the least considered by the agent or the studio or the theatre in the so-called 'publicity budget.'"[41] When Louise Beavers, who starred in *Imitation* as Delilah, shrugged off Universal's snub, she drew the ire of Fay Jackson, the ANP's most prolific Hollywood correspondent. "There is something pitiful and futile," thundered Jackson, "something despicable and ignoble, something suicidal, certainly something that strikes awfully at the very base of the colored man's economic status and racial self-respect when our own people forget their identity and perpetuate the policies that make them the butt of ridicule and enslavement by other races of the world."[42] Beavers's brush-off was not just a personal affront to Jackson and the other individual reporters who were shut out of covering the premiere; her dismissal represented a betrayal of the whole race.

Because they wrote regular columns for their newspapers on the celebrity beat, a handful of black journalists formed relationships—albeit some healthier than others—with celebrities, replicating in some cases the same symbiotic relationship that mainstream news institutions had with Hollywood publicity machines even as they were segregated from press junkets and film premieres.[43] When personal relationships between correspondents and stars became fractured, as was the case when Romeo Dougherty and Bill "Bojangles" Robinson got into a verbal altercation at a Harlem benefit show, the newspaper itself suffered greatly. There was no institutionalized agreement between the star (or his publicist) and the publication; all access and subsequent "plugging" relied simply on goodwill. This did not mean that black journalists covering Hollywood stars bowed to them; in fact, as always, these stars were held to high community standards.

Black press journalists often judged the merit of film celebrities on the attention they paid to their communities. They were the most sympathetic to celebrities who answered calls to collective action. In the wake of the Depression, activism often meant helping communities in need that had been left behind by municipal relief programs. For example Bill Robinson was lauded for his charitable contributions. After bit parts in *Dixiana* and the race film *Harlem Is Heaven* in the early 1930s, Robinson made his breakthrough as one-half of Hollywood's first "acceptable" interracial couple—the team of "Bojangles" and Shirley Temple. In

1935 the duo released two films, *The Little Colonel* and *The Littlest Rebel*, both produced by Twentieth-Century Fox. Viewed from a historical perspective, these films (particularly *Rebel*, which posits that the Union army was the ultimate threat to a peaceful and happy southern lifestyle equally revered by slaves as it was by white freemen) are problematic. However, in their own time, they operated as vehicles in which a black man could be on equal terms with—and even be entrusted to care for—America's sweetheart, and for that the black press was largely uncritical of their content. Instead, they heralded Robinson's "great tenderness and grasp of child psychology" and newly minted status among Hollywood's elite: "Everybody knows that 9/10s of the stories emanating from Hollywood are exaggerated truths, but if anyone says that Bill (Bojangles) Robinson is the toast of Filmland, take it from me, it's no fib," wrote Fay Jackson.[44]

Robinson, in contrast to fellow comedian Stepin Fetchit, seemed poised to step outside his film roles to act as a race representative off set. While Fetchit was notorious for behaving badly, Robinson spent most of his time promoting *Colonel* by discussing the social issues plaguing the black community.[45] As *Courier* correspondent Bernice Patton noted, "[His] theme throughout the interview chose the course of the unfortunate and needy Negroes in Harlem, more than the expected theatrical routine. No wonder he is 'the mayor of Harlem.'"[46] From paying for stoplights to be installed in a Richmond intersection, to performing at countless benefits, to subsidizing a Harlem community swimming pool so that neighborhood children could cool off, Robinson had, as one journalist put it, "a heart as big as the Empire State Building."[47] Robinson set a template for off-screen social activism that influenced black journalists' perceptions of other popular race actors. For example this scathing critique of the otherwise popular Ethel Waters, which accompanied a front-page photo in the *Philadelphia Tribune*, is telling: "Ethel Waters, who 'went Hollywood' on a benefit performance at the Lincoln Theatre here recently. Other national performers did their bit practically gratis for sweet charity's sake, but La Ethel wouldn't warble a note until cold cash was in sight."[48]

However, representational politics still mattered. If a celebrity became involved with a project that was not viewed as a positive representation of the race, he or she was criticized for it. When Waters—negotiating her own leap from the stage to the screen—signed on for a role in the short film *Rufus Jones for President,* which harped on "coon" stereotypes, Ralph Matthews wrote Waters an open letter asking her, "As one who is anxious that you always remain our most beloved darling of the stage, a true successor to Black Patti, Aida Walker, Flo Mills, as a favor to me won't you exercise a little more care in your selection of vehicles and songs?"[49] Actor Paul Robeson "was bitterly denounced by his formerly best friends and supporters" for not being more active in getting the word "n——r" removed from the *Emperor* screenplay.[50] Celebrities were continually the subjects of news stories that combined ordinary studio-lot gossip with broader discussions of race representation and activism, though by the 1930s many writers had abandoned explicit "uplift" rhetoric.

Celebrity journalism became prevalent in black urban weeklies during the Depression decade. And unlike the celebrity coverage that had been published earlier in the century that explicitly held accountable notable black figures for uplifting the race, this more modern form of celebrity journalism reflected a perspective more befitting the period—which meant greater emphasis on personal narratives, greater efforts to engage the public, and, of course, gossip. To argue that black weeklies replicated sensationalism, though, would be an overstatement: lack of financial resources prevented most of these newspapers from printing high-quality visuals, and they continued to prominently feature on their front pages serious political discourse that mainstream sensationalism had displaced.

"Imagined Intimacy" with Jazz Age Superstars

The development of celebrity journalism in black weeklies during this period suggests that the shifting social mores of the period were finding their way into newsrooms, as journalists began to speak openly about romantic relationships (read: sex). Tenor Roland Hayes drew unwanted attention when he began an affair with an

Austrian countess, though his hesitation to settle down and marry caused Ralph Matthews to openly question his sexuality.[51] Track star Jesse Owens, too, experienced the same close scrutiny when he found himself in the middle of a love triangle. "The discourse of scandal," according to Erika Spohrer, "creates a disjunction, in its very existence, between 'image' (the imaginary) and 'truth.'"[52] The more about a celebrity's personal life—including the person's romantic foibles—that readers knew, the more accessible and relatable the celebrity became. Attention to stars' bedroom affairs had obvious gossip appeal, but it also created for readers an "imagined intimacy" (no pun intended) with these public figures.

Roland Hayes's personal life garnered nearly as much attention as his professional life; as it did not only with Owens but also with Jack Johnson, Josephine Baker, and Paul Robeson, the black press paid particular attention to his complicated love affairs. It appears that he was engaged or possibly engaged three times before his eventual marriage to his cousin, Alzada: first to a woman he met in Boston in the early days of his career, Crystal Byrd; second, to a Viennese countess, Ileno Kolerado; and third to a New York debutante whose identity was never uncovered.[53] Of particular interest in late 1926 was the sordid affair of Hayes and Countess Kolerado. According to a series of articles published in the *Afro-American*, the *Pittsburgh Courier*, and the *Chicago Defender*, Hayes apparently found himself in a love triangle. Rumor had it he had become engaged to Byrd, with whom he became involved in Boston "beginning in the obscure, poor days of both."[54] This account, the *Afro-American* acknowledged, was unconfirmed: "Two years ago, friends of Mr. Hayes denied the rumors that he and Miss Byrd were to be married soon. Hayes was then on the high seas en route to Europe alone. Miss Byrd had just resigned her National Y.W. Secretary's work in order to study abroad."[55] The *Courier* also dismissed the engagement rumor.[56] Though the rumors were not substantiated, the *Afro-American* reported that Hayes had paid Byrd $35,000 in "heart balm" in an effort to remedy the fact that "he was responsible for her long spinsterhood."[57]

Coverage intensified at the end of that year when a Jewish newspaper in Vienna published a report suggesting that Hayes was having an affair with Kolerado. Rumors had swirled about Hayes and the countess as early as November, but the report from the *Jewish Forward* blew up in the black press. The *Philadelphia Tribune*, which unlike the *Afro-American*, the *Courier*, and the *Defender* often resisted the urge to report on sensational celebrity gossip, got in on the story then, reporting: "Countess Ileno Kolerado at one time heard and saw the Negro tenor and she fell head over heels in love with him. Since that time she did not miss one of his concerts. Later she invited him to her house and the Negro sang for her and the Countess was sitting at his feet and swallowed him with her eyes. She confessed her love for him. The Negro tenor accepted her love and told her that he loved her, too." The article continued by recounting the discovery of the affair by the count, with whom Hayes allegedly engaged in a "fist fight" over the countess. Though the author of the article tried to distance himself from its content with a disclaimer—"Due to the difficulty of literally translating Hebrew into English we are not printing a reproduction of the article ad literatim, but are merely stating the alleged facts as appearing in the *Jewish Forward*"—it is clear that the purpose of the article was to scandalize readers; it even made the front page of the Christmas issue.[58]

In 1931 a rumor that Hayes was once again romantically involved—this time with a New York debutante—appeared and just as quickly disappeared from the *Afro-American*. Two years later, in 1933, upon the singer's return to Baltimore to perform, columnist Ralph Matthews devoted an entire story to Hayes's failed love life. Forty years old at the time, Hayes had experienced a series of affairs that Matthews pegged as "end[ing] quite disastrously." Matthews assessed a series of scenarios that could have prevented Hayes from settling down, including the trouble he might find in "select[ing] one as artistic and famous as himself." Matthews even suggested that Hayes suffered "the bitter disillusionment of a man who has paid too dearly for the one taste of romance that he did enjoy that has turned him against femininity?"[59]

Jesse Owens was a young, attractive, likable rising track star in the summer of 1935 when a persistent rumor began to circulate that he had jilted his childhood sweetheart, Minnie Ruth Solomon, and had become engaged to the daughter of a family friend, Quince-lla Nickerson. Black weeklies scrambled to compete for the story, which quickly became less about who Owens actually planned to marry and more about which newspaper would go the furthest to get an exclusive angle. Both the *Defender* and the *Afro-American* broke the story the last week of June 1935. "The big surprise was sprung by Leon Washington, [a] young newspaperman," wrote the *Defender*, who snapped a photo of Owens and Nickerson in an "intimate pose" at a Cleveland train station.[60] The infamous photo was reprinted in most of the leading black press papers. The *Defender* promised in its June 29 issue that an interview with Nickerson would be forthcoming. A week later the *Atlanta Daily World* picked up the story, and journalists from the paper not only called his mother for comment but also convinced Solomon—Owens's original girlfriend—to call the track star and have their conversation recorded by the newspaper. "A newspaperman, anxious to get first-hand information regarding the rumored engagement," wrote the *Daily World*, "called Owens long-distance in San Diego and had Miss Solomon talk with him."[61] A few weeks later, staff reporter Bill Crain approached Nickerson outside her work and subsequently reported: "Last Tuesday afternoon as Miss Nickerson was leaving the insurance offices where she was employed as a secretary, this writer approached her and fired a number of questions to find her attitude on the matter."[62] By late August the rumors had died down, and Owens had married Solomon. However, that did not stop the *Afro-American* from boasting credit for the story; "The AFRO! Oh it was your paper that messed me up!" declared Owens when he ran into contributor Flo Collins at an event.[63]

Scandal, no doubt, helped to sell newspapers. In contrast with earlier news stories of this nature, such as Jack Johnson's high-profile romances with Etta Duryea and Lucille Cameron, far fewer moral judgments were directed at celebrities in the 1920s and 1930s. The "moral vacancy" of the Jazz Age seemed to have wormed its way into the mind-set of these journalists, who had come to appreciate a juicy bit of gossip without fretting (at least too much) over its implications for the race collectively. The middle-class values that many of these papers espoused became eclipsed by this sensational turn. It is tempting to dismiss these shifts in reporting as serving only the economic interests of the period, when gossip and scandal worked well to move newspapers. And certainly, to some extent, this refocus on sensational reporting practices *did* help many black weeklies survive, particularly during the tumultuous Great Depression, when many of these papers saw steady circulations fall. These shifts served another function, though. Celebrity coverage has the ability, particularly in times of upheaval, to create an "imagined intimacy" between the star and his or her public by building "social integration and shared rituals."[64] This was especially true in the depressed urban spaces of the early twentieth century, where a disparate strangers were forced to live in close quarters with little in common but their desire for a better future and their need to escape their bleak reality, if only temporarily.

In February 1931 Cab Calloway took over Ellington's post as the Cotton Club's house musician. Calloway was only twenty-four at the time, but he quickly settled in as Ellington's successor. Calloway was born on Christmas Day 1907 in Rochester, New York, to Eulalia and Cabell Calloway II. Around his fifth birthday, his family relocated to Baltimore, Maryland. In 1913, just a year after the family's relocation, Cab's father passed away. He and his siblings were raised by their mother; their stepfather, John Fortune; and their birth father's extended family.

Cab's older sister, Blanche, was a successful entertainer, and in 1923 she joined the cast of the all-black revue *Plantation Days*. The revue was one of many that followed in the wake of the success of *Shuffle Along*. Cab joined his sister as a member of the Hollywood Four backing quartet during the revue's tour in the summer of 1927. Blanche was annoyed by the presence of her acerbic younger brother during that summer, and the ensuing attention he would earn as he emerged from her shadow likely irritated her as well.

Calloway spent the late 1920s touring not as a bandleader but nominally as an actor, dancing and singing in cabarets and nightclubs in Chicago and New York. He did a short stint as a member of the *Hot Chocolates* and provided vocals for the Alabamians. Calloway met Louis Armstrong in 1927, and he was immediately captivated by the elder performer's distinctive vocal style. "Each of Louis's phases was a thing of beauty on its own," he recalled. "You listened to Louis—you didn't listen to the band." Calloway became convinced that he, too, could develop a vocal style as unique as Armstrong's, but in contrast to the cornetist, who performed center stage with very little movement, Calloway had also adopted the physical stage presence of Bert Williams, who had passed away only a few years earlier. Calloway learned quickly how to bring together sonic elements and physical performativity so that it was his *interaction* with his band that created a compelling stage show. In May 1930 he participated in the "Million Dollar Affair in Musical Talent" contest at the Savoy Ballroom. Charles Buchanan, the manager of the Savoy, plucked Calloway from the Alabamians, fired the Missourians bandleader, and appointed Calloway in his stead. "The Missourians had a leader and vocalist called Lockwood Lewis, and during the battle I outdid Lockwood Lewis, but the Alabamians were outplayed by the Missourians," Calloway told music critic Steve Voce in 1958. "So the manager decided to put the Missourians and me together."[65] The Missourians had enjoyed a residency at the Cotton Club, so when Duke Ellington announced that he was going on tour, the band and its dynamic new leader were a natural fit.

By most accounts Calloway did an admirable job, though his band was vastly different from Ellington's. "Cab Calloway not only held down this big undertaking," wrote the *Tribune*, "but was looked upon by the patrons and the show world as a new idol and stands alone as master of ceremonies."[66] The *New York Amsterdam News* observed, "If Mr. Ellington's music is a syncopation of savage rhythms, it is much more musical than Calloway's." "But have no fear," the review continued in the next paragraph. "For the playing of his orchestra is savage enough to satisfy our most aboriginal instincts."[67]

Under the direction of big-time manager Irving Mills, Calloway signed a record deal with NBC. Mills was a performer himself before transitioning to front-office management of musical acts, and he developed into a canny businessman with well-documented ties to the New York mob but also a valuable asset in the studio, where he cowrote many of Calloway's most successful records, including

"Minnie the Moocher." The Mills Artists' Booking Agency oversaw both the touring and the recording schedules for Mills's artists, later formalized through his acquisition of the American Recording Company. Often Mills would draw visibility to one act by leveraging it with another. For a venue to book Duke Ellington, it would also have to agree to sign a contract with Calloway or the Blues Rhythm Band. "Calloway, under the direction of Irving Mills, white, who is sponsoring him, is the new star in the orchestra firmament at the present moment, and there is every reason for believing that this brilliant young leader is well on his way to becoming the outstanding orchestra sensation of the year," wrote Ralph Matthews in one of his earliest articles on the up-and-coming young singer.[68]

Calloway quickly garnered the favor of star Baltimore columnist Matthews. In one of the first Looking at the Stars columns to survive in the *Afro-American* archives, Matthews chronicled Calloway's rise to fame. The profile began by noting, "Few people have been able to shape their dreams into reality as he has. And it all came about through one formula. He wanted to be different from anybody he had ever seen and with that paramount goal in view he reached the heights. Dreaming was only half the battle. The rest was hard work." Matthews continued, "When Cab leaves the stage after each performance he is so wringing wet that his valet has to change his clothes from skin out, and wrap him in a lounging robe to keep him from catching cold. He puts all he has into each performance."[69] There is some indication that Matthews had followed Calloway since Calloway was a member of his high school marching band.[70] Matthews's coverage of Calloway betrayed an almost paternal attention to the young musician, whom he described as a "brilliant young orchestra leader . . . well-known in both theatrical and radio circles."[71] Stories about Calloway—both by Matthews and by other journalists—routinely emphasized his youth, using the descriptors "boy," "juvenile," "young man," "young orchestra leader," "darling," and others. Calloway embodied the myth of American meritocracy. "If you have talent," he told a reporter, "cultivate it to the fullest extent; if you haven't, then do the best that you can."[72] The emphasis on Calloway's hard-earned success, which stood in stark opposition to the struggles of the black weeklies' readership, served as a salve to readers' growing concerns about the effects of industrial capitalism and the perpetuation of Jim Crowism.

To reinforce the link between Calloway and his listeners, black journalists emphasized his "ordinariness." "Such ordinariness," argues sociologist Joshua Gamson, "promoted a greater sense of connection and intimacy between the famous and their admirers."[73] Despite Calloway's newfound fame, George Murphy assured his readers that Calloway was still "an unsophisticated boy that Baltimore knew a few years back. He still yearn[ed] for more space in which to live, good home-cooked meals, and the peace and quiet of a small bungalow for his wife and himself."[74] Oliver Smith made sure his readers knew that the young maestro was "not at all snobbish"; in fact, according to another reporter, Calloway was "one of the most likable chaps around town."[75] Articles about Calloway often included lists of his favorite things, which included baseball, brown suits, French fried potatoes, crabmeat salad, steak, his Studebaker, and "a little" alcohol.[76] "From in front of the footlights the man who climbed the ladder of success with the famous Hi-De-Ho rhythm, is a glamorous person in a characteristically emphasized stage costume," wrote Rilious Reed for the *Defender*, "but back stage, and more particularly, back home, he is just a big-hearted and obliging pal, weighing 170 pounds."[77]

Duke Ellington's backstage persona was similarly emphasized in news stories about him. "Edward Kennedy Ellington, whose music weds the cosmopolitan suavity of a Park Avenue tea to the savage strangeness of the Congo at midnight, stands revealed as a man fond of gin highballs, contract bridge, adventure stories, and the movies," began Frank Marshall Davis's profile of the musician. "For even the Duke—an internationally famous figure in modern-era composition and interpretation is a normal human being, even as you and I."[78] The more believably ordinary a celebrity seemed in print, the more likely it was that audiences would form tight parasocial attachments to him or her. The "revelation" of Ellington's downtime hobbies was a deliberate publicity strategy meant to curb suspicion that the images presented by him were inauthentic.

In reality these performers, due to the influence of Irving Mills, who had significant control over their careers, had carefully constructed their personas. Ellington, in contrast with other stars whose personal lives were splashed all over the gossip pages of race weeklies, carefully guarded the fact that he was carrying on an affair with actress Fredi Washington, possibly during the time in which she was engaged to a member of his band. Calloway was notoriously obsessed with appearance; he reportedly tore apart clothing belonging to band members if it had a tear or stain on it.[79] During a visit to the *Atlanta Daily World* offices in September 1934, he scolded a staff photographer for trying to take a candid shot of him and his band. "Sakes man," he reportedly said. "I don't look like a guy who needs a picture made right now. Heck, I'm attired for comfort."[80]

Young sports stars, such as Owens and his contemporary and friend boxer Joe Louis, had similarly controlling public-relations teams who closely guarded their public personas. Louis in particular garnered an immense amount of attention during the second half of 1935. Louis was previously considered a gifted young boxer with some promise, but his decisive victories over Primo Carnera (June), King Levinsky (August), and Max Baer (September); his engagement to Marva Trotter (the two were married immediately after the Baer fight); and a highly orchestrated public persona made him the most popular and frequently covered figure in the press that year—and certainly the most unilaterally celebrated athlete of the period.

There is little doubt that Louis's emergence was a transformative moment for the black community; as the *Amsterdam News*'s Edgar Rouzeau summarily noted of Louis's attributes: "A fighting man straight up and down his spine, and not a comedian, is this modest, baby-faced, fairly good-looking, self-effacing, Bible-loving young giant whom the critics have been raving so much about—the 21-year-old super-fighter they have labeled the greatest discovery since the days of Jack Johnson."[81] The *Daily World*'s Ric Roberts maintained that Louis was "a perfect human with no reprehensible habits, a man who ma[de] his white contemporaries look like a pack of thugs when it [came] to morals and the straight path."[82]

He was routinely featured on the front page of the weekly editions; the *Afro-American*, for instance, ran nearly thirty front-page stories on Louis in fifty-two issues. At times the *Courier*'s front page was so crammed with Louis-related coverage that it was nearly impossible to identify the masthead.

Louis's demeanor fascinated reporters; for example, after his victory over Max Baer, the *Tribune*'s Orrin Evans "marveled over" Louis's "lack of outward jubilation over his victory."[83] The *Defender* ran a photo of Louis right before the Levinsky fight "showing one of his very rare smiles."[84] When compared to Jesse Owens, with whom he had often make public appearances, Louis appeared introverted; upon meeting the two men, the *Afro-American*'s Florence Collins noted that Owens was "less shy" than Louis, who did "not hesitate to talk, though he [was] not loquacious." Collins also noted that Louis seemed "timid" around young girls.[85] In reality Louis's demeanor was a highly orchestrated attempt by his handlers to distance the young contender from associations with other headline-grabbing black athletes, in particular, Jack Johnson, who they believed had tainted the public's view of blacks in general.

Nonetheless, Louis's celebrity status only grew. In fact the *Afro-American* ran a series of articles in which staff reporters Bill Gibson and Russell Cowans reported not on Louis but on the fan mail he received daily, which numbered fifty to seventy-five letters a day "from all parts of the globe."[86] "The majority of them," Cowans wrote, "are from girls and women of all ages, many of them pouring out endearing messages of love and idol worship."[87] In another article he noted, "The unprecedentedly large volume of fan mail coming to the Brown Bomber must have been a shock to the mail man. . . . But he would have received a greater shock if he could have opened some of the letters and read the contents."[88] When Louis wed Marva Trotter, the *Afro-American* declared that she was "the type of girl his public would have wished for him," though noting that many of his female fans would have preferred he not marry at all.[89] Trotter, for her supporting role in Louis's celebrity narrative, was demure and passive, and their public-relations team very quickly managed any reports of marital strife between the pair. She was as much a part of Louis's mythic narrative as Louis himself.

Celebrity profiles helped to build parasocial relationships between stars and their audience, a connection that was increasingly important as black entertainers began to garner the attention of mainstream audiences, pulling them further and further from the everyday reality of their fan base. Whether it was salacious (love triangles!), mundane (favorite foods!), or idealized (storybook romances!), these stories helped to forge a relationship between stars and their fans that was more relatable than previous modes of uplift had offered to readers.

The Social Functions of Celebrity Mythologizing

Though journalists were complicit in developing celebrity mythology, it was the public—or so they claimed—that held ultimate control over them. The "celebrity-as-public-servant" model displaced important questions about American meritocracy and afforded audiences the illusion of power. In 1931 the *Courier*'s Floyd G. Snelson Jr. spearheaded the "Most Popular Orchestra Contest." For the cost of a two-dollar subscription to the *Courier*, readers could cast a vote for their favorite musical artist of the year. Over fifty thousand votes were reportedly cast in the inaugural contest, which crowned Duke Ellington as the "King of Jazz." Cab Calloway came in third, and Louis Armstrong, who spent 1931 in "obscurity in comparison to his activities of former years," placed seventh.[90] Female readers were likely as invested in the results of Snelson's "Most Popular Orchestra" contest, though they might have been disappointed to see that only one female bandleader made the cut: Cab's sister Blanche. This was far more than a scheme to boost subscriptions; readers sent in votes and letters detailing why Fletcher Henderson or Noble Sissle or the Blue Rhythm Band deserved recognition. Recognition of their favorite big band signaled to the public that they were stakeholders in public discourse not only on celebrities but on civic life more generally.[91]

During the 1930s black weeklies' attention to celebrity reporting performed an important social function that built on the foundation of its previous attention to collective representation: it forged bonds between readers, inculcating them with a sense of comfort and control of which lingering Jim Crow politics and Depression-era economic hardship nearly robbed them. The race celebrities who emerged during this decade stepped into the national spotlight as a "constellation" against a cloudy sky. In many ways the stars of Harlem were built for this type of exposure: they embraced the technological modernity and social progressivism of the period. They courted fame and reveled in it. They were highly visible to both black and white audiences without compromising race consciousness. And for many fans, they were a symbol that black citizens too could live the "American dream."

5

The Marginalization of Black Female Celebrities as Race Representatives

"Mrs. Calloway is a Buffalo girl and met her husband in Chicago," noted the *Afro-American*'s George Murphy. "She played for a time in *Hot Chocolates*."[1] Celebrity profiles typically included information on spouses; this practice, of course, was all part of building with readers imagined intimacy with their favorite stars. Calloway's wife, Wenonah "Betty" Conacher, was a dancer, though shortly after her marriage to Cab, she gave up her role in *Hot Chocolates* to set her sights on a middle-class lifestyle. She told Murphy, "Cab does not like me to play in the shows, and I am glad to stop."

Like her sister-in-law Blanche, Conacher had professional aspirations that were overshadowed by Cab. These women were not the only ones to be overshadowed by their male counterparts. Lily Armstrong, Louis's wife, led a big band of her own, and though she consistently received credit for molding her husband into a charismatic performer, she herself received very little attention for her work as a bandleader. Isabel Washington, actress Fredi Washington's older sister, gave up a promising acting career early on to marry Adam Clayton Powell Jr. Eslanda Robeson, an Ivy League–educated woman and aspiring artist, made as her primary responsibility the successful managing of the career of her husband, Paul.

Black women who became stars in their own right, such as Josephine Baker, Florence Mills, Fredi Washington, and Louise Beavers, were subjected to the insistent male gaze of the staff writers of black urban weeklies, who revealed a blind spot when discussing the intersectional politics of the Harlem Renaissance.[2] Alain Locke, author of *The New Negro*, was notoriously "anti-woman"; similarly, James Wheldon Johnson, Walter White, and others routinely funded and supported male writers over female writers. The Harlem Renaissance, for all its progressivism, was a male-dominated movement.[3] Lingering Victorian moral ideologies influenced the ways in which black journalists framed female celebrities, while the burgeoning consumer beauty industry created a gulf between these celebrities and their female fans, who rarely saw their own images reflected in the pages of black weeklies. The "New Negro Woman" was shrouded by a veil of both racism *and* misogyny. Through the persistent male gaze of black journalists, she was objectified, written out of the grand race progress narrative.

As Gloria Hull and Barbara Smith observe in their essay, "The Politics of Black Women's Studies," "The opportunities for Black women to carry out autonomously defined investigations of self in a society which through racial, sexual, and class oppression systematically denies our existence have been by definition limited."[4] Accordingly, the black female celebrities discussed in this chapter had very few opportunities to define independently their own racialized identity. Rather, through the gaze of a male-dominated black press, these women were often trivialized or condemned on the basis of their sex.[5] Journalists during this period used two discursive strategies to mitigate the influence of female race performers: they trivialized them on the basis of their looks, imposing white, imperial discourses on their black bodies, and they condemned and punished them for violating norms of femininity that dictated how they were supposed conduct themselves privately and perform publicly. In so doing black journalists evoked respectability politics to define the terms of black womanhood. These New Negro Women were marginalized by coverage that emphasized their looks over their artistic contributions, which threatened to eliminate them from discourses of race pride and uplift.

Selling Black Women's Citizenship

Consumer culture evolved within the established institutions that black citizens relied on in their daily experience. Improvements in transportation, the growth of national advertising campaigns, and the increasing popularity of magazines—combined with increasing economic freedom—all contributed to a burgeoning consumer culture that was closely tied to industrialized leisure and entertainment. Scholars of American advertising and consumption have noted the gendered dimensions of consumption; generally, labor (including activism) where considered a masculine domain, while consumption (tied to the efficient running of the household) was a feminine task.[6] According to Charles McGovern, the very act of consumption was translated by advertisers into women's "labor"; running a home became akin to running a business.[7]

Consumer purchasing became a legitimate way to enact ideals of citizenship, and marketers played on consumers' desire to assimilate in order to sell products. National discourse through the 1920s and 1930s from disparate political corners including organized labor and Franklin Delano Roosevelt began to describe citizenship in terms of "equal opportunity in the marketplace."[8] This ethos resonated particularly with the black middle class. Booker T. Washington's National Negro Business League, Marcus Garvey's UNIA, and the NAACP all evoked similar rhetoric in their collective push to encourage economically mobile black citizens to patronize black-owned businesses. Also black citizens put an enormous amount of pressure on white-owned businesses by enacting boycotts against stores in which they themselves could not seek employment. The first of these boycotts occurred in Chicago's Black Belt in 1929, and it became the template for the "Don't Buy Where You Can't Work" and "Spend Your Money Where You Can Work" campaigns of the 1930s. Black newspapers, such as Harlem's *New York Amsterdam News*, played an instrumental role in organizing and promoting these new, highly effective forms of protest. The increasing purchase power of the black middle class became one of its fiercest political weapons.[9]

Black women were especially effective consumer advocates. Through participation in organizations such as the Detroit Housewives' League, the Housewives' Cooperative League in Pittsburgh, and the Dunbar Housewives' League in Harlem, and national mainstream organizations such as the Consumers National Federation, the Cooperative League of America, and the New York

Consumers Council, black women fought and won victories against job discrimination and advocated for the rights of consumers against unfair pricing. "Consumer activism among African Americans was less of an exclusive female activity than among white," writes Lizabeth Cohen of early consumer-based activism, "but black women's organizational skills and experience certainly ensured its success, propelling it more into the mainstream of politics in African-American communities than in white ones."[10] Despite being effective consumer activists, black women had a far more difficult time escaping the ideological messages embedded in the advertisements (and much of the editorial content) that they read in black press publications—even those of the very black-owned businesses and products for which they so staunchly advocated.

Black women's bodies were transformed in popular culture and advertising into discursive planes of racist, sexist, and classist ideologies. Stereotypes of black women included the "jezebel," an overtly sexual black woman who served as a convenient excuse for whites who sought to turn a blind eye to the spate of antebellum rapes of black slaves by their white owners; the "tragic mulatto," who as the product of "a divided racial inheritance" is emblematic of the "problem" of miscegenation; and the "mammy," a robust older woman who often acts as comedic counterpoint to the male coon character or as nonsexual companion to the Uncle Tom character.[11] The overtly sexualized jezebel and the doomed tragic mulatto figure were symbols of sexual deviance—the former a lascivious and conniving feminine figure that fed into whites' interest in perversely objectifying black women as sexual objects and the latter the product of the forbidden sin of interracial sex. The mammy stereotype faired no better; stripped of all femininity, the mammy stereotype was an asexual black woman.[12] Both the jezebel and the mammy figures were marginalized vis-à-vis their dark skin. Colorism—the implicit or overt favoring of light over dark skin internalized by black and other communities of color—ideologically positioned dark-skinned black women as somehow less feminine, less valuable, and more threatening to the dominant patriarchal social order.[13] Evelyn Brooks Higginbotham has noted that the gulf between white and black female sexualities was even larger than that between black and white men. While contests of hypermasculinity could be won or lost on the battlefield or the playing field or in the bedroom, "Black womanhood and white womanhood," she observes, "were represented with diametrically opposed sexualities." There could not be, in the view of one 1904 newspaper column, "such a creation as a virtuous black woman."[14] Skin color defined hegemonic conceptions of womanhood to the detriment of everyday black women.

Black women, like the rest of the country, could buy citizenship— but that status could come only with the quite literal disavowal of their own racial identity. To be a true citizen, so the typical ad pitch suggested, one need only buy this product to lighten skin or straighten or lengthen hair. For instance Rozol Skin Whitener promised to produce "a remarkable satisfactory, youthful, whole-some and whitened complexion."[15] Rozol, Dr. Fred Palmer's Skin Whitener Preparation, and Snow White Bleaching Cream, Snow White Hair Beautifier, Black and White Hair Dressing, and East Indian Hair Growth were frequently advertised in black press periodicals. Though the middle-class women of the church and club movements of the 1920s did their best to shift their peers away from the frivolity of buying their identity on department store credit, they were also the intended targets of many of these ads because they were the women with disposable income to pay for such products.[16] In an article published in the *Messenger* in 1918, author Louis George estimated that the women of New York spent nearly $5 million annually on beauty-care products ranging from skin cream and blush to "lip rouge" and nail polish. Howev-er, as George argued, the price was well worth it: "The girl's hair attractively arranged, her skin manifesting a soft, velvet texture, her polished and clean nails, her pearly teeth—are admired and appreciated by everybody. Even these extreme race loyalists artfully avoid the unkempt, unimproved hair and the poorly 'attended-to' skin."[17] The implication of the last sentence is, of course, that even the most ardent race activist adhered to whitewashed gender ideology. In her study of advertisements in black press newspapers, Amoaba Gooden has argued that the black press was complicit in undermining its female readership through its persistent publication of these ads: "The Black press were clearly sharing that class attainment played a role in Black women's ability to define themselves as beautiful and feminine. The nuances of the ads and the degree of advertisements demonstrated that the Black press targeted middle class Black women who were able to invest in the bleaching creams."[18] Elite publications, such as the *Crisis*, celebrated the achievements of black middle-class women through cover photos that emulated whites of the same status, while black urban weeklies embraced the exploitation of women by becoming preoccupied with chorus-line girls. Most of the discursive and visual framing of women took place in newsrooms dominated by men who sometimes implicitly and sometimes overtly suggested that black women's self-worth could be bought and sold.

The Trivialization of Cabaret Performers

Shuffle Along, Hot Chocolates, Chocolate Dandies, and Lew Leslie's *Blackbirds* revues were among the most successful black musicals of the 1920s. These musicals borrowed heavily from Harlem cabarets, which "pleased Broadway producers for whom a Harlem nightclub proved a less expensive tryout venue than a playhouse out of town," notes Larry Stempel in his cultural history of Broadway theater.[19] One of the largest draws at these cabarets was their chorus line, which featured scantily clad female dancers. Positions in chorus lines were so coveted that, at times, white dancers would attempt to pass as black just to get an audition.[20] Betty Conacher, Florence Mills, Josephine Baker, and Fredi Washington all appeared in chorus lines for these wildly successful shows. Prior to the advent of the chorus-girl-driven revue, though, few female performers had garnered the attention of black press writers. Unlike the full-figured and regal Black Patti of the previous era, chorus girls were more often than not waifish and light-skinned—almost mirror images of the "flapper" type that graced mainstream magazines of the period.

Broadway musicals became a space for black women to garner public attention, though instead of being recognized for their actual talent, they were objectified by male journalists, as reasons "why men go broke," to quote the *Philadelphia Tribune*.[21] What made black women in theater newsworthy was their looks, which subscribed to white, Western notions of beauty. Irvin C. Miller, one of the few black theater producers at the time, even put together a revue called *Brown Skin Models* in 1925, designed to "glorify" women of color from all parts of the country by featuring them on stage in "the most gorgeous costumes produced by the leading European modistes in Broadway reviews." The women who starred in the revue bore little resemblance to the ordinary black women of Harlem.[22] In particular the women featured on cabaret stages were noticeably light-skinned.

Advertisements aimed at black female consumers emphasized the importance of straight, flowing hair and (artificially) light skin tone. A'Leila Walker, one of Harlem's leading socialites, made her fortune by promoting a hair-straightening serum. Josephine Baker promoted skin-lightening cream. Most beauty products available implicitly suggested that making these women look white rather than black would enhance their attractiveness. The cover girls featured in newspapers and as illustrations in magazines reflect the prevalence of artificially enhanced beauty. In his review of *Chocolate Dandies* for the *Messenger,* Theophilus Lewis wrote of showgirls Valaida Snow and Lottie Gee: "The show does not offer them much opportunity to display what qualities they possess. But that's all right, they don't have to do anything. They're just that good-looking."[23] The caption accompanying Alice Coleman's promotional photo in a May 1924 edition of the *Philadelphia Tribune* said of Coleman: "Who helps make Hartwell Cook's Hurry Along review the idyl [*sic*] of youth and beauty that it is. Bobbed hair and the charm that enhances beauty are this little lady's glories."[24] Her perfectly coifed bob justified her place on the front page, as similar physical traits did for many young aspiring models who appeared on the front pages of black urban weeklies, often with little or no information to identify or describe their intellectual or artistic contributions to the race.

Any talent that these performers might have possessed seemed to be a secondary concern. As a part of its sensationalist overhaul, the *Afro-American* began to include on its front-page portraits of noteworthy black women. By 1924 it was common to see a "starlet" grace the front page of any black press newspaper, often with only a caption and no feature story attached. Some of these women were famous, while others simply paid to have their photographs published. Either way their perpetual presence on the front page was no doubt a way for the paper to garner more (likely male) readers. The lack of meaningful information attached to the photographs in black newspapers hints at a larger truth about their function in the black press, on the stage, and in society at large: the "New Negro Woman" was there only to be "good-looking," not because of talent, intelligence, or personality.

As Carolyn Kitch notes of W. E. B. Du Bois's *Crisis* cover girls of the same period, the "whiteness" of the figures pictured "sent female readers a disempowering message" despite the fact that they were supposed to be visual markers of racial uplift. Photographs of female college graduates, physicians, attorneys, and other "Talented Tenth" representatives all subscribed to whitewashed imagery, even down to the way in which these cover models were posed. The overall effect of those photographs was to "insert black faces into white ideals and therefore assume part ownership of those ideals."[25] The representation of black chorus girls in urban weeklies of the period similarly trivialized the physical beauty of their female readership, who bore little resemblance to the women who graced their pages. Black journalists failed to see that the promotion of these women compromised the idea of racial pride for their female readership.

What little correspondence exists from the newsrooms of black weeklies suggests a bit of a "locker room" mentality among male staff members. "Now that arrangements are made with Hertzel Brown, do you still want pictures of pretty girls?" *Defender* contributor Alfred Smith once inquired of Metz Lochard. "Plenty enough of them around here."[26] Even Du Bois, in a letter to Robert Vann, asked him to have "that attractive clerk in your office . . . find the facts and send them to me."[27]

The Condemnation of Eslanda Robeson

Black women were not only trivialized in journalistic discourse; when they challenged the gender ideologies presented by (overwhelming male) journalists, they were condemned and punished for violating those norms. In 1931 rumors began to circulate that Paul Robeson had taken up with a white socialite, with whom he was living in London. The ordeal played out in the press, with sensational headlines like "'Tired of Each Other'—Robesons" and "'Paul Does Not Need Me Anymore'" blazed across the front pages of black newspapers. Robeson, for his part, was hardly coy; regarding his affair he told the *Atlanta Daily World*, "It has not been much of a secret abroad. . . . When I was in London last we were seen together much of the time and made no bones about our attachment."[28]

Amid this tumultuous backdrop, news of the making of the *Emperor Jones* began to spread; the *Amsterdam News* and other papers began to run promo shots for the film in anticipation of its release. Robeson commanded the role of Brutus, giving the deeply flawed character depth and humanity—traits that were all but absent from black-centered films during this period. Robeson's physical stature was emphasized throughout the film. He loomed over every other actor in nearly every frame and is alternately referred to as "big boy" and one of the "big men." He daydreamed about the meeting the president on the steps of the capitol to tell him, "Well Brutus you sure is much of a man." In contrast with other popular black actors of the period—like Clarence Muse or Stepin Fetchit, who filled bumbling comedic roles—and counter to the impressions of blacks that *Amos 'n' Andy* was promoting on the radio, black journalists read Robeson's Jones as a redefinition of black masculine identity. As Rob Roy of the *Defender* noted when the film was released in 1933, "Where Robeson has to speak of another race he always says 'white man' and then in a tone that suggests contempt and not an admission of fear and complex."[29] Not since Jack Johnson (who is fleetingly referenced in the film) had a black entertainer garnered so much attention so vehemently on his own terms. Journalists celebrated Robeson's interpretation of Jones as an overtly masculine protagonist as subversive.

Robeson had met Eslanda, often referred to as "Essie" in press coverage, at Columbia University in 1920, and the couple married a year later. Though she was an Ivy League–educated woman who had also hoped to break into acting, she set aside her own professional aspirations to manage her husband's early career. She ensured that Robeson received adequate pay for his stage role as Brutus Jones, and when the script was adapted to film, she ensured that he would receive top billing there, too. The *Courier* credited her with having "guided hubby to fame," though her shrewdness contrasted unfavorably with her "girlish looking body."[30] Despite all she had done for Robeson, she quickly became an object of disdain for many journalists. Some critics implied that Essie was manipulative, using "the feminine cleverness which she ha[d] so often demonstrated" in negotiating contracts on Robeson's behalf.[31]

When their marital strife became public, J. A. Rogers of the *Courier* chided fellow journalists for detracting attention from Robeson's *Emperor* performance. "Divorce suits and love affairs are, or ought to be, the private concern of the individuals personally involved," he wrote. "In a civilized world the public would keep its nose out of the domestic life of a noted personage, thereby making it easier for him to render to the public the fruits of his genius and talent."[32] Readers were outraged by all the negative attention Robeson courted as a result of the alleged affair. Ralph Matthews reprinted a letter he received in his weekly Looking at the Stars column that charged: "We the Negro press, blinded [Robeson] with the wrong kind of publicity, and left a bewildered, shattered man instead."[33] The *Atlanta Daily World* sent a correspondent to New York to gauge Harlemites' reactions to the news. The reactions, which the author framed as a split between genders, were revelatory.

The author reported, "An unofficial canvas of Harlem Sunday and Monday revealed that colored women were almost unanimous in the opinion that Robeson is ungrateful for the very valuable assistance his wife has given him in his struggle to reach the top," while many men that were interviewed claimed "if a Negro wants to rise to true heights of greatness at some point he must quit being a Negro and be a man" and noted that many successful black men "did not marry Negro women."[34]

Despite the allegations leveled at Robeson, Essie received the brunt of the criticism, while he emerged as the victim of overzealous gossip. The condemnation of Eslanda Robeson in the context of her husband's affair revealed underlying attitudes about the social value of black women. As one reader of the black press suggested, black women were hindrances to upwardly mobile black men, meant to be cast aside as their male counterparts rose through the ranks. Eslanda, by virtue of the fact that she had taken on a leadership role in shaping her husband's career, had violated the gender norms of other famous spouses who happily and passively stepped aside to let their husbands enjoy the spotlight. She was publicly condemned, despite the fact that she was guilty of nothing more than having an unfaithful spouse.

Mills/Baker, Madonna/Whore

"If that truth must be told the triumphs of John Barrymore, Jane Cowl, Doris Keane, Paul Whiteman and all the rest," wrote the *Courier*, "pale into insignificance before the knockout of two colored girls—Florence Mills and Josephine Baker."[35] As female performers cracking a male-dominated entertainment field, Mills and Baker signified on both racial and gender stereotypes. As journalistic subjects they were framed antithetically—one a nostalgic return to Victorian (white) moral purity and the other a fetishized "object" on whose body were inscribed imperial racial ideologies and Victorian sexual ones. In discussions about each race performer in the black press, this dichotomy worked to both help and undermine each star—coverage of Mills was overwhelmingly flattering but not as voluminous as coverage of Baker, which was sometimes flattering but often critical and sometimes overtly sexist. While Mills was "sweetly magnetic," Baker represented something far more dangerous to (mostly male) journalists.

Mills and Baker—who toured France together briefly in 1926 as part of the *Blackbirds* cast—regularly drew comparisons with each other, and some accounts suggest that they were friends. Baker was known for her provocative yet comedic dance routines, namely, her "banana dance," during which she wore only a skirt of bananas, while Mills was an elegant and charismatic, if not conservative, performer. When Lena Horne was asked to compare the two, she replied, "that Josephine seemed to the French like a 'fabulous child of nature' who reminded them of lions and tigers and the jungle, whereas Florence was like a waif they could cry over and pity."[36]

Mills's career started at the age of four as "Baby Flo" performing on various vaudeville stages, including the Williams and Walker Company's *Sons of Ham* and as a pickaninny in *Bonita*. As a young girl, she took dancing lessons from Bill "Bojangles" Robinson. Mills was no doubt a part of the legacy that had begun with Black Patti and continued with Aida Overton Walker (to whom she was often compared); Mills not only performed with Walker directly (in *Sons of Ham*), but she also tried out for (and possibly won) the chance to perform as part of the Black Patti Troubadours. Mills took over Gertrude Saunders's role in *Shuffle* in the summer of 1921. Mills represented a "new kind" of Broadway star, "a black female singer and dancer who could deliver everything that black entertainment was renowned for, but with an added gamine delicacy . . . pathos and humor in a blend that was uniquely her own."[37]

Shortly after joining *Shuffle*, she was discovered by a cabaret promoter who would become the "pioneer of the Negro nightclub revue"—a Russian Jewish man named Lew Leslie. Leslie's mission was "the discovery and promotion of black female talent"; his vision was to promote black showgirls the same way that Ziegfeld promoted white ones.[38] In April 1922 Leslie offered Mills a three-year contract with a salary of $500 per week, "the best ever given to a colored woman, both as to terms and as to salary," pending her release from *Shuffle*.[39] Leslie's *Plantation Revue* opened in the Winter Garden Theatre in New York, with Mills as its star. Salem Tutt Whitney, writing for the *Defender*, praised Mills as "wonderfully talented, fascinatingly vivacious, sweetly magnetic," noting, "Florence Mills sings, dances, and talks her way into the inner most recesses of one's heart than be tilled by no other."[40] Mills's reputation grew steadily from 1923 through 1927: upon her return from a European tour with *Plantation Revue*, she starred in the Greenwich Village Follies; turned down an offer to become part of Ziegfeld troupe; and starred in two more Lew Leslie productions, *Dixie to Broadway* and *Blackbirds*. Along the way she became a staple of Harlem society but spent much of her time participating in charity events all over the country. J. A. Jackson of the

Afro-American noted, "She has the distinction of being the least 'up-stage' woman in the profession and has never been too busy to help any worthwhile benefit by donating a personal appearance, oftimes with her whole show."[41]

She had also managed to avoid becoming the object of gossip in the press; Mills had been happily married to Ulysses "Kid" Thompson, of the Thompson and Covan vaudeville duo and the Tennessee Ten, since 1921. The *Afro-American*'s theatrical editor quickly squashed rumors of Mills's infidelity on the *Plantation* tour: "Those knowing that Miss Mills is happily married to U.S. Thompson . . . can all but smile at this distortion of the truth." When *Plantation* came to Baltimore, he wrote, "Folk can attest that [Mills and Thompson] were together at all times when the show played this town."[42]

Mills's squeaky-clean image contrasted sharply with her *Shuffle* costar, a replacement chorus girl named Josephine Baker.[43] In 1922, with little stage experience under her belt, Baker auditioned for a role in the chorus line, but she was rejected. During her audition Noble Sissle dismissed her as "too small, too thin, too dark."[44] Undeterred, she became a dresser for the show and learned all the routines so that when a chorus girl fell ill, she was the obvious replacement. In 1924 Baker joined Sissle and Blake's *Shuffle* follow-up, *Chocolate Dandies*, where she received modest attention. "She seems as pliable as a rubber band," read an early review of her performance. "Her gyrations are comic to the last degree," noted the *Amsterdam News*. "Some people call her the chocolate edition of Charlotte Greenwood and there are others with long memories who say that she is a bronze counterpart of a celebrated French eccentrique, Pasquerrette, who came to this country years ago."[45]

After *Chocolate Dandies'* run ended, she continued to perform in Harlem's Plantation Club, but her big break came abroad, on the French stage as the star of the provocative *Le Revue Négre*, which opened in October 1925 at the Théâtre des Champs-Elysées in Paris. Baker's *Négre* performance was noted by stateside black press newspapers, especially in 1926, by which point her stardom abroad had been firmly established. Headlines like "Josephine Baker Goes Big in Paris," "Josephine Baker Now Is a Parisian

Craze," and "Josephine Baker Hit in Paris" were common in 1926 black press entertainment news sections. Even though the mainstream press had very little use for Baker, the black press paid close attention to her.

Historian Stephanie Leigh Batiste has argued that through her provocative performance style, Baker "exude[d] oversexed, primitive savagery and animalism in the service of colonial fantasies about blackness and at the same time the gorgeous desirability of an uncontained black difference."[46] Comments by the white American poet e. e. cummings were reprinted without comment in black urban weeklies in New York and Chicago: "She resembled some tall, vital, incomparable fluid nightmare, which crossed its eyes and warped its limbs in a purely unearthly manner—some vision which opened new avenues of fear, which suggested nothing but itself. . . . It may seem preposterous that this terrifying nightmare should have become the most beautiful (and beautiful is what we mean) star of the Parisian stage. Yet such is the case."[47] At once "terrifying," alien, and seductive, Baker was the embodiment of imperial racial discourses that desired at the same time to understand, control, and violate black female bodies.

In June 1927 Baker become the object of mass speculation when, at twenty-one years old and already divorced twice over, she married an Italian "count," Pepito di Albertini, in Paris. Frustrated by the fact that no Paris newspapers had carried news of the union, *Philadelphia Tribune* correspondent J. A. Rogers traveled to Paris to investigate the marriage reports for himself (despite his protestations about the Robeson affair), and what he found was quite disappointing. In an article titled "Is the Star of the Folies-Bergere Really Married?," which was reprinted in the *Tribune*, the *Defender*, and the *Courier*, and other papers, Rogers reported that the marriage had actually been an "advertising stunt," and further that the "count" was actually "only a cabaret dancer and a no-Count." Rogers charged that the publicity stunt came as a result of Baker losing favor on the Parisian stage. "The truth is that Miss Baker has been steadily losing vogue in Paris," he wrote. "When I visited the Folies I was much disappointed to find that it was not her, but an English dancer, Jack Sanford, who was the hit of the show." Rogers added, "Her dancing was not as good as that of many girls I have seen at the Lincoln or the Lafayette in New York, though I heard that her dancing last year was very good."[48]

This news was immensely disappointing to black journalists who had believed that Europe was a welcoming environment for black performers, and who had subscribed to the myth that Baker was a "Brown Cinderella."[49] As the *Defender* pointed out, "In America the legal union of these two persons would have created national pandemonium and Count de Albertini would have found that the only way he could feel free to have the woman of his choice—if her skin was dark—would be in the disgraceful and unholy state of concubinage when he would still be received as a gentleman in the best white families."[50] Black journalists continued to traffic to their readers an idealized version of Europe as a hub of both cultural refinement and racial tolerance. The *Plaindealer* asked, "Is Europe heaven for sepia theatrical stars?" citing the success of Baker, Robeson (who at the time was experiencing great success on the London stage in the title role of *Othello*), and a slew of lesser known actors and actresses who had found steady work in Europe after being snubbed in America. The author of the article argued, "Opportunity plus ability is perhaps the most logical reason for the tremendous success of Negro actors and actresses abroad. In America, the talent of colored theatrical stars is well recognized but the opportunity is not commensurate with their ability."[51] In 1932 Robeson claimed that he was prepared to leave America permanently to pursue social equality in England. "I desire above all things to maintain my personal dignity," he told the *Philadelphia Tribune*. "If this stirs up race prejudice I am prepared to leave this country forever. I am assured of a following in England. . . . Abroad you are only another artist and must stand on your merits."[52]

It was unclear at the time the news of Baker's engagement broke whether Albertini was a real count, and his status was a point of debate in the black press, whose writers wanted desperately to believe that Baker had become a countess—European royalty—as the ultimate proof that Europe was indeed more tolerant than the United States. Baker and Pepito had become romantically involved in late 1926; he soon became her manager. Pepito, however, was not a count; rather, he was a former stonemason and sometimes gigolo who, when visiting Paris, liked to call himself "Count Pepito de Albertino" (or sometimes "Abatino") because it "had more class."[53] To many writers the story of Baker's marriage to the "count" must have sounded like an integrationist fairy tale come true.

Rogers was clearly determined to get to the bottom of the "no-count" controversy, and it is fair to suggest that his skepticism over the arrangement was fueled at least in part by cultural anxieties resulting from women's social mobility during the 1920s. Divorce was a relatively new phenomenon during this period, when rates nearly doubled. In 1906, public records indicate that there were 84 divorces per every 1,000 households; by 1928, that number increased to 166. More women were finding their independent voices in the workforce, in education, and in the voting booth. Backlash against early feminists was reflected in mainstream celebrity journalism, where male journalists felt threatened not only by the popularity of "shallow, good-time girl flappers" but also by the growing numbers of female journalists hired to cover them.[54]

There is evidence to support the argument that male journalists writing for black urban weeklies felt threatened by the women's movement. In an article titled "Forgotten Husbands: What Happens to the Mates of Famous Women?," the *Afro-American*'s Ralph Matthews investigated the fates of celebrity husbands who had been overshadowed by their celebrity spouses. To research the piece, Matthews reached out to Jimmy Gentry, a Chicago-based theater critic who had "unearthed a forgotten husband of Josephine Baker"; that is, Gentry had tracked down Baker's second husband, a fellow vaudeville entertainer named William Howard Baker, whom she had married when she was fifteen years old. It is not clear when Josephine and William separated, though when she left for Paris in 1925, they were still legally married. William told Matthews in an interview that he had not immediately followed his wife to Paris because he "did not want to be dependent on her." Yet he maintained that "the correspondence with [his] wife continued without cessation until the startling news in summer 1927 that she had married Count Pepe Abertino." We may never quite know the intimate details of the Bakers' romantic separation, but Matthews clearly framed the story as a cautionary tale to male readers, warning that their wives might desert them if they became too financially independent, like Josephine.

Matthews's article, using language similar to commentaries in mainstream rags such as *Motion Picture Classic* and *Photoplay*, commented on the growing concern about the "new woman"—dangerous in her independence, her fickleness, her economic mobility, and her sexual desire. "And so it goes," chided Matthews, "if the wife wins fame, the husband is forgotten." Though, he noted, this might be preferable for most men in that position, for "many husbands prefer to be forgotten altogether than to go through life known as 'Mr. Ethel Waters,' 'Mr. Blanche Calloway,' or 'Mr. Aida Ward.'"[55]

Just as Josephine Baker's personal life was being placed under a microscope, the "Mills as saint" trope was being crystallized upon her premature death from appendicitis in November 1927. She was only thirty-two years old at the time. The *Courier* framed Mills as an agent of racial uplift. "But Florence was more than an actress," an anonymous journalist wrote. "She and the entire Negro race felt that she was an ambassador of good will from the blacks to the whites; a potent factor in softening the harshness of race feeling; a living example of the potentialities of the Negro ability when given a chance to make good."[56]

An series of tribute articles originally published in the *New York Evening Graphic* and reprinted with permission in the *Philadelphia Tribune* whitewashed Mills's legacy by using racial ideology and implicit jabs against Baker to conflate Mills's "cleanliness" and moral purity with racial whiteness. Noting that she brought her Bible with her everywhere ("the thumbmarks show how studiously 'the Little Blackbird' read it") and was a devoted wife to her husband ("If I had nothing but his love," Mills once said, "I'd still be rich"), the articles seemed to draw an implicit contrast between Mills and Baker, whose "wicked nudity" prompted a Baltimore-area church to hold vigil three consecutive days "in atonement for outrages on morality."[57] The tribute read in part: "In Europe—especially in Paris—there had been an avalanche of what was termed 'wicked' dances. There were gyrations that at best could only be classed as animal. And into this populace with its hectic appetite fluttered the 'Little Blackbird' to croon herself to stardom and portray what the critics declared as a good, fine, clean American dancing." The author's use of "wicked," "gyrations," and "animal" were no doubt obvious clues to the reader that he was referring to Baker—whose "danse savage" evoked exactly these responses from white audiences, both titillated and horrified by her overtly sexual stage persona. In contrast the author employed paternalistic language to describe Mills as a fragile creature (the "Little Blackbird"), "fluttering" to the stage offering "clean" entertainment. "Cleanliness" was such an important motif in commemoration of Mills that it was mentioned again three times in this article alone: she was "always clean, deodorized of the slightest suggestiveness," and later the author noted that she "kept her mind and body clean." Cleanliness was evoked in this article, whose author was white, as analogous to "whiteness." The author even stated that Mills was "impeccably white in thought and deed." "White" in this passage carried two meanings: moralistically "pure" and racially white. Jim Crow ideology, after all, rested on puritanical morality concerning women's bodies and the need to "defend" them from being "sullied" by miscegenation. Whatever the members of the *Philadelphia Tribune* editorial board were thinking when they reprinted this piece, they unwittingly undermined Mills's role as a race representative in favor of selling to their readers a lesson in whitewashed morality.

The Madonna/whore trope emphasized in this *Tribune* article was characteristic of coverage of Mills and Baker generally, and it undermined both of their roles as race representatives. Mills could only truly achieve narrative closure by being repositioned in death as a white, rather than a black, figure. By stripping her of her racialized identity, she could only then be truly mourned. Conversely, Baker embodied in many ways the spirit of the Harlem Renaissance. During this period cultural output was often discussed in the black press in terms of "primitivism," including allusions to Africa and the "jungle." Inherent in the movement was a celebration of African heritages as a source of racial solidarity and pride.[58] Baker's performances certainly reflected a celebration of African womanhood (albeit an exaggerated version); however, the fact that she was a financially independent and sexually liberated woman did not appear to work in her favor. Baker's artistic contributions were dismissed at the time as "black exotica" that was easily consumed by whites and quickly dismissed by blacks. When Baker returned in 1935 to the United States to star in the *Follies of 1936*, the *Afro-American* noted that "the chic, sophisticated Baker of today [was] a very different person from the wild, irrepressible Jo Baker of ten years ago." The author declared that "the exotic dancer of yesterday is dead," and he seemed truly relieved at the thought.[59] Baker could not transcend the male gaze of black urban weeklies. Race representation was simply not fit for a woman wearing a banana skirt.

Body Politics in the Critical Response to *Imitation of Life*

"The story is great; the directing marvelous and the acting almost unbelievable. 'Imitation of Life' is a film that brings facts home to you in drama that is superb. See it," wrote the *Chicago Defender* about a Hollywood film starring two black women that would end up finishing as the highest grossing of 1934, at the height of the Great Depression.[60] *Imitation of Life* was in many ways a reflection of the heightened social consciousness of the Depression years, during which the film industry, albeit clumsily, attempted to rectify its previously unfair treatment of blacks. The film was very much a product of the Harlem Renaissance; the author of the novel on which the movie was based, Fannie Hurst, was one of Zora Neale Hurston's white patrons, and she had invited her fellow author to live with her as her secretary, friend, and "driving companion." Hurston was the inspiration for Hurst's novel.[61]

The film was driven by the performances of Fredi Washington as light-skinned Peola trying to pass for white and of Louise Beavers as Delilah, Peola's dark-skinned mother. It wasn't necessarily a rejection of racial stereotypes, however; Beavers as Delilah embodied "the part of a loyal and plump family cook," typical of the "mammy" figure, while Washington as Peola fell victim "to her desire, as a tragic mulatto, to be accepted as white."[62] In the story two mothers—Bea, who was white, and her black maid, Delilah—went into business together to promote Delilah's family pancake recipe as a means to support their daughters. Though the pancake mix became a great success that allowed both women to live comfortably, Delilah stayed on as Bea's maid. Delilah's light-skinned daughter, Peola, resented her own blackness and disowned her mother in a vain attempt to live as a white woman, only to return to mourn the death of the deserted and heartbroken Delilah.

Black critics celebrated the performances of Washington and Beavers; upon its release in late 1934, a still from the film appeared on the front page of the *Courier* with the caption, "The critics are loud in their praise of the sepia stars, declaring their drama is the most poignant."[63] The *Kansas City Plaindealer* called Beavers's role as Delilah "one of the most important ever held in a picture by a sepia artist."[64] H. S. Murphy of the *Atlanta Daily World* commented, "Undoubtedly Louis Beavers and Fredi Washington steal the whole show from Claudette Colbert and Warren William in 'Imitation of Life.'"[65]

The search for the right stars of the film started years earlier, when director John Stahl began visiting black nightclubs and venues looking for potential actresses. Beavers was chosen relatively quickly from a pool of actresses that included Hattie McDaniel (who later became the breakout star of *Gone with the Wind*). The role of Peola took much longer to cast; Stahl was determined to cast a light-skinned black actress—rather than a white one—to play the delicate role. He feared that a white actress in the role of "the daughter of a colored mammy . . . would simply not 'go down' with theatre audiences." Stahl considered over three hundred actresses before settling on Washington, who had previously starred opposite Robeson in *Emperor Jones* and opposite Cab Calloway in a Universal Pictures short. For her role in *Emperor*, she had to be "darkened . . . for fear that audiences might think Robeson was playing romantic scenes with a white actress."[66]

Imitation was a film composed of what Washington called "borderline roles," which tackled the taboo subject of interracial relations. Washington relished the opportunity to use her fame to advocate for blacks, which she did through her filmic performances, interviews, and involvement with organized labor. "You know," she told Ralph Matthews during a radio interview, "I have to wait so long between pictures for roles suitable to my type."[67] Like Washington Beavers was deeply invested in *Imitation* as a vehicle for social change. She told George Hall of the *Tribune*, "I personally believe that such pictures will do more to bring about race equality than politics and associations such as the NAACP and the Urban League."[68] Beavers had made sure that the word "n——r" was taken out of the *Imitation* screenplay; she reportedly told screenwriter, William Hulbert, "It is a fighting word," and refused to use it. The screenwriter complied with her wishes.[69] "In almost every successful picture now," she told the *Afro-American*, "you see one or more non-white characters. True, they may have only a maid or servant part, but even that shows advancement over the slapstick and African Zulu parts to which they were once confined in the 'Trader Horn' and 'Tarzan of the Apes' type of drama."[70] Washington hoped that *Imitation*'s critical success would give producers "courage" to cast more actors of color in dramatic roles.[71]

Coverage of Fredi Washington was typical of previous coverage of starlets: it focused largely on her looks. She was described as "pretty, talented," "talent plus looks," "a picture in beauty," and visual representations of her almost always accompanied even the smallest tidbit or news story.[72] Washington, however, had more than just looks working in her favor; she was, as the *Atlanta Daily World* bluntly put it, "beautiful but not dumb."[73] Hilda See of the *Defender* seemed quite surprised that Washington was "particularly interesting" and "easy-going but clearly expressive . . . both on stage and on the street." See thought Washington was "quite a person."[74]

Washington was indeed "quite a person." In addition to her acting career, she was a labor activist. Beginning in the second decade of the century, blacks who worked in the film industry began to organize into labor unions. Black theater employees who worked as projector operators began to unionize and demand better pay and working conditions. The International Alliance of Theatrical Stage Employees and Moving Picture Machine Operators of the United States supported their efforts, and walkouts in Philadelphia, Washington DC, and Baltimore took place in the mid-1930s. In

1937 Washington spearheaded the formation of the Negro Actors Guild of America, which included among its ranks Noble Sissle, Bill Robinson, and Duke Ellington. The guild fought for equitable compensation for black actors and more and higher-quality roles for them in major Hollywood productions. Washington organized meetings, protests, and boycotts; handled correspondence; and performed treasurer duties for the guild into the 1970s.[75]

During her press tour for *Imitation*, Washington began work on *One Mile from Heaven*, which was released by Twentieth Century Fox in August 1937. In that film she plays the mother of a young mixed-race girl who becomes the subject of a newspaper exposé by a local newswoman, played by Claire Trevor. The film was a box-office flop, much to Washington's chagrin. She chided the *Courier*'s film critic, Porter Roberts, for overlooking the film. "I take the trouble to write," she began in a letter to him, "because I have noticed you have criticized almost constantly parts taken by colored actors in pictures, advocating that they demand parts void of any 'n——rism.' Well, exactly that, happened in 'One Mile from Heaven' but you over-looked it entirely or is it that you get a bigger kick out of criticism than praise?"[76]

If coverage of Washington betrayed a certain disturbing element of "surprise" over the idea that she could be both beautiful and intelligent, coverage of her costar, Beavers, was even more insulting. Coverage of Beavers focused on her physical countenance; her full figure was hardly celebrated the way in which, say, Black Patti's was in the early 1900s.[77] Instead, it became an object of judgment and, at times, ridicule. Beavers was "quite plump and jolly" and "buoyant"; her diet habits were also a focus—she "endorse[d] bananas and cream as a diet ace" and (believe it or not!) ate "no sweets."[78]

Even female journalists covering Beavers disproportionately focused on her looks rather than on her talent. In "Nothing Delilah-Like in Real Louise Beavers," the *Afro-American*'s Lulu Jones Garrett began her profile by introducing Beavers as "far better looking than her Delilah make-up would lead you to believe."[79] For any readers concerned about Beavers's lack of a husband, Garrett offered the following assurance: "[Beavers is] too busy just now to consider marriage, though she admits that interest in her career is all that takes her mind from men and matrimony."[80] Throughout the article Garrett focused her attention on describing for readers Beavers's physical countenance and beauty habits: "She has no beauty ritual, lets her companion, Irene Hill, select her wardrobe, and uses very little makeup, even on the stage."

The narrative arch of *Imitation* is the conflict between Peola and her mother, defined and separated by their skin color. Accordingly, black journalists covering Washington and Beavers on their press tour for the film seemed unable or unwilling to separate each actor from her role in it. The colorism that defined the narrative arch of the film also defined the dominant narrative assigned to each woman. Washington, so exasperated with questions about "passing" for white in her private life, told one journalist, "Why should I pass for anything . . . but an artist? . . . I don't want to 'pass' because I can't stand insecurities and shams. I am just as much 'Negro' as any of the others without presuming to over-rate my abilities."[81] Though Beavers received heaps of praise for her portrayal of Delilah, she also received pushback from critics who resented the "mammy" overtones of the character. "People don't seem to understand that I am not personally Delilah," the embattled Beavers told the *Amsterdam News*'s Roi Ottley. "There are plenty of scripts which I personally do not agree with, but can I be personally responsible for what a Hollywood writer puts in his story?"[82] When a staff writer from the *Afro-American* inquired if her contract stipulated that she was to play only maid roles for Universal, she "vigorously denied" the charge.[83]

Black press journalists, in celebrating Washington's and Beavers's star turn in *Imitation*, betrayed overtones of colorism in their descriptions of the women, linking skin color with idealized conceptions of femininity and in the process undermining the social value of each actress. Washington's career stalled almost immediately when *One Mile from Heaven* flopped in theaters. Louise Beavers, favored to play the role of Mammy in *Gone with the Wind*, lost out to Hattie McDaniel. Though Beavers continued to have a film career through the 1950s, she never broke out of the mammy stereotype assigned to her as a result of *Imitation*. In the case of the stars of *Imitation of Life*, their gendered-typed roles objectified them, preventing them from expressing or representing anything other than a "tragic mulatto" and a "mammy figure."

The Crisis of Masculinity in Black Press Newsrooms

Though coverage of female celebrities in black urban weeklies was as voluminous as that of male celebrities, there was a deep disconnect between the women who received attention in the black press and the lived experience of the press's female readership. The popularity of cabaret stars and their significant presence on the front pages of both black-centered newspapers and magazines undermined black femininity by transposing white ideals onto black bodies, as Kitch has argued about the *Crisis* cover models. Female readers likely felt marginalized by images that "reinforce[ed] the desirability of mainstream ideals," which necessarily meant that black women were symbolically written out of womanhood altogether.[84] Even in the cases of more famous celebrities such as Florence Mills, Fredi Washington, Josephine Baker, and Louise Beavers, coverage of these noteworthy women was also problematic, often judging their sexual expression (Mills and Baker) or focusing on their physical appearance (Washington and Beavers). This occurred despite their efforts to align with prevailing political ideologies of the time. Had Mills been a man, she would have been heralded by black press newspapers as an uplifter, as would Baker, as a Harlem Renaissance icon, and Washington, as a pioneer of organized labor. The roles of female celebrities as race representatives were compromised by the sexist attitudes of the male (and in some cases, female) journalists covering them.

The crisis of masculinity reflected the gender ideologies of the news institutions themselves. The Jazz Age, with its evolving sexual mores, was a real threat to the stability of black families, and independent women became the scapegoats for its decline. The uptick in American divorce rates was alarming to middle-class black uplifters, for whom the sanctity of marriage was paramount. In the early 1930s, James and Eloyce Gist, black evangelists who also dabbled in filmmaking, shot two films that condemned the sins of the Jazz Age: *Hellbound Train* (1930) and *Verdict: Not Guilty*

(1933). In *Hellbound Train* a devil-horned figure takes a terrifying cabaret tour, condemning its patrons at every stop along the way. In *Verdict* a skull-faced jailer in a nun's habit serves as judge and jury over a young woman, who is forced to confess her sins. Though it is unclear just how large an audience these films might have garnered as part of the Gists' evangelical tours, they reflect the perceived social threat of the "New Negro Woman."

Things were changing in the black newspaper industry, too. The popularity of film among audiences gave female journalists an opportunity to truly make a name for themselves in the black press. In addition to Ralph Matthews, Lester Walton, Sylvester Russell, and other established entertainment writers of the period, one Associated Negro Press writer, Fay Jackson, emerged as the source for celebrity gossip, Hollywood casting decisions, and exclusive interviews with stars. Her Hollywood Stardust column rivaled Matthews's Looking at the Stars column in the pages of the *Baltimore Afro-American*. Jackson was as much a "personality" as the celebrities she covered; according to Donald Bogle, she "wore her hair closely cropped, favored tailored suits, carried a briefcase, and puffed away on unfiltered cigarettes—not the standard attire or look for a young woman in the movie capital [Los Angeles]."[85] By 1940 the male-dominated newsrooms of black press weeklies experienced growth in female contributors, including Hilda See of the *Chicago Defender* and Lula Jones Garrett at the *Baltimore Afro-American*. Though institutional records no longer exist to reflect the exact demographic changes that took place in these newsrooms, the names that appear as bylines in entertainment sections of black press weeklies hint at a real sea change. As attention shifted to celebrity coverage, as it did in the mainstream press, women were increasingly both news subjects and newsroom colleagues. Though the Atlantic Ocean separated these newsrooms from Josephine Baker's banana skirt, there is still little doubt that the influx of female celebrities that took place during the 1920s and 1930s prompted a crisis of masculinity in many black press newsrooms.

The words of bell hooks—that the "dominant tendency in Western patriarchal minds to mystify women's reality by insisting that gender is the sole determinant of women's fate"—ring out.[86] Black female race performers were marginalized in journalistic discourses that were predominantly controlled by men. Belittled for their appearance, punished for their assertiveness, and undermined professionally by virtue of their sex, these women were written out of the narratives of race representation, uplift, and activism in which they played an integral part.

In 1940 Hattie McDaniel became the first black actor to win an Academy Award for her portrayal of Mammy in *Gone with the Wind*. Her achievement received little press; only a handful of newspapers covered the win, and even fewer treated it as front-page material. "The Academy Award given to Hattie McDaniel for her superb acting in the film: 'Gone With the Wind,'" wrote one *Atlanta Daily World* journalist, "deserves more than just a passing notice."[87] Yet the achievement failed to make the front page of any of the major black urban weeklies of the time. Black journalists had found better race representatives on whom to expend their energy, celebrities who represented both racial equality and the restoration of beleaguered masculinity: *sports heroes*.

6

National Heroes, Foreign Villains, and Unhyphenated Americans

"Joe Louis killed Nazi supremacy theory," Associated Negro Press reporter William Patterson declared. "Joe Louis did this by fighting. Not singly, for he had the moral support of 13,000,000 of Negroes and millions of whites who hate fascism and its injustices. Jesse Owens did it by fighting. He fought every step of the 100 yards of cinder path to win."[1]

Writing on the heels of Louis's victory over German champion Max Schmeling in 1938, Patterson's words rang in the minds and hearts of millions of black sports fans for whom the mid-1930s were a defining period. Track star Jesse Owens emerged in 1933 and in the subsequent four years set world records in an array of track and field events, capped off by a dominant performance in Hitler's 1936 Berlin Olympics. Louis, a favorite of black press sportswriters charmed by his humble demeanor, celebrity good looks, and tenacity in the ring, provided the ideal mythic narrative as he established himself as a worthy heavyweight contender in the mid-1930s only to be sidelined by a brutal loss to "villain" German prizefighter Max Schmeling in their initial matchup in 1936, which set the stage for one of the most compelling and heroic comeback stories in sports history.

Together, Owens and Louis—contemporaries, friends, and de facto political symbols—defined 1930s racial activism in sport by fighting symbolic battles on an international stage. Conflicts in Ethiopia and the rise of Hitler in Germany underscored the global nature of the color line, and when Owens and Louis emerged as

American celebrities, they did so without prefix or hyphenation. They were symbols of both racial progress and hypocrisy, and the sports staffs of black urban weeklies framed them as both accordingly. It is difficult to contemplate the civil rights gains that were to take place after World War II without first acknowledging the fact that the first Americans to stand up and be counted, despite being Jim Crowed at home, were black athletes. Jesse Owens and Joe Louis, in particular, radically redefined what a black public figure could represent to the nation, to the world, and most importantly to their own embattled communities.

In sports coverage black journalists routinely expressed hopefulness that achievement in sport would "level the crests of race prejudice." Black athletes' public triumphs differed from the achievements of other categories of black celebrities in crossing racial barriers. In theater, film, and music, it was simple for white mainstream audiences to act as culture vultures, consuming the celebrity personalities they found most appealing, while black journalists had to actively frame for black audiences the cultural meaning (and value) of one performance over another. Arguments about high and low culture, assumptions about class and gender, and competing philosophies on the function of African American artistic expression muddied conversations about what constituted "positive" and "negative" race representation. The notion of "winning" was much simpler for audiences of both races to process. The trampling of the color line in sports was an easy narrative for journalists to describe and promote and for readers to understand and relate to, during a time when American versions of heroes ("us") and villains ("them") were deceptively simple to understand. During times of crisis, the mythologizing of sports serves to perform a critical social function: it unites communities against a common "opponent" or foe.

Sports historians David Wiggins and Patrick Miller use the term "muscular assimilationism" to describe the ways in which black athletes' achievement in sports became circumscribed as civil rights acts.[2] Black journalists harnessed these achievements and aggressively translated them into symbolic victories needed in the fight against Jim Crowism. Black sportswriters used classic narrative conventions to frame sports victories of the 1930s. They relied on heroic tropes to frame their favorite sports celebrities (and themselves), and they used the playing field as a metaphor for civil rights. With the help of public-relations teams well versed in constructing a black celebrity persona that was attractive to white audiences, both Jesse Owens and Joe Louis rose to become national heroes. The celebrities covered in this chapter represent some of the first "unhyphenated" black Americans—seemingly superhuman athletes whose tenacity on the field and in the ring became a metonym for American democratic power against the looming threat of fascism in Europe.

Sports Heroes Save Black Newspapers

The Depression threatened to cripple the black newspaper industry, as its main subscribers—working-class, urban blacks—were among the most adversely affected by the stock market crash. The mighty *Defender*'s circulation dipped to less than seventy-five thousand— nearly a third of what it was at its highest. These papers found a way to survive, though, following the lead of the *Courier*, which shifted its focus almost exclusively to coverage of prizefighter Joe Louis to sustain the interest of its readers. Louis's emergence had a significant impact on the black press, which implemented new, cutting-edge news-gathering and reporting strategies in covering the young celebrity. "The year 1934," declared Ric Roberts in the *Atlanta Daily World*, "will long live in the memories of every colored citizens [*sic*] of these United States of America. Just when the race was in need of some sort of stimulation . . . just when it began looking like we were to have no more Fritz Pollards, Paul Robesons, DeHart Hubbards, Howard Drews, Jack Johnsons, Sam Langfords, Tiger Flowerses and Slaters; just when we had commenced forgetting about Eddie Tolan and Ralph Metcalf, things started happening."[3] Indeed, during the 1930s the newsrooms of black urban weeklies began to pivot coverage and resources to sports reporting, and race athletes became popular news subjects. As Patrick Washburn has noted, the *Courier* began to rival the *Defender* in popularity in part by promoting itself as the "Joe Louis newspaper" in the 1940s, but its evolution to that point started several years earlier, in 1935, with the Carnera and Levinsky bouts.[4] The *Courier* distinguished itself as the black community's leading authority on African American sports; it developed the decade's preeminent sportswriting staff, and it allocated financial resources to cover national and international sports stories. It was the only black press weekly to send a reporter to the 1936 Olympics, while the rest of its competition relied on the Associated Negro Press wire service for reports from Berlin.[5]

The exaltation of sports heroes coincided with a wave of patriotic sentiment linked with the threat posed by Hitler's expanding European conquest. Black journalists were among the first American writers to frame contests between American and German athletes as metaphors for the tension between American democratic values and European fascist aggression.[6] During the previous decade, black journalists repeatedly extolled the virtues of Europe at the expense of America; the idea that Europe was a place where race prejudice did not exist and where black citizens could have increased opportunities and freedom was repeatedly evoked.[7] As the *Afro-American*'s Frank Marshall Davis surmised, "It seems Europeans, because of a different cultural background, have a general understanding and appreciation of art not found on these shores."[8] Eurocentrism was bolstered by the proclamations of Josephine Baker, Paul Robeson, and other popular celebrities who repeatedly gave interviews praising European audiences as racially tolerant. Yet the rise of fascism in Italy and Germany quickly signaled to black communities across the country the global nature of the color line. In January 1933 Hitler became chancellor of Germany and began to implement his National Socialist policies, which relied on both antisemitism and junk scientific theories of racism that were developed first in the United States. Eugenics had drifted to Europe, where Hitler—in collaboration with U.S. funding sources, like the Rockefeller Foundation—continued research into the development of a "master race." As John Hope Franklin asserts, "African Americans were among the earliest and most energetic Americans to condemn fascism . . . and quickly learned to hate Nazism and its Aryan doctrines."[9] Black urban weeklies across the country similarly condemned Italy's 1935 invasion of Ethiopia and subsequent military occupation. Mussolini, wrote the *Courier*, was akin to the "Jew-hating Hitler."[10]

Reporting on issues of national and international interest was bolstered by the development of new technologies and new modes of transportation that put journalists in the center of the action. New technologies meant that the newspapers with the largest circulations and highest revenues could obtain exclusives more quickly than other papers. It also meant increased opportunities for staff reporters—who previously had to rely on reprints from other newspapers and releases from the Associated Negro Press and mainstream wire agencies—to travel to sporting events and become a *part of* the story. Sportswriters took on greater roles as *characters* in the narratives that they created. For example when *Defender* sports editor Al Monroe—who attended Louis's training camp in Pompton Lakes, New Jersey, in preparation for the Baer fight—boasted, "Never before in history has a sports writer been singled out at an important camp and permitted to watch a private drill," he was not only reporting on Louis's training; rather he too became a heroic character in this mythic story.[11] One week before the Carnera fight, the *Courier* informed its readers, "When Joe Louis . . . crawls through the ropes in Yankee Stadium arena next Tuesday night to battle Primo Carnera, The Courier's Big Four of the reportorial staff will be on hand to give Courier readers a graphic account of the big fight." The "Big Four" included Chester L. Washington, sports editor; William G. Nunn, city editor; Lonnie Harrington, boxing critic; and Floyd J. Calvin, New York correspondent.[12] Even the headline, which began "Courier Writers with a 'Punch,'" emphasized not Louis's ferocity but the reporters'.

Immediately after the fight, which ended with a technical knockout after six rounds, Nunn declared, "I feel that the race's prayers were answered"; however it was unclear if this declaration was related to Louis's victory or to the speed with which the *Courier* was able to break the story. Nunn continued (ostensibly typing from a prop plane taking him from New York back to Pittsburgh), "Special plane wing through night and thus makes glorious history for Negro journalism!" The editor's note that accompanied Nunn's rundown of the fight read: "This story was written by William G.

Nunn, city editor of the Pittsburgh Courier, as he rushed back to Pittsburgh via special plane, with the FIRST pictures of the Louis-Carnera fight. ONE HOUR after he arrived, the 'O.K.' was given, and the Courier presses started turning out the greatest edition in the history of America's best weekly." Six weeks later Louis struck another victory, again by technical knockout, over King Levinsky. The fight lasted only one round, during which Levinsky went down four times. The *Courier* won that night again, as well: "Once again the PITTSBURGH COURIER has scored with a direct Western Union wire from the ringside at Comiskey Park, in Chicago: with a Postal Telegraph teletype clicking the stories of the fight and side lights as they happened 500 miles away, The Pittsburgh Courier 'marched ahead' once more to make glorious newspaper history." The speed with which the report made it to the presses was again emphasized: "THE COURIER PRESSES WERE RUNNING ONE HOUR AND SIXTEEN MINUTES after the knockout."[13] Excitement over technological innovation pervaded reports of Louis's victories as much as sentiments about race pride did. These writers self-mythologized, creating for themselves and their institutions public personas that shared the spotlight with their famous news subjects.

Defeating "Cheese Champions"

"When we examine the records we find that in every sphere of sport in which the Negro engages he has more than made good," wrote Romeo Dougherty in 1935. "His road has been made doubly hard by the obstacles which he has been forced to surmount in reaching the place he occupies."[14] The color line had made it nearly impossible for many black athletes to even receive the opportunity to compete in their field. As Wiggins and Miller have noted, "Although Blacks shared an impressive vitality and sense of self-worth in creating sporting communities of their own, they continued to protest again segregation and discrimination at every opportunity and made the most of the occasional exception to the prevailing pattern of exclusion."[15]

The "pattern of exclusion" in sport came in various forms. The color line had been officially or unofficially drawn in the majority of college and professional sports at the time; for instance,

Fig. 4. Black weeklies around the country celebrate race hero Joe Louis. The *Courier* was the first to buy in to the craze. *Pittsburgh Courier*, August 10, 1935, front page. *ProQuest Historical Newspapers–Black Newspapers.* ProQuest.

baseball was officially segregated (which led to the formation of separate Negro Leagues in 1920 by former Cuban Giants pitcher Rube Foster). Segregation in college football depended on how progressive the culture of the institution was. The success and longevity of the Howard and Lincoln football programs led to the recruitment of black athletes by schools like the University of Michigan, though once the players arrived, they were often subject to discrimination and humiliation at the hands of their coaches, teammates, and rival schools. In 1934 Georgia Tech refused to take the field against Michigan if it played end Willis Ward, only the second black player to integrate Michigan's football team; in response Ward was forced to sit out of the game.

"Occasional exceptions" came most frequently—though not frequently enough—in boxing. Boxing was segregated to the extent that individual white fighters—depending on their success and the clout they carried—could simply refuse to take on any black fighter they chose. Black athletes' opportunities to compete at a high level were scarce, thanks in large part to the flamboyant antics of Jack Johnson during his championship reign. Black sportswriters seemed almost embarrassed by Johnson and did what they could to distance themselves from the troubled champion. By 1920, however, attitudes toward boxing as a legitimate sport had changed drastically. Government deregulation, combined with the establishment of the National Boxing Association, widespread coverage of sporting events in urban newspapers and on the radio, and depictions of boxing in film all contributed to the destigmatization and booming popularity of the sport.[16] Previous debates about boxing's "propriety" as a sport in which black athletes should engage were outmoded; rather, the black press simply celebrated any contender who seemed have a shot at holding a title. For instance the *Defender* called for Harry "Black Panther" Wills to "whip this big over-rated fellow [champion Jack Dempsey] to a frazzle" and to "treat [him] rough."[17] Concerns about black men engaging in "uncivilized" activity—at least in the ring—seemingly disappeared.

The *Courier*'s Chester L. Washington wrote of the "deeds of daring and courage of the mighty men of the mighty art" of boxing, which held deep cultural significance in the 1920s.[18] Boxing had become increasingly popular over time, and the heavyweight title held symbolic power. Heavyweight champs were "genuine sports heroes."[19] By 1920 only one black boxer—Johnson—had received a shot at the heavyweight title, and he had won decisively not once but twice, though his victories were marred by racial strife and personal missteps.

To risk a black man holding the title was, for many, to risk the inherent superiority and thus future dominance and legitimacy of the white race itself. As William Gildea, Joe Gans's biographer, notes, "Boxing's subtext has always been America's subtext: race."[20] In the 1920s several black contenders rose through the ranks but were denied a shot at the title simply because boxing served as a microcosm of life under Jim Crow—the color line followed these men from all forms of public space, including transportation, schools, and restaurants, and into the ring, where they were often allowed to challenge only other boxers of their own race. For instance one of the best contenders to emerge, Sam Langford, fought Sam McVea fifteen times, Joe Jeanette fourteen times, and Harry Wills twenty-three times in lieu of fighting white contenders in his weight class for a title.[21]

Frustrated, black journalists hurled some of their harshest critiques at the "color line" in boxing. The ring seemed to symbolize life under Jim Crow, where whites regularly marginalized blacks. Tex Rickard, the most successful fight promoter of the period, was accused by the *New York Amsterdam News* as the force that "[brought] Jim Crow stuff into boxing."[22] The *Defender*'s Juli Jones lamented, "Taking everything in consideration, the present crop of fighters have had the roughest road to travel that could be made. They were Jim-Crowed and everything else done to discourage a boxer. Yet they have kept on."[23] The *Courier*'s Ira Lewis dismissed both John Sullivan (who dodged Peter Jackson) and Jack Dempsey (who dodged Harry Wills) as "cheese champions" not worthy of the heavyweight title.[24] The contention of black newspapers was that no white champion could rightfully call himself a "champion" if he refused to fight legitimate contenders based solely on their race.

By 1930 it seemed as though any great hopes that may have shown potential during the 1920s had faded away. Battling Siki, a

Senegalese lightweight whose only notable victory came in 1922 against Frenchman Georges Carpentier for the world title, was murdered on a Harlem street corner in 1925. Heavyweight contender Harry Wills had spent the 1920s chasing Dempsey, but after being shut out of the title shot, he had lost the chance to reach his full potential. Sam Langford, another notable heavyweight, lost his vision and needed assistance raising the funds to receive surgery. His blindness forced him into early retirement. Tiger Flowers, the middleweight champion, had passed way from complications from a seemingly routine surgery to remove scar tissue from around his eye. Sam McVey, George Godfrey, and Joe Jeannette continued to fight exhibition matches, but none of them came close to a championship shot. And Jack Johnson was simply too old to restart his career.

Jesse Owens and the Slow Death of Eugenics

Sportswriters were not at a loss for news to report on during this period, though; Negro League baseball and collegiate football and basketball were all popular among black sports fans, but stand-out superstars in those sports emerged only decades later.[25] Rather, sportswriters began to become excited over an increasingly popular collegiate sport that, like boxing, emphasized individual achievement: track and field. As the *Afro-American* noted, the two sports had much in common: "If grit, gall and determination are needed to win success in the prize ring they are also needed just as much on the field and track."[26] "Grit, gall and determination" led four young men to the Olympic Games in the summer of 1932—Eddie Tolan, Ralph Metcalfe, Ed Gordon, and Cornelius Johnson. Tolan placed first in both the one-hundred-meter and the two-hundred-meter dash; Metcalfe placed second in the one-hundred-meter dash and third in the two-hundred-meter dash; Gordon placed first in the broad jump; and Cornelius Johnson placed fourth in the high jump. *Atlanta Daily World* sportswriter Edwin Henderson offered "a very optimistic prediction that in the not-too-distant future this same ill-considered athletic world [was] going to do much to level the crests of American race prejudice."[27]

Black athletes consistently challenged and undermined prevailing attitudes about the inherent physical "inferiority" of the black race. Pseudoscientific theories sought to explicate taxonomies of human difference based on "evidence" ranging from the size and shape of one's head to theories about extra foot bones. Black sportswriters were keenly aware of the harsh stereotypes that pervaded mainstream imagery of black men, and they feared the double-edged sword of physical achievement. For instance *Chicago Defender* sportswriter Juli Jones Jr. lamented, "When a Black man wins a big victory in the ring, some of the big writers compare him with an African gorilla and cartoon him as the most terrible beast in the jungles—an unfair picture and comparison."[28] In covering Senegalese fighter Battling Siki, writers routinely tried to underplay his African heritage as indicative of some sort of "lack of civilization."[29] Despite his status as a national hero, Joe Louis was covered by mainstream dailies as alternatively the "animal-like, aggressive black man" and the "confused, childlike Negro."[30] When Howard University sponsored a physical exam in an effort to prove that there was "no evidence to support the widely-published theory of white sports authorities that Owens's speed as a sprinter was due to an extended heel bone common among African tribes," the *Afro-American* covered the story on its front page.[31] The newspaper even ran a photo of Owens on the exam table.

In response to these strange theories and the negative attitudes they perpetuated, sports journalists took every opportunity to emphasize the physical beauty, strength, and superiority of their athletes. By 1933 the "Four Fastest Humans" on earth—Ralph Metcalfe, Eddie Tolan, Jesse Owens, and Jimmy Johnson—were sportswriters' favorites. "I am thankful that the beautiful body of our new world's champion," wrote Henry Edwards of 1932 Olympic gold-medalist Tolan, "is clothed in a beautiful, dark, ebony skin. I am grateful because this fact leaves no room for conceited arguments by some of our Nordic-superiority-advocates."[32] Owens was far from "subhuman"; to black press journalists, he was *super*human: "The star leapt through space 24 feet 9 5–8 inches in the broad jump, 7 inches better than the established world record," wrote Vernon Williams of the athlete's Big Ten breakout performance.[33]

These athletes' achievements were celebrated extensively by the black press, which framed such stories as a call to young black Americans to "get into the game of life. . . . [When you do] you will smash race prejudice." At the same time, New Deal youth programs, like the National Youth Administration and the Civil Conservation Corps, targeted civic participation for black teenagers. They taught wartime and environmental trades, decreased illiteracy rates among black children, and even allowed participants to continue their education upon completion of the program. Nannie Burroughs of the *Afro-American* charged, "It is high time that Negro youth were becoming obsessed with the desire and a burning passion to enter the game [of life] and win."[34] In particular Tolan and Metcalfe's victories emphasized the American dream ideals of discipline, determination, and hard work: "Thank God for Tolan and Metcalfe, with their heads back and eyes shining and feet flying. . . . This triumph over the world is heartening to the entire Negro race," wrote Burroughs.[35] Photos and illustrations of the pair were commonplace front-page items. Harry Edwards wrote in the *New York Amsterdam News*, "I am . . . grateful to Edward Tolan for the inspiration he has given to thousands upon thousands of colored American youths, and I am confident that he has awakened a similar echo in the hearts of many in far away Africa and the East."[36] Tolan, Metcalfe, Owens, and Johnson were young superstars who, perhaps, symbolized to many families the possibilities inherent for their own children.

Owens in particular was exemplary: he was "a likable young star," "a modest boy who never trie[d] to make a show of himself just because he [was] a celebrity," a devout Christian, and a momma's boy.[37] Owens accepted a position on Ohio State's track team, despite protestations that the school was notorious for race prejudice; in two years' time, he was named team captain.[38] In spring of 1935 at the Big Ten Track and Field Championships in Ann Arbor, Michigan, Owens tied the world record in the 100-yard dash and set the world record in the long jump, the 220-yard dash, and the 220-yard low hurdles.

Owens's Big Ten performance served three symbolic functions for the black press: first, it gave sportswriters fodder for expressions of racial pride, as the 1932 Olympic team had three years previously; second, Owens's relationship with his white coach, Charles Riley, and teammates helped to promote racial integrationism as a legitimate political strategy; and third, it cemented Owens's celebrity status.

Sportswriters routinely framed Owens a "credit to the race." "With high hopes and bounding hearts," wrote the *Atlanta Daily World,* "Negroes everywhere in America . . . must contemplate with deep satisfaction and pride the athletic prowess of Jesse Owens."[39] For conservative newspapers, such as the *Afro-American,* Owens was a respite from the edgier celebrities who graced their pages. They delighted in his devotion to the church. "Religion is an integral part of family life," wrote one anonymous journalist. "It should not be considered a bit of maudlin sentiment to relate that through his school days the boy prayed that he might never 'get the swelled head.' You must talk to him to realize how well his prayers were answered."[40] Other writers emphasized his devotion to his education, underscored by his father's choice early in his son's life to relocate from Decatur, Georgia, to Cleveland, Ohio. The Owens family was a Great Migration success story, and Jesse himself was framed as an uplifter. "The success of these boys," wrote Williams of Owens and his Olympic teammates, "has been a credit to the race as well as to themselves."[41]

Many black sportswriters were especially impressed by the fact that Owens had seemingly become "a favorite of both races." His Ohio State team celebrated his Big Ten wins "as if they had been received by members of their own race." His relationship with Riley, according to the *Afro-American,* was "one of the finest examples of mutual affection in the annals of track, growing out of a genuine admiration which transcends race and color."[42] The *Atlanta Daily World* happily reprinted comments made in mainstream Atlanta dailies about their favorite race athlete, asserting those sportswriters had "exhausted their vocabularies in stories telling of our own Jesse's glory."[43] Owens's functional relationship with his white coach and teammates provided support for the integrationist agenda that many black weeklies promoted in their pages.

Owens's status as a celebrity fundamentally changed the way the press approached covering him. When he visited Los Angeles's

City Hall, for example, it was Fay Jackson—the ANP's Hollywood correspondent—who covered the story, rather than one of the staff sportswriters. There was, of course, controversy surrounding the Nickerson affair, though Owens's handlers had addressed the matter by quickly marrying the sprinter to his childhood sweetheart, Ruth Solomon, to whom he remained married for the rest of his life. Despite his athletic feats, Owens was "in deed and truth, 'just one of us.'" Owens did "not smoke cigarettes nor drink, but he like[d] to dance and play bridge."[44] The *Afro-American* so embraced its wholesome new star that it published a weekly column about his life for the summer of 1935.

Owens's success had real implications for the race, as his feats in the Big Ten began to chip away at eugenic theory, which sought to rationalize the global economic, social, and political oppression of people of color. The *Oakland Post Enquirer*, one of William Randolph Hearst's West Coast dailies, commented, "Owens's easy superiority in so many foot races . . . gives rise to interesting speculation about the more important question of superiority among the human races. IS the white race superior? If so is its superiority THREATENED?" The author continued: "Certainly there was not much of a margin of superiority between Jesse Owens of Ohio and George Anderson of California in SPEED last week."[45]

"Racial prejudice and tolerance," the writer concluded, "examined in the cold light of science do not have much basis for existence."[46] As journalists in the newsrooms of black press weeklies, such as the *Pittsburgh Courier*, which reprinted this valuable nugget, scoured mainstream dailies for news of their race stars, they must have noted with great satisfaction the slow death of eugenic thought.

"Americans" without the Hyphen

"Joe Louis has a problem," wrote the *Defender*'s Al Monroe from the prizefighter's Lakewood, New Jersey, training camp. "It is getting rid of weight, but Joe Louis doesn't figure to have much of a problem getting rid of Max Schmeling on the evening of June 18 at Yankee Stadium."[47] Excitement over the matchup between Louis and German champion Max Schmeling for a title shot against James

Braddock dominated the sports pages of black urban weeklies for the first six months of 1936, and no wonder. Louis was a race hero. "He symbolizes the latent power of his people," wrote Ted Benson, "the clenched brown fist." He continued, "When Louis defeated Max Baer, the Negroes of the cities identified themselves with his victory and celebrated nationally. That dynamite concealed in his muscles released pent-up desires to be free from the chains of economic slavery and to escape the prison walls of national discrimination."[48] Joe Louis's early summer 1936 battle against German Max Schmeling—a prelude to the historic 1936 Olympic Games—became not a contest of black against white but rather of American hero against German villain. Louis was favored to win the bout against Schmeling by odds of 5–1 by knockout, and the match was to exceed $1.5 million in receipts. Accordingly, the tickets priced out many black fans eager to see their champion crush the "Nazi Aryan hope."[49] "Pawn shops have been raided for field glasses and any other long-distance seeing apparatus," reported *Courier* sports editor Chester Washington the night before the fight, "because, folks, those $5.75s are awfully far back!"[50]

So certain were sports journalists that Louis would "kill" Schmeling that Washington, reporting from Lakewood in the days before the fight, imagined Louis, tucked in his bed, "closing his eyes and visualizing his victory dreams of honors and wealth and a world championship [against Braddock] looming on a rosy horizon."[51] The certainty of his victory was only fueled by the Germans' trepidation in allowing Schmeling to fight a black contender. "The feeling here is that if Joe Louis, idol of the American people, defeats Max Schmeling, the 'Aryan,'" reported a *New York Amsterdam News* correspondent from Berlin, "the national pride will be sorely hurt, and will cause serious repercussions, which would find its outlet in stricter laws against competition against non-'Aryans.'"[52]

So when Louis went down in the twelfth round of the fight, after allowing Schmeling to lead the subsequent rounds, American boxing fans and most acutely black communities around the country were simply devastated. "Even from the very start of things," lamented the *Defender*, "it was evident that this was another race's party with little attention and thought for the Joe

Louis blood and kin and as it turned out for Joe Louis himself."[53] On the sports page of the same issue, Enoch Waters posited that Louis's defeat "was more than just a personal loss. It was a defeat which 12,000,000 black souls felt as keenly as the Black Bomber himself." "What the race lost in money was as dust to diamonds," he continued, "compared with the loss suffered in hope."[54] As historian Lane Demas notes in his study of the American press's reaction to the loss, black sportswriters struggled with "coming to grips with the risky nature of hero construction—that tenuous process by which the hopes, aspirations, and dreams of the entire community are embodied in one man."[55]

In the days after Louis's loss, track star Jesse Owens set one more world record, this time at the NCAA's annual track and field meet, in the one-hundred-meter sprint. Owens "was out to set aright the prestige the Race had sustained in the fall of Gladiator Joseph Louis Barrow on the night of June 18, as everyone no doubt recalls," read an article in the *Defender*'s sports section right alongside Waters's heartbreaking account of Louis's defeat. Owens and Louis were friends; they had done promotional tours together in the years preceding 1936, and there was a certain harmony in the idea of Owens picking up and carrying Louis's torch straight to Berlin.

Owens arrived in Berlin weeks later already a national celebrity and already under the watchful eye of reporters, who had assigned to what were supposed to be apolitical games crushing symbolic weight. Hitler declared that the Olympic Games would not allow African Americans to participate. The United States Olympic Team that year included seventeen African American athletes, twelve of whom (including Owens) were track and field competitors.[56] Black sportswriters were outraged by Hitler's Olympic ban and debated how athletes should respond to the snub. The *New York Amsterdam News* was the most vocal in its opposition to participation in the games. In August 1935 the newspaper published on its front page an open letter it had sent to Olympic hopefuls Owens, Eulace Peacock, Ralph Metcalfe, Cornelius Johnson, Willis Ward, James Luvalle, and Ben Johnson asking them to refuse to participate in the games. The letter read: "The Amsterdam News begs you to refuse to participate in the Olympic Games in Germany in 1936.

We beg you to demonstrate a courage which, so far, has been lacking in the guiding spirits of the American Olympic Committee. We beg you to display that spirit of self-sacrifice which is the true mark of all greatness." The newspaper's request was made "in the name of the 204,000 Negroes in Harlem, the 12,000,000 Negroes in America and the countless darker exploited colonials throughout the world."[57] The athletes were asked to make a determination based on their obligation to the African diaspora in the United States and Europe. A few months later, the *Afro-American* joined the *Amsterdam News* in its call for a boycott.[58] Reporters repeatedly sought information from Owens's trainers and managers to see where he stood on the issue. Owens often downplayed the controversy or refused to respond to inquiries about it altogether.[59]

Despite continuing protests from civil rights groups, including the NAACP, the Amateur Athletic Union approved American participation in the games in mid-December 1935. That month the athletes responded not to the *Amsterdam News*'s letter but to the American Olympic Committee, requesting the opportunity to participate in the games. Eustace Gay of the *Philadelphia Tribune* wrote a polemic condemning the "hypocrisy" of American Olympic boycotts: "What is more inhuman than lynching human beings? How would America like to have a leading German Government official make a speech in which he declared that 'no true sportsman should accept hospitality from any American government so long as it continues its inhuman treatment' of the colored minority?"[60] Black sportswriters actively debated the gains that would be made if black athletes participated. Would their participation be an opportunity to display on a global stage their inherent equality with all other races, or would it be a hypocritical move to boycott a country that, as Gay pointed out, carried out similar practices of oppression and inhuman treatment that America did? There was no clear answer.

On August 3 Owens struck his first blow, winning the one-hundred-meter sprint just one-tenth of a second ahead of his American teammate, Ralph Metcalfe. The next day he won the long jump and the day after the two-hundred-meter sprint. On August 9 he and Metcalfe became the last-minute replacements on the four-by-one-hundred-meter relay team, in which Owens won his fourth gold medal and set a team world record in the process: 39.8 seconds. As Pamela Laucella notes in her study of mainstream coverage of Owens's 1936 Olympic performance, white sportswriters "continually reinforced racially separatist ideologies" by positing that Owens possessed some biological trait that led to his physical dominance—rather than skill or intelligence or character or training.[61] The racial blind spots exhibited by mainstream sports journalists were countered by black press sportswriters, who framed Owens's achievements in the purview of not only Nazism but also of the hypocrisy of American sportswriters who condemned Hitler's refusal to greet Owens while failing to acknowledge their own racism.[62]

"But what if Jesse Owens toured Georgia, Florida, Alabama, Texas or anyplace 'behind the sun'?" wondered Joe Richards, writing for the *Chicago Defender*. "He would meet the same old prejudices and jim-crowism: have to tread alleys and ride freight elevators to radiocast; he'd find himself behind sign-boards on the street-cars, sign-boards captioned 'colored' or 'Negro'; he'd sit in the galleries of the picture-palaces and hear himself called 'n——r' on every hand, and if he so much as attempted to shake hands with one of the female Nordic members of the Olympic team, he'd be 'strung up.'"[63] Richards's alternate vision of Owens as a victim of American, rather than German, racial prejudice must have resonated with readers experiencing those very same Jim Crow exploits as they rejoiced in Owens's charming, quirky smile splashed across both black weeklies and mainstream urban dailies.

Not all sportswriters were as cynical as Richards, as justified as his cynicism was. Raymond Jackson, for instance, was heartened by the observation that white sportswriters' reactions to Hitler's snub rivaled in outrage those made by his race contemporaries: "As the texture of the comments made by leading columnists and sportswriters sounded similar to the travestying of superiority complexes made by Negro editors and Negro writers in general." What if, he wondered, "race prejudice doesn't belong in the category along with the misunderstood husband and wife, the poor tired businessman, the crooner and the saxophone."[64]

The August 8, 1936, cover of the *Pittsburgh Courier* led with editor Robert L. Vann's account of Owens's historic performance. As it had done with coverage of Louis's earlier victories, the editors in charge of designing the issue's layout shifted the masthead right and shrank it considerably, so that the most distinctive element on the page is the huge banner headline, "HITLER SALUTES JESSE OWENS." "Our Jesse" is pictured left, below the banner, and Vann's story—broken into three sections—dominates one side of the front page, while the other side is dedicated to Italy's invasion of Ethiopia. Increasingly, as a result of its spectacular coverage of its sports stars, the *Courier* had an operating budget that allowed for the funding of foreign correspondents; it was the only newspaper to send a correspondent (Vann himself) to Germany to cover the Olympic Games while staff writer J. A. Rogers was making a name for himself with his coverage of the Ethiopia crisis.[65]

"It is deeply gratifying," wrote Vann, "to note that colored American athletes now doing their bit for the United States at the Olympic Games in Berlin have achieved a status abroad that it is scarcely suspected is theirs when in their native land," echoing criticisms shared by other black press journalists on the subject. Yet Vann's editorial tone was hardly cynical; rather, he saw Owens's victory as a teachable moment for white audiences tuning into the games: "Radio broadcasters have pictured them, not as Negroes, but as Americans. That is what they are, Americans, without hyphens, with roots deep in American soil. It is indeed good for America as a whole to learn that there are Americans named Owens and Metcalfe and Johnson and Albritton and Woodruff, just to name a few, in Germany today, upholding the good old stars and stripes."[66]

Curiously, Vann also claimed to have seen for himself Hitler salute the track star: "I saw Jesse Owens greeted by the Grand Chancellor of this country as a brilliant sun peeped out through the clouds. I saw a vast crowd of some 85,000 or 90,000 stand up and cheer him to the echo. And they were mostly Germans!"[67]

Meanwhile, Louis's reputation sustained a brutal blow when he hit the mat that June 1936 evening—so much so that the *Defender*

Fig. 5. In the *Courier*'s first issue after Jesse Owens's historic 1936 Olympic performance, editor in chief Robert Vann tries to convince readers that German chancellor Adolph Hitler saluted their hero. *Pittsburgh Courier*, August 8, 1936, front page. *ProQuest Historical Newspapers–Black Newspapers*. ProQuest.

ran a "contest" asking readers to weigh in on who would win a hypothetical match between Louis and the disgraced Jack Johnson, and readers were split. "Now that Louis has given the fans their first big disappointment, the contest voters are rallying to support Jack Johnson in the 'greatest of the great' contest," read one February 1937 entry.[68] Attitudes about representation were shifting, and Johnson, though semiretired and certainly past his prime, was still a strong celebrity presence, and at least temporarily, seemed to be favored as such over the once-untouchable Louis.

Louis quietly worked to regain his reputation, winning five of his next bouts by knockout. When "Cinderella Man" James Braddock, under pressure from politically active Jewish groups threatening to protest if he took on Schmeling in a title defense, broke his contract with Madison Square Garden, it finally opened up an opportunity for a black heavyweight contender. Unwilling to chance losing his title to the German "villain," Braddock signed on to fight Louis for the title at Comiskey Park in Chicago. The Garden retaliated by filing an injunction to prevent the fight, but the New York State Athletic Commission did little to intervene, and the injunction was quickly overturned. The judge in the case "stressed particularly the point that demanding Braddock not to fight Joe Louis with no given time as a maximum would mean curtailment of the champion's chances to earn a living at his chosen profession."[69] Schmeling was effectively frozen out of a shot at the title, and for the first time in twenty-two years, an interracial heavyweight championship match was to take place.

As they did in the lead-up to Louis-Schmeling I, black urban dailies with large enough budgets to accommodate the arrangement sent reporters to Louis's training camp to chart his progress. *Courier* city editor William G. Nunn, part of the team that so heroically reported on Louis's early victories, wrote from the fighter's Kenosha, Wisconsin, training camp:

> To Courier readers and to hundreds of thousands of idol-worshippers of the youth, we say to you: DON'T Worry!
> We know you've heard stories and tales about Louis' lack of a spark—about his indolence—about his escapades—and

about every ugly rumor that can touch a man who is knocking at the door of ringdom's "Hall of Fame."

... Again we say to you—DON'T WORRY![70]

Rumors about marital woes had swirled around the press, particularly in the wake of the Schmeling defeat. Some sportswriters, including Nunn, had even blamed Marva for distracting her husband in the crucial days leading up to the fight. Nunn dismissed these concerns. "The Joe Louis we saw here this afternoon," Nunn promised, "is the Joe Louis of the pre-Carnera and pre-Baer fight days."[71]

Nunn's assessment proved to be accurate. On June 22, 1937, Louis bested Braddock over eight rounds to claim the heavyweight title—nearly thirty years after Jack Johnson had first won the title from Tommy Burns in Australia. The *Defender* and the *Courier*, Louis's most steadfast supporters, dedicated nearly all the space on their front pages to the victory. The *Defender* featured as one its most striking visuals of the period Louis's singular fist with the caption, "It was the second time in the history of pugilism that a brown fist had won the highest honor of professional boxing and the world's heavyweight title." The *Courier* proclaimed, "LOUIS WORLD'S CHAMP" but juxtaposed the victory with news out of the Senate: the Costigan-Wagner Bill had reportedly passed through the Senate Judiciary Committee in a 12 to 3 vote.[72] The juxtaposition of those two stories on the *Courier*'s front page was striking, given the history of postfight violence that had plagued Johnson's 1910 title defense. Their presence together on the front page of the *Courier* underscored just how much times seemed to have changed—interracial celebrations had replaced riots and lynching. The "leveling of race prejudice" seemed to actually be happening.

"Whites are not sour. Blacks are glad," wrote Nunn from the jubilant streets of Chicago. The fear of racial violence that had accompanied the Johnson-Jeffries fight nearly thirty years earlier was replaced with what Nunn described as a "friendly, but barbarous tribe, white and black, which strains at the leash to make this one unforgettable night." He offered a vivid description: "Swirling, careening, madly dashing from house to house . . . yelling, crying,

Fig. 6. The *Defender*'s iconic front page celebrating Joe Louis's victory over "Cinderella Man" James Braddock portrays Louis as a powerful brown fist—an image that would be crystallized years later with the construction of the monument to Joe Louis in downtown Detroit. *Chicago Defender*, June 26, 1937, front page. *Black Studies Center*, Chadwyck-Healey, ProQuest.

laughing, boasting, gloating, exulting . . . slapping backs, jumping out of the way of wildly-driven cars . . . whites and blacks hugging . . . the entire world, this cosmic center of the world tonight, turned topsy-turvy, this is the Southside of Chicago."[73] While whites' reactions to a black heavyweight champion were overall muted, this was not necessarily an indication of increasing racial tolerance. Rather, Louis had worked hard to operate within the purview of behavior accepted by whites, and his willingness to fulfill their expectations of a humble, self-effacing champion simply made him more palatable to them than Jack Johnson had been.

Nonetheless, to Nunn the peaceful reaction to Louis's victory was reason itself to celebrate. "A deeply rooted desire for retribution, which has almost become an obsession, is burning within the very soul of the world's fistic king," wrote Chester Washington after a conversation with champion Louis, who despite his new title was still smarting from his defeat against Max Schmeling. "With all the larceny in Joe's heart, if only his fists are honest, he'll take the Teuton!"[74]

And so he did, on June 22, 1938, in New York City, in only 124 seconds. In what became one of sport history's most lauded symbolic victories, Louis knocked out Schmeling in the first round of their rematch, effectively putting to death the notion of Aryan superiority and venting the frustrations of millions of Americans increasingly concerned with Hitler's ever-expanding European conquest. "Joe Louis killed the idea of Nazi supremacy," wrote William L. Patterson for the ANP. "He laid to rest the idea of the supremacy of any racial of national group over another."[75]

Leveling the Crests

This analysis of sports coverage in the black press agrees with previous scholars' assertions that sport was a particularly productive site in the symbolic struggle for civil rights, emphasizing the role that black journalists played in framing sports heroes as race representatives. According to black sportswriters, "leveling the crests of American race prejudice" would occur in two specific ways: first, achievement in sports would undermine prevailing notions of physical "superiority" held by whites as a result of pseudoscientific theories that, during this period, gained particular traction with the eugenics movement; and second, equality between the races on the playing field would undermine inequality elsewhere. The achievements of Jesse Owens and Joe Louis critically undermined prevailing attitudes toward the physical "inferiority" of black citizens generally. No one could frame their victories as anything but the result of talent, hard work, and determination. These accomplishments made these two athletes not just race heroes but national heroes as well. Sports journalists repeatedly argued that success in sports could lead to a decrease in racism—that it could not only uplift the black race but also influence the hearts and minds of white audiences. Globally, both black and white audiences were symbolically united in their celebration of black athletes who represented the United States. Accordingly, sports celebrities such as breakout track track-and-field star Jesse Owens and prizefighter Joe Louis were framed by sports journalists as race representatives, changing the conditions of the *real* by using common-denominator representational politics that cast Americans as a united "us" against the German "others."

Jack Lule, in his study of the mythic functions of news reporting, found that sporting events provide ideal fodder for the construction of hero myths. Sports have an inherent sense of conflict and suspense, which are resolved through public spectacle. Fans choose sides; they assign to an athlete or a team the labels "heroes" and "villains." Like mythic heroes athletes perform seemingly superhuman feats of strength and agility. "In portrayals of right and wrong, good and evil, success and failure," writes Lule, "myths of the sports hero reflect and reaffirm core values and beliefs."[76] The need to reify extant core beliefs comes at times of upheaval, when those values are threatened with attack.[77] The individual physical feats of sports heroes were translated by their fans into collective feats of heart, soul, and will. Under the crushing pressure of Jim Crow oppression, the Great Depression, and international turmoil, the victories of Joe Louis and the 1936 U.S. Olympic Team seemed to represent to black communities all over the country hope that conditions for the race could change for the better.

1

Journalistic Commemoration and the
Construction of a "Felt" Past

Lightweight champion Joe Gans was "truly a master at the game. . . .
His equal in the fine points of boxing is yet to be found," read
the *Defender*'s August 1910 obituary.[1] Gans, who passed away from
tuberculosis only one month after watching Jack Johnson defend
the heavyweight title against Jim Jeffries, was the first athlete to
cross the color line in sports. Though he was effectively ignored in
black press weeklies, which during his championship reign (1902
through 1908) were predominantly concerned with racial uplift, in
the months and particularly the years after his death, he became a
venerated symbol of racial progress—an exemplary figure to which
the rest of the race could aspire. In death Gans was discursively
transformed from a man and an athlete to a cypher on which black
journalists could encode evolving attitudes toward the sport of boxing as well as strategies for civil rights activism. In this way Gans and
other deceased celebrities became symbols of *mnemonic resistance*,
discursive constructions created by, in this case, black press journalists to "resist encroachments of a powerful dominant memory" that
challenged the era's resistance to venerate notable public figures of
color.[2] Entrenched in mediated public memory preoccupied with
glorifying the Civil War, reconciling southern white racial aggression, and erasing the trauma of slavery, American collective memory
during this period became a terrain of struggle as black journalists
opposed officially sanctioned ways of narrativizing the past.

Individual personalities are often the symbols through which
major historical events, such as the struggle for freedom, are

remembered. Memory and identity are mutually constitutive.[3] Stories about the past build community and a collective sense of identity. They guide judgments based on a community's shared moral vision. Stories about the past also offer cues for social order and particularly to individual aspiration. Carolyn Kitch has argued that celebrities play that role in death just as they do in life. Journalistic narratives, she observes, "construct celebrities in a way that endows them with sacrificial symbolic status that allows them to live and die for all of us." A celebrity death is "an unstable public moment in which people feel compelled to assess their identities and beliefs—to the meaning any major celebrity holds for any social group."[4] The reclamation of the past that black journalists undertook during Jim Crowism was a key identity project informed by the veneration of those they regarded as their most enduring and most important public representatives. It should come as no surprise that celebrities served this function in death just as they did in life.

The evocation of dead celebrities was characteristic in coverage that emerged during this period, which serves to underscore the growing importance of celebrity culture to black communities as the product of growing leisure and entertainment industries. Over a four-year period, 1910 through 1914, the world lost Joe Gans, George Walker, Samuel Coleridge-Taylor, and Aida Overton Walker, and black journalists honored each with more coverage than he or she had garnered during their lifetime. George and Aida Walker together were remembered as pioneers of black theater. George's untimely death in 1911 after suffering a year in a New York sanatorium made front-page news in the *Afro-American*, which—though it had basically ignored his career—described the comedian as "one of the most dignified in the profession."[5] The *Defender* dedicated one-quarter of its front page to his death.[6] Walker's legacy as a civil rights pioneer emerged only posthumously. Sylvester Russell declared that "the name of Williams and Walker is still fresh in the pages of American stage history; so fresh that we can scarcely afford to stand aside and see that name go to waste; that name which means so much prestige and so very much asset to the Negro professional."[7] Aida, who died three years later at thirty-four years old, was also remembered fondly. The *Defender* ran a photo of Walker dressed in her stage costume with the caption, "The Chicago Defender publishes this picture of the lamented stage favorite at the request of her friends and associates who consider this one of her best poses when she was at the zenith of her career."[8] The flattering posthumous coverage of the Walkers seems to suggest that the Williams and Walker Company was a regular fixture in the pages of the black press, though coverage of the troupe's stars began to amplify only after George Walker ceased performing and then focused only on Bert Williams's Follies turn.

When Coleridge-Taylor passed away in early September 1912, he was recast in memory as a symbol of the black American freedom struggle, despite the fact that he was actually British and possessed no family history of bondage. The *Crisis* dedicated several pages of coverage to his life and work in both the October and the November issues, even publishing a lengthy poem written by Alfred Noyes in his honor.[9] To the *Crisis* Coleridge-Taylor's work was "true Negro music," capturing the "melancholy beauty, barbaric color, charm of musical rhythm and vehement passion" of the African American folk song tradition.[10] The *Gazette* reprinted remarks from Coleridge-Taylor's student and friend fellow composer Clarence Cameron White, who said, "Mr. Coleridge-Taylor's life and work meant more to the young Negro musician and music student here in America than can be told in words. . . . Coleridge-Taylor will live as long as there is a boy or girl with Negro blood in his or her veins who has the 'spirit of song' in his or her heart."[11] Coverage of Coleridge-Taylor's echoed the Pan-African sentiments that had characterized the contemporary writings of his friend, Du Bois, who published a eulogy to the composer called *Darkwater* in the months after his death.

As World War I came to a close, the world lost two more of its iconic stars: ragtime pioneer James Reese Europe and superstar actor Bert Williams. The eulogizing of both performers and the nostalgic invocation of other greats of the past reflected the changing political philosophies of the period. The war had been long, violent, and impersonal. There were few public heroes, and the end of the war was punctuated by escalating racial tensions.

The Harlem Renaissance commercialized black culture, but it also signaled to many a growing sense of agency (read by some as "militancy") in black communities, especially in urban areas. Accordingly, journalists used stories from the past to build a collective sense of experience and identity as a way to cope with critical changes in public life for many of their readers. Hegemonic, whitewashed narratives were challenged in these tributes as they were in other aspects of black-centered journalism. To maintain a coherent sense of African American identity and experience, black journalists—and especially sportswriters—framed contemporary challenges through the lens of the past. In so doing they began to crystallize a mythic, usable past that had not previously existed in public discourse about the collective experiences of black and African Americans.

Nostalgia for Uncle Tom

Journalistic recognition of celebrities served an important purpose in black public life. Commemoration of celebrities after they died was a strategy through which black journalists constructed what Thomas Cripps, in writing about the history of blacks' participation in narrative film, called a "usable black past."[12] The reclamation of the past was an urgent project for black communities robbed by bondage of the cultural reference points that constitute communities' shared, unifying sense of memory. Mediated public memory dredged up the ghosts of slavery by presenting imagery of an idealized antebellum society in which black slaves were complicit, and even satisfied, with their own violent subjugation. Commemorative practices, as they were embraced by journalists writing for black urban weeklies, represented a struggle to work through black citizens' communal sense of a shared traumatic past.

The sense of nostalgia that pervaded Civil War memory in the decades following Emancipation was a hollow but persistent public story that circumvented the suffering of millions of African Americans traumatized by the emotional and physical scars of slavery. Writing about the Civil War commemorative events of 1883, David W. Blight describes the ironic celebration of black Union soldiers: "The clanging of medals on a black veteran's jacket at the parade, the freedom anthems sung at commemoration, or the swarming crowds at black exhibitions about racial 'progress' sometimes rang hollow against the screeching realities of lynching, the degradation of blackface minstrelsy, the bleakness of poverty, and the insults of segregation."[13] Slavery had not ended with Emancipation. The racial ideology espoused during that period was simply transposed into Jim Crow legislation; very little had changed in white Americans' collective mind-set toward the social status of blacks. Rather than recoil at antebellum memory, white audiences across the country embraced in disparate forms public celebrations of the southern way as the American way.

Minstrel renditions of *Uncle Tom's Cabin*, based on the novel by Harriet Beecher Stowe, became popular in the mid 1880s. *Uncle Tom's Cabin* was especially attractive to white audiences not because of its abolitionist narrative but rather because it tapped into what Daphne Brooks has called the "spectacle of suffering" inherent in early mainstream depictions of black Americans, masked as a progressive celebration of black Emancipation.[14] These productions began as somewhat faithful renditions of the book but soon devolved into "Tom shows," "transform[ing] a moral drama into an entertainment at times resembling nothing so much as a minstrel show."[15] Tom shows consisted of a combination of gimmicks—from showcases for black musicians and dancers to live animal acts—that were meant to loosely "illustrate" the novel. Indeed, the "Uncle Tom" figure—a "submissive, stoic, generous, selfless, and oh-so-very kind" type that is seemingly content with his inferior position—gained traction in early film, where popular actors such as Clarence Muse and Bill Robinson were relegated to roles that emphasized their characters' subscription to antebellum values.[16]

In the *Little Colonel*, Robinson plays Walker, the butler, who along with maid Ma Beck (Hattie McDaniel), coddles "Miss Lloyd" (Shirley Temple) as she navigates the uneasy relationship between her crotchety southern grandfather and her more progressive parents. In one scene, right before showing her a "new way to go upstairs" to bed (tap-dancing hand in hand), Walker assures Miss Lloyd that her grandfather, who regularly hurls verbal abuse at his servants, was just "cranky." In the Civil War film *The Littlest*

Rebel, Robinson's role as Temple's protector goes even further when Virgie's (Temple) father (a Confederate soldier) is imprisoned in the North and leaves his young daughter in the sole care of "Uncle Billy" (Robinson), one of the house slaves. Uncle Billy "can sing and dance and climb trees—he can do anything in the world," according to Virgie. "Anything in the world," by the end of the film, includes saving Virgie's father from Union soldiers and scrounging up enough train fare to deliver a letter to none other than Abraham Lincoln on behalf of Virgie's father.

In both films Temple's southern family laments the way in which the war has disrupted their way of life. Audiences were invited to empathize with white southerners who considered themselves collateral damage from the war. Black characters in the film were not vilified, but they were not sympathetic either; they function in the narrative as stereotypical tropes that justify mourning the "southern" (white) way of life that was lost as a result of Emancipation. In addition to the popularity of the Robinson-Temple collaborations, bastardized filmic versions of "Uncle Tom" were vestiges of American public memory that sought to reconcile the horrors of slavery. "America just can't let Uncle Tom die," lamented Associated Negro Press celebrity columnist Fay Jackson in 1935.[17]

James Reese Europe, Public Mourning, and the Paradox of Memory

The Unites States' intervention in World War I and its aftermath of domestic racial strife were also tinged with the painful realities and broken promises of Emancipation. Though the "emancipationist vision" of increased educational and economic opportunities for blacks seemed evermore possible because of the war, the racist realities of an emboldened Ku Klux Klan, the class anxieties of a displaced sector of the white working class, and eugenic pseudoscience contributed to continued antipathy by many whites toward black citizens.

U.S. intervention in Word War I opened up legitimate opportunities for blacks, and accordingly coverage in black weeklies shifted sharply away from entertainment-driven news. When the United States entered World War I in the spring of 1917, the black press had little interest in discussing celebrities. Instead, these journalists and editors turned their attention to covering the war effort, advocating for the right of black men to enlist in the military and reporting on occupational advancements of blacks at home in industrial and manufacturing jobs. Accordingly, coverage of entertainers sharply dropped during this period in favor of coverage not only of the war but also of the advances being made by black workers at home. Entertainment coverage during this period declined sharply across all black press papers, but especially in the *Baltimore Afro-American*, the *Chicago Defender*, and the *Cleveland Gazette*, which, more than their contemporaries, valued entertainment culture as particularly newsworthy.

The Great War had yielded many black war heroes, and black newspapers venerated them accordingly. More than 360,000 black citizens enlisted in the military and were sent overseas, including a group of young Harlem men who became the Fifteenth New York Infantry.[18] The 369th Regiment, which comprised the Fifteenth Regiment and James Reese Europe's infantry band members, lost hundreds of soldiers who were either killed in action or as a result of injury or disease from participating in the war effort.[19] The *Cleveland Gazette* praised the Fifteenth: "That the Afro-American soldier is in the thickest of the fray, giving a good account of himself, is attested by high French officers, who have nothing but words of praise for the valorous conduct of their Black brothers in one common cause."[20] French soldiers had nicknamed the infantry the "Harlem Hellfighters."

Prominent New York bandleader James Reese Europe (along with a young soldier and fellow New York musician Noble Sissle) was commissioned to pull together an infantry band, which combined with the Fifteenth and became the 369th Infantry. Europe was initially hesitant to assemble the regiment orchestra. As a first lieutenant, Europe owed his first allegiance to his soldiers, not to a musical outfit. Europe, who had relocated from Mobile, Alabama, to Washington DC, and finally to New York in 1899 at only seventeen years old, had enlisted in the Fifteenth because he simply respected the notion that black Americans should "close ranks" as W. E. B. Du Bois had suggested in a controversial *Crisis* editorial and assist with the war effort. As Jeffrey T. Sammons and John H. Morrow Jr. recount in their cultural history of the Hellfighters, Europe relished his role as a lieutenant in the army, telling Sissle, "I'm in it now! I'm real stuff now!" When Colonel William Hayward, the ambitious and embattled leader of the Fifteenth, approached Europe to request that he take over as band director, the musician bristled, and seeking to find a way out of the obligation, he made a list of demands that he hoped were unreasonable enough to force Hayward to ask someone else. Europe asked for compensation for band members, twice as many members as was usual for a military infantry band (sixty as opposed to the twenty-eight members who had constituted the regiment band previously), and he wanted to recruit his members from outside New York. These demands would require a massive cash infusion, which Hayward found by way of a $10,000 donation by friend Daniel Reid, a director of the U.S. Steel Corporation and American Can Company. Europe, floored that his demands had actually been met, agreed to serve as the infantry bandleader.[21]

As a collective of musicians, the Hellfighters combined elements of ragtime and jazz music to create something that Europe described as "music which was [theirs]—not a pale imitation of others."[22] The *Defender* described the music Europe made: "[It is] rhythm that is sustained throughout every number, the unique instrumentation, which consists of banjos, mandolins, clarinet, cornet, traps and drums, makes a class of music that has set the society and wealthy people wild. . . . Wealthy society leaders in New York never think their functions are complete without Europe's orchestra playing."[23] The band "mixed syncopated songs, ragtime, blues, plantation melodies, and French songs" and delighted American and French regiments stationed all over Germany and France.[24]

Europe had rose to prominence in Harlem as the bandleader for dancers Vernon and Irene Castle and the director of the Clef Club. In 1910, frustrated with the disorganization and exploitation of black New York musicians, Europe had founded the Clef Club, an organization of Harlem musicians, which operated as a labor union and as a central booking agency exclusively for black musicians. Because of his efforts, Europe was named "Man of the Month" in the June 1912 issue of the *Crisis*. The magazine noted, "Fully to appreciate the worth of James Reese Europe to the Negro musicians of New York City, one would have to know how the Negro entertainers in cafes, hotels, at banquets, etc., were regarded before the organization of the Clef Club, and how they have been regarded since. Before, they were prey to scheming head waiters and booking agents, now they are performers whose salaries are fixed to contract."[25] The *New York Age* described Europe's professional association of musicians as "a clearing house for the Negro musician, who not only found it possible to secure more work but to get better pay."[26]

Europe and his band returned to the States after the war in the spring of 1919 and immediately embarked on a successful stateside tour. Upon Europe's return, the *New York Age* declared, "Jazz music is now all *the* rage throughout the United States: Since the return of colored military bands from France to these shores the country simply has gone wild about jazz music. . . . Lovers of syncopation are indebted to the Negro for what is known as ragtime, and despite the false claims of some white writers, the Negro musician is primarily responsible for the introduction of jazz music."[27] Though jazz music would become a point of contestation in the black press, this early article conveys the excitement that Europe brought home to America with his ragtime band. He spent the first week of May 1919 in Chicago, where he was "treated as a celebrity and as a musical authority"; the *Defender*'s Abbott even entertained Europe in his home.[28]

However, his success after the war was cut tragically short. A week after his Chicago visit, band member Herbert Wright, angry over a critique Europe had made of his performance that evening, fatally stabbed Europe with a penknife after a show at Mechanics Hall in Boston. In attendance backstage during the fatal attack were members of the black society, including tenor singer Roland Hayes, who reportedly witnessed the tragic incident.

Europe's public visibility as both a lieutenant and a bandleader drew the attention of both white and black patriots, and the subsequent commemoration of his passing was perhaps the first commemoration of a black war hero since 1888, when a monument to Crispus Attucks was installed on Boston Common. The City of New York gave Europe an official funeral—he was the first black American in the city's history to receive the honor—and commemoration of him occupied the front pages of not only black urban weeklies but also the *New York Times,* which heralded the late bandleader: "Ragtime may be negro music, more alive than much other American music; and Europe was one of the Americans who was contributing most to its development."[29] The *New York Age* called the funeral "one of the largest ever held in New York for a member of the race."[30]

Black newspapers covered the funeral extensively, as throngs of New York residents came to mourn the bandleader. The size and scope of the funeral constituted a public mourning event that few blacks had witnessed or even thought possible. The *Philadelphia Tribune* wrote, "Not since the day that Jack Johnson came into town bringing the world's heavyweight championship with him has New York's colored population turned out in such numbers eager to pay respect to the memory of Lieut. James Reese Europe . . . who made jazz music famous the world over."[31] "If Chicago ever received a real shock it came last Saturday with the information of 'Jim' Europe's passing," wrote Nahum Daniel Brascher of the *Defender.* "The only comparison at all was the news of the passing of Booker T. Washington and Theodore Roosevelt."[32]

"'Jim' Europe lives!" continued Brascher in his tribute to the fallen bandleader. "He lives, of a truth, in the hearts of those who love him. Do you remember about John Brown? Remember the song? Let's bring it up to date: 'Jim' Europe's body lies molding in the clay, but his soul goes marching on!"[33]

It was an odd juxtaposition—the bandleader war hero who introduced the United States and Europe to ragtime, a dedicated labor organizer and civil rights activist but hardly a militant radical, venerated by both races compared with a white failed abolitionist insurgent, hated by whites and met with suspicion by many blacks, who was hung at the gallows for an operation that many knew was doomed to fail at its outset. Brascher's tribute to Europe reflects what Blight has called the "paradoxical memory" of slavery and emancipation: "It was a world of real experience, one complicated by relationships with whites that were both horrible and endearing and enriched or traumatized by their own family and community relations."[34] The specter of slavery necessarily overshadowed all commemorative practices by blacks in collective, public mourning. The evocation of John Brown in a tribute to Europe reminds readers of the struggles of slavery and the journey to emancipation—trauma and triumph that made it possible for Europe to both live and die as he did and a way to resolve the tension inherent in the fact that scores of whites took part in mourning for him. Black newspapers' emphasis on the ritual mourning practices enacted by whites (his funeral procession, tributes written by whites, and mainstream newspaper coverage) also reflects an investment in an integrationist vision that was not at all a part of black Americans' shared past but could play a role in their future. Public memory is, after all, as proscriptive for contemporary struggles as it is reflective of past sorrows.

"Assassinated," concluded Brascher, "he has but fired our hearts, that were already filled with his music, to prepare, prepare, thoroughly, and give to the world the lasting, everlasting rebuke to prejudice."[35]

"Old Master" Joe Gans and the Shifting Modes of Exemplarity

American journalism has treated celebrities as characters through which myths are formulated and shared across news stories and other forms of media. Memory often uses individuals as "exemplary models" to represent the shared cultural ideals and values that are reflected in narratives of past events. The evocation of "exemplary models" through public commemoration "can signal to a society what is important and what is not, how to act and how not, who is worthy and who is not."[36] Through public discourse, individuals become imbued with lasting symbolic significance. They are no longer men or women, fathers or mothers, sons or daughters, but rather symbols designed to signify the characteristics of the past most "worth" remembering.

Joe Gans, in death, became an exemplary figure, a tool through which to "unify strangers together" by "blend[ing] the public and

private spheres together by conferring historic events with significance for the individual, and by constructing a chronological
history."[37] Born Joseph Gant in Baltimore, Maryland, in either
November or September 1874, Gans had—just like his younger
contemporary Jack Johnson—spent his youth participating in
"battle royals," street spectacles that consisted of young black boys,
blindfolded, sometimes dressed flamboyantly and sometimes bare-
chested, punching each other senseless until the final boy stand-
ing was deemed the "winner." These spectacles were organized
on city streets and docks all along the country, and they were one
more way that racist whites stripped blacks of their basic dignity
for their own amusement. "Blindfolded, I could no longer control my emotions," recalled Gans. "I stumbled about like a baby
or a drunken man. . . . A glove connected with my head, filling
my mouth with warm blood. It was everywhere."[38]

In 1902 Gans challenged and beat reigning lightweight champion
Frank Erne for the title, which he held until 1908. Gans, who had
knocked out Erne with a simple punch in a bout that lasted one
minute and forty-eight seconds, was the first black boxing champion in any division.[39] Journalists writing in the years after Gans's
death heralded his defensive skills, his brilliance, his agility, and
his comportment both in and out of the ring. "Like a majority
of great fighters—the truly great fighters of the ring—Gans was
too methodical to be spectacular. In action he always worried,
always fretted about things," wrote the *Courier* in 1929. And yet,
the article continued, "No man ever conquered a tougher field
than did Gans in winning the title. . . . You had to be good to go
through that field."[40]

During his lifetime Gans's noteworthy achievements were criticized because they seemed to overshadow the work of the uplifters. In a 1902 editorial in the *Baltimore Afro-American*, the writer
lamented, "Mr. [Joe] Gans gets more space in the white papers
than all the respectable colored people in the state."[41] In general
the black press ignored Gans's championship reign, for it served
very little tactical purpose for them. The rhetoric of racial uplift
emphasized artistic achievement, genteel manners, emotional
restraint, and cultural refinement. Punching someone in the face

for a living hardly meets any of these criteria. Wrote Gans's hometown paper in 1933, "A long time ago the AFRO AMERICAN, which in those days, was not kindly disposed towards fighters, as were none of the Uplifters in fact—spoke of the fact that to be mentioned in the white press a colored man had to be a criminal or a prize-fighter."[42]

The *Cleveland Gazette* was the only black press paper to give Gans's victory over Frank Erne any play, and this overall lack of coverage might in part be because the fight was short and uneventful. As the *Gazette* recounted, "After a minute of futile sparring, Gans tapped Erne once on the face, dazing the Bizon, after which the Afro-American landed a blow on Erne's jaw and sent him down and out. Gans was hardly touched in the mix-up. One minute and forty seconds were consumed in reaching a decision."[43] Gans's 1906 bout with Battling Nelson received a greater amount of attention but again only in the *Cleveland Gazette*. The coverage was less about celebrating Gans's victory and more about the aftermath of the fight, which ignited a firestorm of racial tension that spilled into city streets all over the country. It is not clear how many casualties resulted from the riots in total, but in Atlanta at least twenty-six people were killed; all but two victims were black.[44] As a result some cities—like Gans's native Baltimore—passed laws prohibiting mixed-race boxing matches. The *Gazette* lamented, "After Joe Gans defeated Battling Nelson, his native city, Baltimore, Md., passed a law prohibiting white boxers from meeting Afro-Americans. Isn't it rich? How very, very silly in the eyes of the entire country, prejudice oftimes makes southerners and frequently the entire south."[45]

Coverage of Gans in the black press during this period is scant, especially as compared with that of heavyweight champion Jack Johnson, who emerged six years after Gans's championship reign began. Gans existed only in Johnson's shadow, who was by all accounts more physically imposing, more flamboyant, and more polarizing than the strong but mild-mannered Gans. Throughout his time as a public figure, Johnson did little to hide his vices, particularly sexual ones. Even before capturing the heavyweight championship title, Johnson was known to travel with a legion of white women, mostly prostitutes, whom he treated to expensive meals and jewelry. This habit only exacerbated negative attitudes toward boxing; Johnson's antics became symbolic of the hedonism of the sport itself and, worse, fed into white visions of the barbaric, sexually predatory black buck stereotype. White sportswriters in particular liked Gans, and he became a particularly convenient foil for their hatred of Johnson. Gans, by contrast, was "the most gentlemanly of all pugs of color," observed one white journalist. "He is entirely different from the Jack Johnson type. Johnson is big, burly, insulting, and has an inflated idea of his own importance. Joe Gans is just the opposite."[46] Meanwhile, black press newspapers, concerned at the turn of the century with whether pugilism was "respectful," overlooked Gans's championship reign almost entirely. Limited coverage of Gans during his championship reign suggests that it was not until after his death that black journalists began to see the value of his quiet contributions to breaking the color barrier in sport.

Gans had spent the beginning of the summer of 1910 sick but determined to travel; he had lined up a few speaking engagements in the Southwest in the lead-up to the Johnson-Jeffries fight, and newspapers in that region had hoped to interview him. His diagnosis of tuberculosis was no secret, but few knew that summer just how badly his health had declined. Gans deteriorated quickly in June and July, and while Johnson was touring the country as the triumphant defender of his heavyweight title, Gans was on a train, bound for Baltimore, unable to stand, walk, or breathe regularly, hoping only to make it to his family home alive. Gans died during the first week of August 1910, at the age of thirty-five.

Upon his death the *Afro-American* and the *Chicago Defender* joined the *Gazette* in remembering Gans. The *Defender* honored Gans with a large front-page illustration of the fighter in the ring with one-time opponent Billie Nolan. The accompanying obituary heralded Gans as "truly a master at the game . . . his equal in the fine points of boxing [was] yet to be found."[47] The *Afro-American* also honored Gans in its August 13 issue, but its depiction of Gans instead focused on his status as "gentlemanly in deportment." The paper declared Gans "a general in the ring with unerring eye and cat-like agility, cool, calm and determined in or out of a mix-up. . . . Gentlemanly in deportment, free from boasting, stranger to brawls and fistfights—to sum it all up he was a gentleman."[48] It ran on its front page a formal portrait of Gans, posed sitting rigidly upright in an expensive suit, rather than a photograph of him in the ring, to drive home the distinction. The photograph could have easily appeared on the cover of the *Crisis,* and it mimicked the formal conventions of that periodical's published portraits of noteworthy blacks. As with the editorial contrasting him with Johnson, this tribute too implies that Gans, who was "gentlemanly in deportment," was the antidote to the flamboyant Johnson, who was quickly wearing out his welcome with black sportswriters across the country. This portrayal might even be read as an effort to recast Gans as an uplifter, for he looked the part.

Gans reemerged in the press's popular consciousness beginning in the mid-1920s, when a string of contenders—including Battling Siki, Tiger Flowers, Sam Langford, and Harry "Black Panther" Wills—began again to threaten to break down the color line. Up to that point, the end of Johnson's championship reign in 1915 had effectively ended the possibility that a black contender could hold a heavyweight title.

In the 1920s boxing, as it had been a decade earlier, was a symbol of larger cultural battles. Postwar discourses surrounding the crisis of masculinity made boxing particularly attractive. It was a nostalgic return to the days when (white) men were "Men." Jack Dempsey, a miserly ex-hobo with an aggressive fighting style, emerged as the star of the ring, and though Harry "Black Panther" Wills chased him for nearly the whole decade, Dempsey drew the color line, refusing to fight any contenders of color. In this return to celebrating hypermasculinity, both Jack Johnson—who was still alive in the 1920s and struggling to make a comeback in public life—and Gans were invoked by nostalgic sportswriters to frame the "weakness" of the modern sport in its unwillingness to confront the color line. Black journalists used these wildly dissimilar men as exemplary models for the same premise—the fight for equality was a masculine endeavor, to take place in a public forum where brutality is not only sanctioned but also celebrated. Recounting Gans's 1909 bout against British titleholder Jabez White, the *New*

York Amsterdam News lamented, "Things have changed since that day twenty-five years ago, and today there isn't an outstanding fighter in any division, black or white, to fire the imagination of the sporting world as did the name of the great little Baltimorean to whom all join in paying their respects though he has been long dead."[49]

Nostalgia pieces on Gans and Johnson appeared in several different forms. Sometimes they would be one-off pieces from sports editors; other times, they would appear as a series of columns written by one of the staff writers. For example, in 1923 the *Defender* ran a six-part series by sportswriter Tony Langston ("who has witnessed more ring contests than any other member of the race") called "Ringside Recollections," designed to revisit some of the race's most lauded moments in the sport.[50] This body of coverage included articles critiquing contemporary fighters by evoking past fighters as frames for their criticisms and articles, cartoons, and illustrations that told stories of great sports victories of the past.

Johnson, as a public figure, newly released from prison and eager to return to the public's consciousness, had an active role in gatekeeping his own memory. Nostalgia was his most powerful public-relations tool. He wrote two memoirs upon his release from prison.[51] He was even tapped by the *Pittsburgh Courier* to author a four-part column series on the various aspects of prizefighting. In all these texts, Johnson self-mythologized. "No one ever taught me that white men were superior to me," he wrote for the *Courier*. "The fact that I lived quite a long time in London and Paris, where there is no color line, aided me in laying aside the inferiority complex that other colored fighters from the South have labored under."[52] According to Johnson, the ring was a replication of North-South racial tensions, with black southern fighters carrying a stigma of inferiority into the ring with them. Invocations of the Mason-Dixon Line evoked the specter of slavery, something of which Johnson, the son of former slaves, was well aware.

Though he was a symbol of nostalgia, Johnson in memory continued to pale in comparison with the more respectable Gans. "Jack Johnson ranks with Peter Jackson among the greatest heavyweights that ever lived," wrote the *Afro-American*, though he "lacked the humility and spirituality of Joe Gans, the greatest lightweight."[53] Posthumously, Gans symbolized what was most laudable about the sport. He became an iconic figure; even Ralph Matthews, the *Afro-American*'s entertainment columnist, wrote of Gans as a "gentlemanly, unpretentious individual."[54] Gans, as opposed to Johnson, simply knew better *when* to be aggressive; in contrast with the hot-tempered Johnson, Gans saved his ire for the ring. "He was at once a pug and a gentleman," wrote Ralph Matthews in 1927. "A ferocious beast in the ring and without a gentle lamb with a manner that made three women love him and marry him."[55]

Then-contemporary fighters who sought to emulate his style began to use "Joe Gans" as a nickname—as in Young Joe Gans and Allentown Joe Gans. The *Defender*'s Juli Jones and a host of other sportswriters routinely used their columns to speak generally on Gans's legacy or as recollections of specific fights.[56] Gans was also specifically evoked to frame discussions about Joe Louis.[57] Juli Jones Jr. was particularly apt to celebrate Gans's legacy; in one article he called Gans "the greatest fighter of all time," and in another he argued that the lightweight champion was consistently popular even among white spectators.[58] Jones also argued that "the name Gans [was] as fresh today in the public mind, through press notes, as it was fifteen years ago," which is ironic because fifteen years previously at the height of Gans's professional success, there was rarely any coverage of him in the black press.[59]

In 1927 the *Baltimore Afro-American* began a fund-raiser to support a Joe Gans memorial for Baltimore's Provident Hospital. Thomas R. Smith, chairman of the committee, promised that Provident would be "managed by Negroes for Negroes . . . and it should prove of great benefit to the entire Negro race in America."[60] This group of black physicians (along with an advisory board of whites), with the assistance of the *Afro-American*, worked together to create a memorial fund specifically designed to finance a research facility dedicated to finding a cure for tuberculosis. Gans, of course, had succumbed to the disease, and it was a common ailment among black residents living in urban tenements with poor air quality. "In his life," wrote the *Afro-American*, "Joe took the count three times. But in his remarkable career[,] never stained by an act of dishonesty or brutality, and which began in the fish hatcheries of and oysters stalls of Baltimore[,] he went to the apex of his class in the squared arena."[61]

The Inimitable "Bert"

Like Gans's passing, the death of his friend Bert Williams became an occasion for black press journalists to pause and assess his ultimate contribution to the race.[62] Unlike Gans, however, whose victory in the ring was—at least in death—a clear symbol of progress, Williams gained fame through a minstrel-derived artistry that was a belabored point of contention during his life. His financial success, which was touted during his lifetime, was framed as Washingtonian evidence of race progress. By the early 1920s, Williams was a bona fide stage star, having transcended the racial barriers of Broadway and overcome the loss of his comedy partner, George Walker. He successfully performed with the Ziegfeld Follies as their first black performer; he enjoyed success as the best-selling black recording artist of the pre-1920 period; and he had toured the United States and Europe extensively behind productions such as *In Dahomey*, *Abyssinia*, and *Under the Bamboo Tree*. Williams's sudden passing in 1922 seemed to represent a symbolic break between the old school of vaudeville performances of the pre-1920 era and a new brand of entertainment influenced by the spirit of the Renaissance. Yet writers needed to offer closure to his legacy, to assign a final assessment to his contribution to African American artistry. So they struggled, in the months and even years after his passing, to determine the appropriate way to honor their quietly embattled superstar.

Initially, the obituaries published in leading black press papers, like the *Defender* and the *Afro-American*, painted a laudatory picture of Williams, focusing on his "remarkable" career and financial success as a stage star. "No performer in the history of the American stage enjoyed the popularity and esteem of all races and classes of theatregoers to the remarkable extent gained by Bert Williams," wrote Tony Langston. "He had a wonderful following and his name in the lights in front of any theatre meant 'capacity' attendance, no matter what the vehicle."[63] A release by the Associated Negro Press vowed that Williams would be "remembered among the illustrious."[64] In the *Afro-American* the author noted that Williams made up to $100,000 a year, and that "on the stage, no colored actor heretofore ha[d] attained the professional or personal standing of the inimitable 'Bert.' . . . His genius made the other race forget the color line."[65] The *Defender* ran a photo of Williams alongside his obituary, sans burnt cork on his face, with the caption, "Celebrated comedian answers final call after remarkable career covering many years upon the stage. Funeral one of the largest ever held in New York City."[66]

A more nuanced analysis of Williams's legacy emerged only in the months and years after his death, and these latter portraits of Williams emphasize his exemplary role in breaking artistic boundaries for black entertainers. Williams's initial success as the first black performer to grace the Broadway stage was especially important in creating opportunities for black producers, writers, and actors a decade later; therefore, his legacy was redefined in the light of this new wave of Broadway performers. In theater the groundbreaking success of Bert Williams and George Walker was reified with the breakthrough of Charles Gilpin, Paul Robeson, Florence Mills, and Josephine Baker, who all received their big breaks in productions such as *Shuffle Along*, *Emperor Jones*, *Showboat*, and other Broadway shows that attempted to establish a cultural aesthetic drawing directly from the tradition that the Williams and Walker Company had pioneered in the first decade of the century.

In the months after Williams's death, novelist Jessie Fauset published a touching four-page tribute to him in the *Crisis*, in which she noted, "His *role* was always that of a poor, shunted, cheated, out-of-luck Negro and he fostered and deliberately trained his genius toward the delineation of this type because his mental as well as his artistic sense told him that here was a true racial vein. . . . His colored auditors laughed but often with a touch of rue,—this characterization was too near to us; his hard luck was our own universal fate."[67] Fauset defended the pathos that characterized Williams's performance as a "Real Coon," thereby distinguishing it for skeptical black readers from the destructive minstrel tradition.

Of the burnt cork Williams wore throughout his stage career to enhance the caricature of his blackness, Fauset wrote, "If the world knew of his great possibilities why had it doomed this stalwart, handsome creature, to his golden skin, his silken hair, his beautiful, sensitive hands under the hideousness of the eternal Black make-up. Why should he and we obscure our talents forever under the bushel of prejudice, jealousy, stupidity." Fauset recalled that upon hearing comedian Eddie Cantor had stopped wearing burnt cork, her "eyelids stung with the prick of sudden tears."[68] Eddie Cantor was a white comedian, who like Al Jolson and others, wore burnt cork during performances to "mimic" blacks. Cantor's retirement of blackface performing was a key transitional moment in the movement away from the practice of white actors mimicking and satirizing black physicality and cultural experience. Perhaps this is the most heartbreaking line of Fauset's tribute—the notion that Williams served as a martyr for his race, sacrificing his authentic blackness to burnt cork so that those who came after him need not suffer the humiliation of minstrelsy.

Williams's reputation as an activist only grew posthumously. In 1925 the *Philadelphia Tribune* wrote, "He was misunderstood greatly; his motive was misconstrued by many of his own people, especially his friends and it hurt him much, but he never wavered in his efforts to bring about an era of better feeling and a clearer understanding between white and colored people in the theatrical world."[69] Williams's role as a representative for the race could only be reconciled by his death. The increased respect bestowed on Williams posthumously is a product of the increased success black entertainers found, whether they liked it or not, on the coattails of his so-called minstrel performances. Black journalists had to acknowledge the possibility that there may not have been a Paul Robeson without first a Bert Williams.

The Construction of a "Felt" Past

Commemorative journalism about celebrities who were overlooked in life but later venerated in death reveals the processual nature of collective memory, especially for blacks as they negotiated the memory work of dominant institutions that celebrated, rather than scorned, the nation's troubled history of slavery.[70] This is not to say that all commemoration of black public figures during this period was fettered by the memory of slavery but rather that public mourning rituals were an important part of what Frederick Douglass described as "*felt* history," narratives of the past that provided the legal and, more importantly, the moral foundation on which to demand full and equal citizenship.[71] The commemorative discourse that framed these celebrities in death suggests that journalists were just beginning belatedly to assess the power of "celebrity"—in celebrating the death, rather than life, of the individual. Indeed, again upon George Walker's death, Sylvester Russell admitted this much, lamenting that "the one man who boldly stood up in his exalted position and made it possible for the Negro thespian of his time, but whom [black journalists] did not really discover until after he had passed away."[72] Articles written about black celebrities in the days, months, and even years after they died may be treated as guides through which the readership was to understand their role in broader culture. Commemorative journalism about celebrities who were overlooked in life but later venerated in death can be thought of as *felt history*—constructed with disarmingly candid prose about the trauma of a shared collective past and with prescient warnings about how the mistakes of the past might continue to hinder progress in the present.

In discussing the entertainment content of the *Chicago Defender*, Mark Dolan suggests that black newspapers and magazines during this period were the "staging ground for African American history."[73] "Memories covering a period of ten years that only this mad newspaper career could have preserved because what others see and forget, the journalist (I flatter myself) must remember," wrote Ralph Matthews in 1934. "Every experience must be tagged and tucked away into a pigeon hole to be snatched out on a moment's notice."[74] This is especially obvious in coverage eulogizing dead celebrities. Black communities during this period lacked a collective "usable past," that is, the idea that, though they had a shared sense of experience among disparate individuals and communities throughout the country as a result of the artistic and cultural traditions packed and carried north during the Great Migration, there was little sense of an established, shared narrative in the entertainment that the community produced. The "great myths" of American self-determination that helped to shape celebrity narratives in the 1920s and 1930s did nothing to reconcile the traumatic memory of bondage. Therefore, revisiting these figures in death was one of the few ways to crystallize a mythic, usable past—a "felt" history from which black communities could draw communal feelings of comfort and inspiration.

8

The Politics of Black Press Celebrity Journalism

The previous chapters have explored how celebrity journalism evolved in the pages of black newspapers and magazines and considered how the concept of "celebrity" reflected the black press's historic mission of advocating for the rights of its readership all over the country against the backdrop of material and economic upheavals and shifting political and social ideologies, particularly for northern and northbound urban blacks. In particular those chapters were concerned with pushing the boundaries of how we as a culture have come to understand the idea of "celebrity" by foregrounding the perspective of black, rather than white mainstream, journalistic coverage of the star system in the early decades of the twentieth century.

Attention to entertainment culture and the idea of "celebrity" emerged in the black press during the latter years of the century's second decade and the early 1920s—distinct from yet contemporaneous with similar developments in the mainstream press. Black newspapers began to steadily incorporate celebrity journalism as a regular facet of their weekly editions. This period was rife with publishers' attempts to increase circulation by relying on "crowd-pleasing features such as simpler language, larger headlines, and more lavish illustrations [and later, photographs] to help expand readership," particularly among the working classes in large urban areas.[1]

These changes were reflected in black urban weeklies as well. As Patrick Washburn has suggested, the emergence of an "African American version" of the yellow press borrowed heavily from the mainstream press, and as a result black newspaper circulation figures skyrocketed.[2] These developments coincided not only with trends in mainstream journalism but also with changing leadership in the black community that had a direct influence on the black press. The "Tuskegee Machine" lost a significant amount of clout in the black newspaper industry upon the death of Booker T. Washington in 1915. Newspapers and magazines alike began to embrace the spirit of the Harlem Renaissance, which created a class of socialites among black residents in Harlem. Celebrities such as Cab Calloway, Louis Armstrong, Bill Robinson (the "Mayor of Harlem"), Florence Mills, Josephine Baker, and Paul Robeson were an important part of the Harlem scene. Though the *Baltimore Afro-American* was at the forefront of early celebrity coverage, it was the *Pittsburgh Courier* that took the black community's preoccupation with celebrity to a new level with its coverage of boxer Joe Louis.

Celebrity journalism in the black press superficially drew on similar narrative devices and thematic elements. Against the backdrop of the Great Depression, the "success myth"—the idea that an otherwise ordinary American could, through hard work, dedication, and talent, become "special"—was as regularly employed in black press coverage of its most lauded celebrities as it was in mainstream coverage of white celebrities. In recounting the stories of their favorite celebrities, journalists in both institutional settings espoused slightly varying but overall uniform versions of the "success myth," working closely with publicists to create "imagined intimacy" between stars and their fans. As in the mainstream press, black journalists and editors expended their energy on reporting celebrity gossip; the tangled love affairs of Roland Hayes, Paul Robeson, Josephine Baker, and Jesse Owens at times threatened to overshadow their professional achievements as reporters competed for who would get the "scoop."

With the evolution of celebrity journalism came a collective of spirited and talented writers whose personalities came alive in the pages of black newspapers and who themselves reached a sort of "celebrity" status. During this period Ralph Matthews's columns Looking at the Stars and Watching the Big Parade were staples of the *Afro-American*, while Fay Jackson's Hollywood Stardust column—written for the Associated Negro Press—was regularly carried in the largest papers, including the *Afro-American* and the *Pittsburgh Courier*. The *Defender*'s Chappy Gardner and the *New York Amsterdam News*'s Romeo Dougherty received regular bylines as well. Sportswriters were also a part of this group of celebrity journalists; the *Courier* boasted of its "Big Four"—William G. Nunn, Chester L. Washington, Lonnie Harrington, and Floyd J. Calvin. Alongside these regular correspondents, celebrity coverage was handled by a group of gifted but anonymous journalists whose contributions played an important part in establishing the tone and mission of the coverage overall, but who did not, for whatever reason, receive bylines on their stories.

Politicizing Celebrity

Over one hundred years ago, films such as D. W. Griffith's *Birth of a Nation* brought to life frame-by-frame imagery that contributed to white Americans' postbellum antipathy toward black citizens. The creators of *Birth*, and indeed any public representation of blacks that debased them, that marginalized them, that contributed to the Jim Crowing of them, bear the responsibility of insidious, ongoing structural oppression that robbed too many black Americans of too many opportunities in too many different ways. In the face of adversity, black journalists around the country but especially in rapidly growing urban areas stood up to Jim Crow racial ideology, rejected the notion that entertainment was a "whites only" enterprise, supported the work of black creators and artists, and framed for their readers just what it meant to be black and free in this new version of America.

The black press played an important role in shaping modes of citizenship for black community members against the backdrop of Jim Crow. Gossip columnists, Hollywood correspondents, theater critics, and sportswriters often connected their stories with larger issues of racism, practices of segregation, and the struggle for equality. These writers, who include Ralph Matthews, Fay Jackson, Harry Leavitt, William G. Nunn, Al Monroe, Chappy Gardner, Theophilus Lewis, and Tony Langston, offered some of the most insightful, incisive, and passionate writing of the period. When Fay Jackson proclaimed that *Imitation of Life* was proof that "Hollywood was growing up," the hopefulness she conveyed no doubt translated to her readers.[3] After all it was Bert Williams who first charmed Broadway audiences and turned his Williams and Walker Company into a veritable proving ground for black theater stars. It was Joe Gans, and then Jack Johnson, and almost Harry Wills, who knocked sense into the white opponents who took them on in the ring. It was musicians such as Duke Ellington, Cab Calloway, and Louis Armstrong who cajoled otherwise fearful white audiences into entering Harlem cabarets, where they drank, danced, and cavorted, often falling in love with Josephine Baker and Florence Mills in the process. It was Jesse Owens and Joe Louis who represented the United States—*their* talents representing the best of *their* country—on an international stage as the threat of Hitler's Third Reich loomed. These were the faces of black-centered entertainment during this period; these were the heroes whom ordinary black citizens could emulate. These were the folks who laid the template for what it was like to be black and free—"free"—in twentieth-century America.

The celebrities that emerged in the pages of black weeklies and magazines were not simply diversionary figures designed to distract from the more pressing matters of the struggle for freedom: they exemplified the struggle, whether they set out to or not. Between 1900 and 1919, there was generally very little coverage devoted to celebrity culture, but what did make the pages of black-centered urban newspapers conveys the sense that journalists realized early on that celebrities had the symbolic power to influence their community as members of the black intelligentsia redefined racial uplift and politicized public and private behavior among the middle and working classes. The participation of blacks in World War I and the emergence of the Harlem Renaissance in American popular culture encouraged black journalists to hold celebrities accountable as "entertainer-activists"—as members of the community uniquely poised to act on behalf of the race collectively.[4]

Scholars have examined the black press's interactions with political leadership in shaping public opinion in the black community and in combating racism and oppression. Significantly less attention has been paid to the content of these newspapers as it influenced the everyday lives of their readers. However, the content that scholars have previously overlooked—in this case, entertainment content—had a significant influence on shaping black citizens' shared conception of what postbellum American citizenship should look like, which necessarily included discussions about how the race as a whole would be represented in entertainment culture. In this way the idea of "celebrity" as it was conceptualized in the black press was intimately connected to the development of civil rights activism.

Black press journalists often tied the idea of "celebrity" to issues related to community building, and the black press's networked journalism model made it possible to share news stories about regional and national celebrities between publications to reach a wide swath of readers. As a way to create "a constellation of recognizable and familiar people," news stories about celebrities built bonds within the black community. The dissemination of entertainment culture was an important way to build bonds within and among communities. The work of Associated Negro Press writers such as Fay Jackson and Harry Leavitt brought the stories of Hollywood to the readers of the *Courier*, the *Tribune*, the *Afro-American*, and other smaller newspapers that subscribed to the wire service. These connections were also fostered by larger newspapers' efforts to integrate technological innovations into their news-gathering practices; of these newspapers the *Courier* led the charge, sending correspondents to report on Joe Louis's early victories in New York and New Jersey, wiring stories back to the home office for immediate publication. The *Defender*, the *Tribune*, and the *Afro-American* also harnessed these practices and increasingly found the funding to allow their correspondents to travel around the country and abroad to report back to their readers happenings in Hollywood, Harlem, Paris, and many other important sites of the African diaspora. Finally, through the publication of letters to the editors (which often included responses from correspondents and columnists), black citizens were able to connect with one another by using the pages of black newspapers as forums in which to debate the merits of their most recognizable celebrities. These newspapers—working in tandem with the national publications, the *Crisis*, the *Opportunity*, and the *Messenger*—brought together black citizens from all over the country. Coverage of race performers provided a symbolic connection between disparate parts of the country that were home to a plurality of black citizens.

The idea of "race pride" was largely contested in the pages of black newspapers as public opinion shifted from the celebration of "professional uplifters" to more overtly race-conscious activists. Black journalists viewed celebrities through the veil of American racism, so news frames that evoked the "enlightenment" or education of the white race through artistic performance were implicit in discussions about representation. Black journalists were aware of mainstream impressions of the race, and they sought to counter those impressions in very specific terms. Coverage of British composer Samuel Coleridge-Taylor, actor Charles Gilpin, and singer Roland Hayes most neatly fit the criteria of Du Bois's Eurocentric "Talented Tenth." Language describing these noteworthy individuals as "assets" to the race or proof of the general "advancement" or "progress" of the race ties in directly with Du Bois's Talented Tenth theory—that a select few noteworthy individuals would be responsible for the collective success of all freed blacks. Discussions about these individuals as representations of the "possibilities" inherent for other members of the race also evoke this idea of racial uplift. Journalists persistently repeated themes to define the public role of race performers that helped to build frames of understanding for black readers. Often the private and public activities of celebrities were framed in terms of whether they constituted "appropriate" behavior for the race as a whole. As Davarian Baldwin had suggested, journalists used popular culture as a site where they could provide guidelines concerning public behavior.

News coverage of celebrities was informed by the struggle for civil rights—even in the most innocuous musings of gossip, in concert and film reviews, and in sports recaps. In theater the groundbreaking success of Bert Williams and George Walker paved the way for Charles Gilpin, Paul Robeson, Florence Mills, Josephine

Baker, and others. As Jessie Fauset noted in her touching eulogy to Williams, theater stars during this period represented a symbolic break from the minstrel tradition, no longer willing to hide their talents behind burnt cork and "under the bushel of prejudice, jealousy, stupidity."[5] Film stars of the 1930s showed mainstream America, and more importantly black audiences, the multiplicity of experiences and identities of black America—as joyful as Bojangles's jaunt upstairs with Shirley Temple, as tragic as the rise and fall of Robeson's Brutus Jones, as frustrated as Washington's Peola, who yearned for "what everybody else had," and as sympathetic as Beavers's abandoned Delilah.

Black celebrities also began to embrace their roles as race representatives during the 1930s, and they focused energy on collective action. They used otherwise routine promotional interviews to lobby for the rights of everyday black Americans, and they used their celebrity status to raise money for underserved communities of color and to increase awareness among whites of Jim Crow injustices. They realized that being famous meant more than being wealthy and well liked. The obligation that celebrities began to feel as race representatives was not exclusively tied to the art that they made; in fact, at times celebrities unabashedly depicted stereotypical behaviors and attitudes. Nor was race representation a product of a public-relations intervention to make a star seem more "charitable," "relatable," or "sympathetic." Rather, the onus to act on behalf of black communities nationally and globally was the brainchild of citizen-activist-journalists who, from their initial coverage of Johnson and Williams through to their exaltation of Louis and Owens, called for black celebrities to never forget the *real* elements of their experiences under Jim Crow.

These findings offer a greater depth of understanding to what the idea of "celebrity" meant in the black press. The definition of a "celebrity," for black journalists and editors, necessarily included an obligation to the uplift of the whole race, which could be achieved by contributing to his or her community; representing the race collectively and in a way that was appealing to white audiences and commensurate with integrationism; and advocating for the improvement of the material conditions of the race publicly. The overarching narrative of celebrity journalism runs in tandem with the fight for civil rights. As accommodationism shifted to activism, and as interest in race pride and an exploration of the community's African roots intensified, the ways in which black journalists framed their celebrities shifted accordingly. If black newspapers and magazines were the "staging ground" for African American histories generally, then celebrity culture played a much larger role in those histories than has previously been acknowledged.

Beyond the Color Line Trope

Works inside and beyond the confines of academia that examine the relationship between race and popular culture in the United States have tended to foreground as their objects of study mainstream newspaper coverage of black celebrities who emerged to cross the color line.[6] The tendency of gatekeepers of public memory (educators, filmmakers, museum curators, and journalists) has been to commemorate "firsts"—hence the substantive commemoration of, say, Oscar-winner Hattie McDaniel, despite a dearth of coverage of her historic win in the black press. Inherent in discussions of the crossovers of black celebrities into mainstream culture is the implication that gaining entry into mainstream entertainment was somehow more prestigious than recognition in its black-centered counterparts. This is not to suggest that historians' preoccupation with heroes like Jack Johnson and Joe Louis in boxing, Louis Armstrong and Duke Ellington in music, Paul Robeson and Bill Robinson in film, among others, is somehow wrong or misdirected; rather, it is to suggest that their accomplishments are only one part of a continuously unfolding story.

The black press is a rich site for information on these forgotten greats, and further work must be done to duly recognize and appreciate their contributions to American culture generally. Several of the most prominent figures covered in this study have been forgotten, overlooked, or undervalued by historians. To date biographical information on Black Patti, James Reese Europe, Charles Gilpin, Harry Wills, Florence Mills, Samuel Coleridge-Taylor, and Roland Hayes is sparse; often information on these important figures is scattered among survey histories or in footnotes or contextual information about one of their more widely acknowledged contemporaries.

For instance one of the likeliest and most lauded contenders during this era of black hopes was three-time World Colored Heavyweight Champion Harry "Black Panther" Wills, whose pursuit of a shot at the title against champion Jack Dempsey has been lost in a flurry of boxing histories that discuss Dempsey's legacy but leave Wills as a mere footnote.[7] In reality Wills's pursuit of Dempsey dominated much of the champion's reign, lasting six years, from 1920 to 1926. Wills was known both for his prowess in the ring and his unwillingness to reveal much of his personal life to the media. One paper called for Wills to "treat [Dempsey] rough . . . just like he did Firpo," adding, "Only we are hoping Jack will have to be carried out of the ring hopelessly knocked out."[8] Unlike the flamboyant Johnson, Wills was hardly willing to create a spectacle around his successes. The *Defender* advised, "Don't put too much on Wills. Put enough on him to make him feel that you love him, are proud of him, wish him well and that the title Jack Johnson brought you Harry will bring back to you."[9]

The black press closely followed Wills's pursuit of Dempsey and along the way both extolled the virtues of the former while eviscerating the latter as "yellow." In the fall of 1915, the *Philadelphia Tribune* described him as "one of the most dangerous Blacks in the business, and perhaps the most promising of the younger generation of Negro pugilists."[10] By 1922 Wills had proved himself the logical contender for champion Dempsey with victories over Fred Fulton (1920), Bill Tate (three times in 1921), Jeff Clark (1921), and Gunboat Smith (1921). Later victories over Bartley Madden (1924) and Luis Firpo (1924) would make Wills a bona fide "cause célèbre" in the boxing community. According to one historian, "[Wills'] size was as impressive as his record; at six feet, four inches, 220 pounds, he was a well-proportioned athlete who could box as well as punch."[11] With these victories as proof of Wills's viability as a heavyweight contender, his manager Paddy Mullins began to apply public pressure on Dempsey.

The black press was unrelenting in its treatment of Dempsey. In one newspaper Dempsey was described as "the poorest excuse that ever drew on a glove," an "ex-hobo," and "simply yellow."[12] Another paper accused Dempsey of fearing Wills's strength: "Wills' tremendous brute strength and the unquestioned force of his hits made Dempsey think twice about meeting him."[13] The Dempsey-Wills-Tunney controversy is a confounding piece of boxing history, involving promoter Tex Rickard, the New York State Boxing Commission and licensing committee, and a group of politicians in Albany who were all concerned about the racial implications of the proposed match. Due to public pressure from Wills and his manager, Paddy Mullins, Dempsey agreed to fight Wills for the title in New York in 1922 and then again in 1924 and 1925. Each time that Dempsey "signed" to fight Wills his manager Jack Kearns or Rickard connived a way to indefinitely postpone setting a date for the fight. By 1926 it was obvious that Dempsey and Wills would never meet in the ring. The New York State Boxing Commission, in opposition to political pressure in Albany to match Dempsey with Gene Tunney (the other logical contender) over Wills, decreed that Dempsey would *not* be able to take on Tunney without fighting Wills first. As a result of their decision, Rickard decided to hold the Dempsey-Tunney bout to Philadelphia in 1926, defying the commission's orders and effectively shutting Wills out of a shot at the title for good.

Harry Wills's saga is a lesson in collective amnesia. Wills's behavior outside the ring was celebrated as a counternarrative to Johnson—a way to redeem the black community collectively from the embarrassment suffered as a result of Johnson's bad behavior. He was a "gentleman" who "has always lived a clean, respectable life" and had been "a credit to the game and ha[d] undone to a great degree the harm caused Negro boxers by Jack Johnson."[14] According to one paper, "The real superiority of Harry Wills as a sporting man and a pugilist lay in his personal character. Undoubtedly there has been no man of his profession, black or white, who was or is as clean and manly, as sober and sane a citizen, as is Harry Wills."[15] No doubt Harry Wills was an inspiration to his community, but because he never received the chance to cross the color line, his accomplishments have been largely overlooked. What made Wills exemplary to his readers? How did his success pave the way for

Joe Louis's rise? What might have happened if he had received a shot at the title after all?

Wills is just one example of a black celebrity who was covered frequently in his own time but has largely been forgotten by gatekeepers of memory. Despite his family's efforts to maintain his legacy, Cab Calloway has been overshadowed in contemporary jazz histories by Armstrong and Ellington, though coverage suggests that the young composer was just as lauded by audiences as his peers.[16] Actress Fredi Washington—a role model for both her race and her gender—has been forgotten altogether. In general the "New Negro Woman" was symbolically written out of the narrative of race progress. In the years since Louis and Owens owned the international sports stage, the collective American memory of their accomplishments remains in flux. The Monument to Joe Louis (or "The Fist") in Detroit, Michigan, is a contested text that carried with it multiple antithetical meanings that underscore perhaps not the *Defender*'s conception of the fist that graced its front page upon the Braddock defeat but rather the isolated and reductive corporeality of a black body. Owens, who quickly fell out of favor with the American popular press upon his return from the 1936 Olympics, raced horses in vaudeville stunt expositions to make ends meet, despite the fact that contemporary films and documentaries laud him as a civil rights pioneer. In 1941 in a letter to sports editor Art Carter, he described looking for professional opportunities once he finished college; in his letter Owens stated that he hoped to "seek his fortune" once he finished school.[17] His accomplishments during that August week in Berlin were willfully forgotten until the 1980s, and he suffered materially and financially for simply wanting to have some control over the trajectory of his own career. Coverage of these stars reveals important insights into theories of exemplarity: Who was considered "heroic"? Who was venerated in life and death? How did those modes of representation change over time?

The stories of icons such as Bert Williams, Paul Robeson, Bill Robinson, Louis Armstrong, and Joe Louis are prominent in contemporary versions of black histories, but their groundbreaking accomplishments are better appreciated with an understanding of the context from which they emerged—which necessarily includes an acknowledgment of those who tried, who came close, who failed, and who never had the chance to make history. By focusing only on black performers' participation in mainstream cultural events— Bert Williams's Broadway debut, Hattie McDaniel's Oscar win, and, later, Jackie Robinson's first season as a Dodger—gatekeepers of public memory have inadvertently marginalized the contributions of many black celebrities who did not have a substantive relationship with the mainstream, white culture of the period. The way in which we as a culture remember and venerate black celebrity pioneers is an important thread in the fabric of civil rights history. This includes an acknowledgment of the ways in which institutional and cultural restrictions placed on these stars because of their race precluded them from reaping the full benefit of their accomplishments in their lifetimes. The ways in which black celebrities live on in contemporary memory reflects a slippage in understanding the multimodal nature of black American histories.

Notes

1. Discourses of Representation

1. Ralph Matthews, "What Does an Artist Owe to His Race?," *Baltimore Afro-American*, June 27, 1931, 14.
2. Baldwin, "Our Newcomers to the City," 163.
3. See, for example, "He Is a Negro, a Singer and a Hero of a Countess," *Philadelphia Tribune*, December 25, 1926, 1.
4. Klapp quoted in Dyer, "Stars as Images," 163; Gamson, *Claims to Fame*, 29; Mendelson, "On the Function," 174.
5. Klapp, "Creation of Popular Heroes," 135.
6. Carroll, "Early Twentieth Century Heroes." For the social functions of hero myth in news discourse, see Lule, *Daily News, Eternal Stories*.
7. Klapp, "Creation of Popular Heroes," 135.
8. Boorstin, "From Hero to Celebrity"; see also Gamson, *Claims to Fame*.
9. Hall, "Spectacle of the 'Other,'" 244.
10. D. Brooks, *Bodies in Dissent*, 5.
11. Batiste, *Darkening Mirrors*, 7. Stephanie Leigh Batiste has defined collective representation as a process "wherein multiple subjects and perspectives together participate in expression of identity, laying the groundwork not only for productive imagination but for the possibility of change and activism."
12. Batiste, *Darkening Mirrors*, 13.
13. Boorstin, "From Hero to Celebrity," 82.
14. Mulvey, "Visual Pleasure in Narrative Cinema."
15. See Cripps, *Slow Fade to Black*, 70–71, 75–89. Black filmmakers attempted to establish film studios to produce and finance what Thomas Cripps has called "race pictures," films that—like their theatrical counterparts *Shuffle Along* and *Chocolate Dandies*—sought to establish some iteration of a "black aesthetic." These filmmakers were met with varying degrees of success. Among the most successful was the Lincoln Motion

Picture Company, established by brothers George and Noble Johnson, which produced race films from 1916 through 1921. Their films "appeared as dark reflections of white models, very much in line with the optimistic assimilationism abroad in the Black ethos of the World War I period" (82). George acted as producer, while Noble carved out a nascent film career as a professional extra. These films, according to Cripps, created "a social absurdity, for they created a Black world without whites in which therefore, Black divisiveness and bungling rather than white cupidity consigned Negroes to the bottom" (155). Though they sought to promote the perspective of everyday black Americans, these films were poor reflections of their actual experiences.

16. Batiste, *Darkening Mirrors*, 13.
17. Marshall, "Intimately Intertwined," 317.
18. Dyer, "Stars as Images," 157.
19. Stacy, "Feminine Fascinations," 253.
20. Spohrer, "Becoming Extratextual."
21. Stacey, "Feminine Fascinations," 253.
22. Woodward, *Strange Career of Jim Crow*; Sitkoff, *New Deal for Blacks*; Taylor and Hill, *Historical Roots*; Wintz, *Black Culture*; Franklin and Moss, *From Slavery to Freedom*. For a historiographic account of African American history, see Dagbovie, *African American History Reconsidered*. For accounts of African American resistance and activism during this period, see Payne and Green, *Time Longer than Rope*.
23. Logan, *Negro in American Life*; Dorr, *Segregation's Science*. Jim Crowism symbolized the rejection of the Fourteenth and Fifteenth Amendments. In 1883 the Supreme Court declared the Civil Rights Act of 1875 unconstitutional. A decade later the Supreme Court handed down the *Plessy v. Ferguson* decision, which institutionalized separate but equal facilities for blacks and whites. By 1890 legislators had tapered off the submission of civil rights bills; by 1900 the active disenfranchisement of African Americans had begun in the South, and Congress and the Supreme Court refused to intervene. Suffrage was challenged by poll taxes, literacy tests, white-only primaries, physical intimidation, and any other strategy that would infringe on the black community's participation in political life. Between 1893 and 1904, more than 100 blacks on the average were lynched each year. Between 1900 and the start of World War I, 1,100 more lynchings took place, and not just in the South; lynching in the Midwest during this period proliferated as well. According to Gregory Michael Dorr, notions about blacks' physical and evolutionary inferiority began as early as 1875, with the publication of R. L. Dugdale's *"The Jukes": A Study in Crime, Pauperism, Disease and Heredity*, which posited that crime, pauperism, and general degeneration were heredity traits. This work, as well as later studies by Charles

Darwin, Louis Agassiz, Henry Goddard, and others, provided the scientific foundation for the eugenics movement, which, according to Stuart and Elizabeth Ewen, sought to "breed out" "socially inadequate" individuals who included "the feeble-minded, insane, criminalistics, epileptic, inebriate, diseased, blind, deaf, deformed, and dependent" (*Typecasting*, 325–26).

24. Van DeBurg quoted in Kern-Foxworth, *Aunt Jemima*, xvii.

25. Gaines, *Uplifting the Race*, vxi.

26. Verney, *African Americans*, 7.

27. Bogle, *Toms, Coons, Mulattos*, 12; Guerrero, *Framing Blackness*, 13.

28. Robert Jackson, "Secret Life of Oscar Mischeaux," 221.

29. Franklin quoted in Bogle, *Toms, Coons, Mulattos*, 15.

30. Verney, *African Americans*, 12.

31. Starr, *Creation of the Media*, 304.

32. "Proprietor and Officials of Moving Picture Placed on Trial for Assault," *Philadelphia Tribune*, October 3, 1914, 1.

33. "Movie Color Line in Superior Court," *Philadelphia Tribune*, March 13, 1915, 1; "First Step Taken to Try to Break Up Practice of Drawing Color Line at Moving Picture Theatres," *Philadelphia Tribune*, March 3, 1917, 1.

34. "First step taken."

35. Bogle, *Toms, Coons, Mulattos*, 4–10.

36. "Step-in-Fetchit Steps Out—Tries Matrimony," *Pittsburgh Courier*, July 13, 1929, 1; "Three Views of the Lazy Actor Who Suddenly Came to Life, Last Week When His Valet and Helper Came to Rehearsal Late," *Baltimore Afro-American*, November 23, 1935, 17.

37. Crafton, *Talkies*; Cripps, *Slow Fade to Black*; Spohrer, "Becoming Extra-textual," 161.

38. D. Brooks, *Bodies in Dissent*, 5.

39. Mindich, *Just the Facts*, 133. There was little systematic investigation into incidents of lynching; rather, claims of theft, murder, or rape perpetrated by lynching victims went unchallenged by local authorities and mainstream newspapers. Black citizens were left to deal with the problem of lynching on their own. Black newspapers like the *Chicago Defender* and the *New York Age* routinely covered incidents of lynching on their front pages, denouncing the practice and the bogus notions of "justice" that disguised what the act truly was: murder. One Tennessee-based black press journalist, Ida B. Wells-Barnett, made it her mission to expose the evils of lynching. Wells routinely interrogated the claims made by mainstream newspapers regarding the circumstances and presumed guilt of lynching victims. She argued that lynching was not about protecting white women but rather was "an excuse to get rid of Negroes who were acquiring wealth and property and thus keep the race terrorized" (120). According to historian David Mindich, Wells employed many of the same

tactics as muckrakers of the period, often visiting lynching sites under-cover and interviewing witnesses. After one of her inflammatory articles resulted in the destruction of the *Memphis Free Speech* press, she moved to New York and gained even greater visibility as a journalist for the *New York Age*, which had a larger circulation. Patrick Washburn has argued that Wells used the *New York Age* as an "official record of the chilling acts of racial abuse." In her first story, "Exiled," published on June 25, 1892, Wells urged blacks to defend themselves against such violence. "A Winchester rifle should have a place of honor in every Black home," she wrote. "The more the Afro-American yields and cringes and begs, the more he is insulted, outraged and lynched" (quoted in Washburn, *African-American Newspaper*, 69). Wells and other members of the black intelligentsia became increasingly vocal about the necessity of armed opposition to lynching violence.

40. Roberts, *Papa Jack*, 91.

41. *Messenger*, July 25, 1925, quoted in Digby-Junger, "*Guardian, Crisis*," 274.

42. Metz Lochard, "The Negro and the White Press," 3, Metz T. P. Lochard Collection, Black Press Archives, Moorland-Spingarn Research Center.

43. Detweiler, *Negro Press*; Farrar, *"Baltimore Afro-American"*; Gonzalez and Torres, *News for All the People*; Pride and Wilson, *History of the Black Press*; Stevens and Johnson, "From Black Politics"; Wilson, *Black Journalists in Paradox*; Washburn, *African-American Newspaper*; Wolseley, *Black Press*; Nelson, *Black Press*.

44. Bunie, *Robert L. Vann*, 80.

45. Richardson, "Platform," 398–99; Beard, "Associated Negro Press," 49; Hogan, *Black National News Service*, 57–87; Washburn, *African American Newspaper*, 74; Wolseley, *Black Press*, 22; Pride and Wilson, *History of the Black Press*, 122; Regester, "Stepin Fetchit," 504; Carroll, "From Fraternity to Fracture." Alissa Richardson has likened the *Chicago Defender*'s reliance on Pullman porters to gather, shape, and transmit news stories to modern conceptions of networked journalism. Pullman porters "achieved modern notions of information crowdsourcing and collaborative news editing, which helped shape and convey political thought in the Black press after World War I" (399). Around 1915 the *Chicago Defender* became the first newspaper to utilize the porters to help to promote its "Great Northern Drive" campaign. Publisher Robert S. Abbott paid porters to bundle and carry copies of the newspaper onto their southbound trains. Porters figured out the best areas to drop the bundles; they aimed for places that were close to community churches, schools, and black-owned businesses. Porters, who had physical access to politicians, celebrities, and other public figures by virtue of serving them on the expensive trains on which they rode, provided the *Defender* with story leads and gossip. In exchange the *Defender* provided the por-

ters with flattering coverage; many porters even contributed content to the newspaper. Soon the *Pittsburgh Courier* adopted this news distribution model, too. The Pullman porters were essential to the *Defender*'s newsgathering and distribution model, but the "networked" nature of the *Defender* and many black press newsrooms went beyond the use of the Pullman porters. By the mid-1920s many newspapers began to subscribe to Claude Barnett's Associated Negro Press wire service, which relied on "executive correspondents" in areas with concentrated black populations. These correspondents were hardly professional journalists; rather, they were citizens whom Barnett and his five-person skeleton staff considered in touch with local community happenings. The ANP headquarters were based in Chicago, but by 1925 the ANP had "executive correspondents" in eleven of America's largest cities, including Los Angeles, where Fay Jackson and Harry Leavitt began reporting on black actors in Hollywood in 1933. Local community leaders—from politicians to clergy to local business owners—also contributed content on a regular basis. It was not uncommon for popular race leaders, such as Booker T. Washington, W. E. B. Du Bois, and others to publish news stories in black press newspapers. Literary authors and performers also contributed artistic works to the papers. Famed actor Stepin Fetchit published a column in the *Chicago Defender* using his real name, Lincoln Perry, as the byline to report on the film industry's treatment of black actors. As Brian Carroll has demonstrated, even Negro League baseball owners, such as Rube Foster, were invited to contribute to black press newspapers, often anonymously and almost always to promote their own business interests and encourage attendance at games.

46. Higginbotham, *Righteous Discontent*, 18.
47. Amistead Pride's newspaper figures appear in Wolseley, *Black Press*, 38.
48. While overall more black citizens were becoming literate, the rate at which inhabitants of rural areas learned how to read lagged. Living in a large city correlated with the likelihood of learning how to read. Wartime opportunities meant that more black students received college educations than ever before and found greater employment opportunities in education, medicine, and law, in addition to industrial production that created a "cultural middle class" of black urban residents. New York's illiteracy rate was 2.1 percent; Chicago's was 2.2 percent; and Philadelphia's was 3 percent. In the South, where illiteracy rates were generally higher, Baltimore's was 7 percent and Atlanta's was 10 percent (U.S. Department of Commerce, Bureau of the Census, *Negroes in the United States*, 239).
49. Farrar, *"Baltimore Afro-American,"* xi.
50. John L. Clarke, "Think This Over," *Philadelphia Tribune*, March 26, 1931, 1.
51. Bunie, *Robert L. Vann*, 44.
52. P. L. Prattis quoted in Bunie, *Robert L. Vann*, 44.

53. Wilson, *Black Journalists in Paradox*, 58; Washburn, *African-American Newspaper*, 112.
54. Farrar, *"Baltimore Afro-American,"* 20–21; Farrar, "See What the Afro Says."
55. Wolseley, *Black Press*, 134; Carroll, "This Is IT!"
56. Fay Jackson, "Movies Want Only 'Uncle Tom' and 'Mammy' Types," *Baltimore Afro-American*, October 12, 1935, 8.
57. Washington, "Biographical Notice," 139.
58. Gaines, *Uplifting the Race*, 77.
59. "'Hit the N——r' New Film Insult," *Chicago Defender*, February 28, 1914, 1.
60. "Bishop Flays Race Citizens Who Laugh at Amos 'n' Andy," *Pittsburgh Courier*, May 3, 1930, 1.
61. Clarence Roy Mitchell, "Amos 'n Andy," *Baltimore Afro-American*, February 15, 1930, 6.
62. "A Birth of a Nation," *Crisis*, December 1915, 86.
63. "Birth of a Nation," *Crisis*. *Birth* lingered in theaters for years after its initial 1915 release. Black publications mounted a boycott again in 1930, when *Birth* was rereleased with sound. As late as 1933, the *Tribune* boasted that it had successfully blocked a screening of the film at the Spruce Theatre in west Philadelphia, having responded to a reader's letter expressing concern over the film.
64. "Rogers Adds Second Slur to Broadcast," *New York Amsterdam News*, January 31, 1934, 1; "Rogers Substitutes 'Darky' for More Offensive Epithet," *Philadelphia Tribune*, February 1, 1934, 1.
65. Floyd C. Covington, "The Negro Invades Hollywood," *Opportunity*, April 1929, 112–13.
66. Covington, "Negro Invades Hollywood."
67. Ross, *Working-Class Hollywood*, 61.
68. "Strike Threat Looms Here in Movie Houses," *Philadelphia Tribune*, November 14, 1935, 1.
69. "Organizing the Negro Actor," *Messenger*, August 1924, 12.
70. Farrar, *Baltimore Afro-American*, xi.
71. Brundage, "Working," 34.
72. Gooden, "Visual Representations of Feminine Beauty"; Lamb, *Conspiracy of Silence*; Carroll, "Early Twentieth Century Heroes"; Carroll, "From Fraternity to Fracture"; Bernstein and White *"Imitation of Life* in a Segregated Atlanta."
73. Carroll, "Early Twentieth Century Heroes"; S. Jackson, "African American Celebrity Dissent"; Regester, "Stepin Fetchit." See also Gallon, "'How Much Can You Read?'"; Lamb, *Conspiracy of Silence*.
74. Carroll, "Early Twentieth Century Heroes," 34.
75. Young, *Embodying Black Experience*, 94.
76. My initial inquiry into the roots of African American celebrity culture began with an inductive reading of black press publications from

1895—against the backdrop of the judicial and legislative rejection of freed blacks' basic civil rights, so-called scientific theories about the "inferiority" of the black race, and the routine lynching of black citizens across the country—through 1935, the symbolic end of the Harlem Renaissance, which coupled with increasing activism over the period, drastically redefined what it meant to be black, American, and "free." The evidence that emerged from this initial reading prompted me to shift the time period for this manuscript by five years. There were nearly no substantive news articles about celebrities from which to draw significant clues until 1900, so the present book does not include any evidence from 1895–99. Also, during my immersion in primary research, secondary sources, archive trips, and visits to public and mediated memory sites, I realized that I could not tell this story without including the developments of the late 1930s: the 1936 Olympics and in particular the victories of Jesse Owens in Germany and Joe Louis at home in the United States and Hattie McDaniel's 1940 Oscar win, to name only a few. The end of the Harlem Renaissance, I discovered, did not signal a shift away from the sensational reporting practices of black press celebrity writers. That critical juncture came later, in the early 1940s, when they began the successful "Double V" campaign at the advent of U.S. intervention of World War II. Therefore, this study includes evidence from 1900–1940. The evidence in support of this project was collected from an inductive reading of the front pages, sports sections, and entertainment sections of each of the publications I have identified as objects of study. Please see the archival section of the bibliography for a complete list of primary sources consulted.

2. Early Crossover Black Celebrities

1. Ward, *Unforgivable Blackness*, 204–12.
2. R. L. Jackson II, *Scripting the Black Masculine Body*, 9–16.
3. Forbes, *Introducing Bert Williams*, 193–205, 112–13.
4. Runstedtler, *Jack Johnson, Rebel Sojourner*, 70.
5. Forbes, *Introducing Bert Williams*, 204.
6. Runstedtler, *Jack Johnson, Rebel Sojourner*, 33.
7. Young, *Embodying Black Experience*, 118.
8. Young, *Embodying Black Experience*, 98.
9. "Jack Johnson Kayoed Jeffries 30 Years Ago," *Chicago Defender*, July 6, 1940, 24.
10. Franklin and Moss, *From Slavery to Freedom*, 271–72 (including Washington's quote).
11. Suisman, "Co-workers in the Kingdom of Culture," 1295.
12. Runstedtler, *Jack Johnson, Rebel Sojourner*, 117.
13. Forbes, *Introducing Bert Williams*, 122–26.

14. Runstedtler, *Jack Johnson, Rebel Sojourner*, 230–31.

15. Cripps, *Slow Fade to Black*, 25.

16. "Bert Williams, Al Jolson Film "Dud," *Baltimore Afro-American*, September 26, 1926, 5.

17. Runstedtler, *Jack Johnson, Rebel Sojourner*, 78.

18. Ward, *Unforgiveable Blackness*, 283n.

19. "Bert Williams Lost to Race," *Baltimore Afro-American*, May 25, 1923, 4.

20. "Bert Williams to Visit Texas Only as an Angel," *Chicago Defender*, December 31, 1921, 3.

21. Ward, *Unforgiveable Blackness*, 8.

22. Sylvester Russell, "The Bert Williams Interview, Its Value and Importance," Musical and Dramatic, *Chicago Defender*, October 10, 1910, 2.

23. Ward, *Unforgiveable Blackness*, 430.

24. Jack Johnson scrapbook, Schomburg Center for Research in Black Culture, New York Public Library.

25. "Bert Williams," *Baltimore Afro-American*, December 22, 1917, 4.

26. Forbes, *Introducing Bert Williams*, 205.

27. Forbes, *Introducing Bert Williams*, 87.

28. T. Brooks, *Lost Sounds*, 105.

29. "Bert Williams," *Baltimore Afro-American*, December 22, 1917, 4.

30. Sylvester Russell, "The Williams and Walker of the Future," Musical and Dramatic, *Chicago Defender*, April 22, 1911, 4.

31. Forbes, *Introducing Bert Williams*, 22–25.

32. Taylor and Austen, *Darkest America*, 12.

33. Taylor and Austen, *Darkest America*, 14.

34. "Bert Williams," *Baltimore Afro-American*, December 22, 1917, 4.

35. Fay M. Jackson, "Glowing Tribute Is Paid to Bert Williams by Cantor," *Baltimore Afro-American*, September 11, 1937, 10.

36. Eloise Bibb Thompson, "Bert Williams Has High Ideals," *Chicago Defender*, March 29, 1915, 1.

37. "Bert Williams to Abandon Comedy," *Baltimore Afro-American*, January 13, 1922, 10.

38. Forbes, *Introducing Bert Williams*, 308.

39. Forbes, *Introducing Bert Williams*, 177–78, 190–98.

40. Lester A. Walton, "Theatrical Life among Afro-Americans Noted," *Baltimore Afro-American*, September 23, 1911, 2.

41. Walton, "Theatrical Life Among Afro-Americans Noted."

42. "Bert Williams," *Baltimore Afro-American*, December 22, 1917, 4.

43. "Bert Williams World's Greatest Living Comedian," *Chicago Defender*, December 26, 1914, 9.

44. "Battling Siki Pays Visit to Defender Office," *Chicago Defender*, February 2, 1924, 9.

45. "Bert Williams," *Baltimore Afro-American*, December 22, 1917, 4.

46. "Bert Williams," *Baltimore Afro-American*, December 22, 1917, 4; "Cantor Calls Bert Williams King of Troubadours," *Baltimore Afro-American*, October 27, 1910, 9.

47. "Dr. Booker T. Washington Likes Bert Williams' Work," *Chicago Defender*, November 19, 1910, 4.

48. For comments about Williams's lack of opportunity, see "Bert Williams To Abandon Comedy"; "Bert Williams World's Greatest Living Comedian."

49. Russell, "Bert Williams Interview," 2.

50. Russell, "Bert Williams Interview," 2; Russell, "Williams and Walker of the Future," 4.

51. Russell, "Bert Williams Interview," 2.

52. "Bert Williams Banqueted," *Baltimore Afro-American*, February 24, 1912, 4; "Glad Hand Given to Bert Williams," *Chicago Defender*, March 9, 1912, 1; "Bert Williams Here with the Follies," *Baltimore Afro-American*, March 9, 1912, 8; Thompson, "Bert Williams Has High Ideals," 1.

53. Lester A. Walton, "More Facts about Bert Williams in Vaudeville," *Philadelphia Tribune*, December 27, 1913, 3.

54. Michaeli, *Defender*, 27.

55. Bill Doherty, "Jack Johnson in Australia," *Ring*, March 1937, 20, Jack Johnson scrapbook.

56. Jack Johnson, "How I Whipped Mr. Jeffries," *Las Vegas Review-Journal Saturday Magazine*, July 4, 1931, 5–6, Jack Johnson scrapbook. "Mr. Corbett, Mr. Abe Attell and the other seconds" refer to Jeffries's cornermen and training team.

57. Johnson, "How I Whipped Mr. Jeffries."

58. Runstedtler, *Jack Johnson, Rebel Sojourner*, 149.

59. Michaeli, *Defender*, 29–30; "canny public relations operator" in Roberts, *Papa Jack*, 139.

60. "Jack Johnson a Hero," *Chicago Defender*, April 23, 1910, 1.

61. "Jack Johnson an Honor to His Race," *Baltimore Afro-American*, December 4, 1909, 3.

62. Untitled article, *New York Amsterdam News*, July 16, 1910, 4.

63. "Ida B. Wells on Why Mrs. Jack Johnson Suicided," *Cleveland Gazette*, November 30, 1912, 2.

64. "Jack Johnson Not Getting a Fair Deal," *Baltimore Afro-American*, November 23, 1912, 6.

65. Starr, *Creation of the Media*, 246.

66. "Bert Williams Going to London," *Philadelphia Tribune*, March 29, 1913, 3.

67. "Bert Williams Took Cakewalk to London," *Baltimore Afro-American*, September 21, 1933, A12.

68. Lester A. Walton, "More Facts about Bert Williams in Vaudeville," *Philadelphia Tribune*, December 27, 1913, 3.

69. Runstedtler, *Jack Johnson, Rebel Sojourner*, 165.
70. Regarding Johnson's claim that he threw the fight, see Lester Bieder-man, "Folks! Ever Meet Lil Artha Johnson?," clipping from unidentified newspaper, Jack Johnson scrapbook.
71. Tony Langston, "Bert Williams, famous comedian, dead," *Chicago Defender*, March 11, 1922, 1.
72. Langston, "Bert Williams, famous comedian, dead."
73. "Bert Williams," *Chicago Defender*, March 11, 1922, 12.
74. Ward, *Unforgiveable Blackness*, 425.
75. "Hear That Small Voice on the Radio? It's Jack Johnson's," *Chicago Defender*, October 10, 1936, 14.
76. Ward, *Unforgiveable Blackness*, 436–39.
77. Washburn, *African-American Newspaper*, 134–35; Orrin C. Evans, "Louis Cool, Silent," *Philadelphia Tribune*, September 26, 1935, 1; "Joe Louis to Honeymoon at Sea," *Baltimore-Afro-American*, September 14, 1935, 1.
78. Jack Saunders, "Jack Johnson, in Cheap Show, Still Belittlin'," *Pittsburgh Courier*, October 30, 1937, 4.
79. "Open Letter to Jack Johnson," *Chicago Defender*, February 22, 1936, 16.
80. Finkle, *Forum for Protest*.
81. Woodward, *Strange Career of Jim Crow*, 114.
82. "The Champions" [caption], *Chicago Defender*, June 8, 2918, 1.

3. Black Celebrities Uplift the Race

1. "Roland Hayes Makes Contribution," *Pittsburgh Courier*, January 17, 1925, 16.
2. T. Brooks, *Lost Sounds*, 444.
3. Brooks and Sims, *Roland Hayes*, 129, 271.
4. "Roland Hayes Makes Contribution," *Pittsburgh Courier*.
5. Gaines, *Uplifting the Race*, xiv.
6. Gaines, *Uplifting the Race*, 21.
7. Gaines, *Uplifting the Race*, 15.
8. Jones Ross, "Preserving the Community," 534.
9. Baldwin, "Our Newcomers to the City," 372.
10. U.S. Department of Commerce, Bureau of the Census, *Negroes in the United States*, 443.
11. Dr. Cobb's comments quoted in "Jesse Owens Just Normal American Boy, Howard University Scientist Reveals," *Baltimore Afro-American*, November 30, 1935, 1.
12. Coit, "Our Changed Attitude," 226–27.
13. Higginbotham, *Righteous Discontent*, 187.
14. Gaines, *Uplifting the Race*, 76.

15. "What Do You Know about Race History? National Negro History Week Will Be Celebrated Next Week as a Racial Uplift Movement," *Philadelphia Tribune*, January 29, 1927, 9.

16. Du Bois, "Talented Tenth," 33–34.

17. Du Bois, "Talented Tenth," 33–34, 75.

18. "Du Bois Lectures," *Baltimore Afro-American*, December 26, 1903, 4.

19. Lewis, *W. E. B. Du Bois*, 49.

20. Lewis, *W. E. B. Du Bois*, 9.

21. "Du Bois Lectures," *Baltimore Afro-American*.

22. Du Bois, "Talented Tenth," 44–45.

23. Alexander, *W. E. B. Du Bois*, 15.

24. Lewis, *W. E. B. Du Bois*, 20.

25. Alexander, *W. E. B. Du Bois*, 40.

26. Alexander, *W. E. B. Du Bois*, 40; Farrar, *"Baltimore Afro-American,"* 142–45.

27. Wilson, *Black Journalists in Paradox*, 53.

28. Alexander, *W. E. B. Du Bois*, 51.

29. W. E. B. Du Bois, letter to Robert Vann, Percival L. Prattis Papers, Moorland Spingarn Research Center.

30. Daniel, *Black Journals of the United States*, 140.

31. Green, *Samuel Coleridge-Taylor*.

32. Du Bois, *Darkwater*, 196.

33. Schenbeck, *Racial Uplift and American Music*, 73–74.

34. "The Samuel Coleridge-Taylor Recital," *Baltimore Afro-American*, December 15, 1906, 4.

35. "Musical Idol of London," *Baltimore Afro-American*, June 6, 1903, 1.

36. Green, *Samuel Coleridge-Taylor*, 53.

37. Green, *Samuel Coleridge-Taylor*, 104.

38. "Samuel Coleridge-Taylor," Men of the Month, *Crisis*, October 1912, 278.

39. Du Bois, *Darkwater*, 205, 217.

40. Brooks and Sims, *Roland Hayes*, 19–29.

41. "Roland Hayes at Carnegie Hall, New Year's Night," *Pittsburgh Courier*, December 29, 1923, 5.

42. T. Brooks, *Lost Sounds*, 448–49.

43. Quoted in "Roland Hayes to Sing with Famous Boston and Detroit Symphony Orchestras," *Pittsburgh Courier*, October 20, 1923, 11.

44. "Roland Hayes Makes Contribution," *Pittsburgh Courier*, January 17, 1925, 16.

45. J. A. Rogers, "Roland Hayes, the Negro Ambassador," *Philadelphia Tribune*, December 22, 1927, 8.

46. Metz Lochard, "The Negro and White Press," 2, Metz T. P. Lochard Collection, Black Press Archives, Moorland-Spingarn Research Center.

47. Jones-Ross and McKerns, "Depression in the 'Promised Land,'" 58.

48. "The Sportive Spotlight," *New York Amsterdam News,* June 10, 1925, 6.

49. Williams, "Vanguards of the New Negro."

50. Jones-Ross and McKerns, "Depression in the 'Promised Land,'" 68.

51. Coit, "Our Changed Attitude," 233–55.

52. Digby-Junger, "*Guardian, Crisis,*" 267.

53. Daniel, *Black Journals of the United States,* 243.

54. Veteran quote from Williams, "Vanguards of the New Negro," 351.

55. Coit, "Our Changed Attitude," 255.

56. Coit, "Our Changed Attitude," 254.

57. Edgar M. Gray, "Critics Disagree over the Art of Charles Gilpin," *Baltimore Afro-American,* February 25, 1921, 1.

58. Gray, "Critics Disagree."

59. Lewis, *W. E. B. Du Bois,* 476.

60. Gwendolyn Bennett, "The Emperors Jones," *Opportunity,* September 1930, 270.

61. Regarding his leaving school to pursue an acting career, see "Charles Gilpin Takes His Last Curtain Call," *Baltimore Afro-American,* May 10, 1930, A10.

62. "Charles Gilpin," *Chicago Defender,* March 12, 1921, 12.

63. "Charles Gilpin," *Baltimore Afro-American,* January 14, 1921, 4; "Charles Gilpin, Actor, Awarded Spingarn Medal," *Chicago Defender,* June 25, 1921, 1; "Charles Gilpin, Star Actor, to Appear in Washington," *Philadelphia Tribune,* March 19, 1921, 12.

64. G. Grant Williams, "Charles S. Gilpin Making New History on Broadway," *Philadelphia Tribune,* June 4, 1921, 2.

65. "Charles Gilpin," *Baltimore Afro-American.*

66. "Charles S. Gilpin, Actor, Awarded Spingarn Medal."

67. "Spingarn Medal Award to Harry T. Burleigh," *Philadelphia Tribune,* May 26, 1917, 1.

68. "See President—Charles Gilpin Does a Handshake with the Big Chief at Washington," *Chicago Defender,* September 17, 1921, 7.

69. "Charles Gilpin, Negro Actor, Not Invited," *Savannah Tribune,* March 5, 1921, 1; Gray, "Critics Disagree."

70. Reprinted in "Charles Gilpin and the Drama League," Who's Who, *Messenger,* March 1921, 203.

71. "Charles Gilpin and the Drama League."

72. "Gilpin Proves Hero of the Drama League Dinner," *Baltimore Afro-American,* March 11, 1921, 1.

73. Will Anthony Madden, "Paul Robeson Rises to Supreme Heights in 'The Emperor Jones,'" *Pittsburgh Courier,* May 17, 1924, 8.

74. "Why Charles Gilpin Is Not Uncle Tom," *Philadelphia Tribune,* October 16, 1926, 1; "In Again, Out Again, Gone Again Goes Charles Gilpin," *Baltimore Afro-American,* December 29, 1928, 9.

75. "Harlem Asking Itself, Why Is Duke Ellington Leaving the Cotton Club?," *Baltimore Afro-American*, January 24, 1931, 9.

76. J. A. Rogers, "Roland Hayes Will Build Institute on Spot Where He Was . . ." *Pittsburgh Courier*, December 24, 1927, 13.

77. Rogers, "Roland Hayes Will Build Institute."

78. Brooks and Sims, *Roland Hayes*, 143.

79. "Roland Hayes, Art and Race Prejudice," *Chicago Defender*, December 19, 1925, A10.

80. Brooks and Sims, *Roland Hayes*, 149.

81. Quotation from "Flay Roland Hayes for Jim Crow," *Baltimore Afro-American*, January 9, 1926, 1. See also "Hayes Deserts Stage; Halts Jim Crow Insult," *Chicago Defender*, January 16, 1926, 1; "Nagging Roland Hayes," *Chicago Defender*, February 6, 1926, A12; "Afro Readers Blame Roland Hayes for Lyric Jim Crow," *Baltimore Afro-American*, January 16, 1926, 10; "Roland Hayes and the Race Rumpus," *Pittsburgh Courier*, January 23, 1926, 10.

82. "Afro Readers Blame Roland Hayes."

83. "Hayes Deserts Stage."

84. "Judge Saves Prisoner from South," *Chicago Defender*, January 16, 1926, 1; "Hayes Deserts Stage."

85. Ethan Michaeli has argued that the *Defender* consistently espoused integrationist, rather than separatist, rhetoric over time. For more on the *Defender* and integrationism, see Michaeli, *Defender*.

86. "Roland Hayes and the Race Rumpus."

87. "Rolling Hayes," *Baltimore Afro-American*, January 16, 1926, 12.

88. Brooks and Sims, *Roland Hayes*, 147.

89. "Afro Readers Blame Roland Hayes."

90. Rogers, "Roland Hayes Will Build Institute."

91. Brooks and Sims, *Roland Hayes*, 215.

4. Mythologizing Black Celebrities

1. Floyd J. Calvin, "Cab Calloway's Rise to Fame Was Sensational," *Pittsburgh Courier*, January 31, 1931, A8.

2. Carney, *Cuttin' Up*; Peretti, *Creation of Jazz*. Peretti notes that blues and jazz have the following elements in common: blues harmony, melismatic phrasing, instrumental improvisation, and roots in New Orleans.

3. Ollie Stewart, "What Price Jazz?," *Chicago Defender*, April 27, 1934, 12.

4. Du Bois, "Criteria of Negro Art," 259.

5. Willis Richardson, "Propaganda in the Theatre," *Messenger*, June 1923, 333–34.

6. Rowena Woodham Jelliffe, "The Negro in the Field of Drama," *Opportunity*, July 1928, 214.

7. Balshaw, "'Black Was White,'" 310.

8. Lewis, *W. E. B. Du Bois*, 476–79.
9. Balshaw, "'Black Was White,'" 310.
10. Wintz, *Black Culture*, 87. The Harlem Renaissance and the New Negro Movement were largely literary movements, though their influence spread throughout entertainment culture. For the most complete compilation of writings by popular African American intellectuals during this period, see Gates and Jarrett, *New Negro*.
11. Wintz, *Black Culture*, 24.
12. Carroll, "From Fraternity to Fracture," 85.
13. Sitkoff, *New Deal for Blacks*, 37.
14. Snorgrass, "*Baltimore Afro-American*," 35–50; Teel, "African-American Press."
15. Bogle, *Bright Boulevards, Bold Dreams*, 104.
16. Hark, *American Cinema of the 1930s*, 1.
17. Jewell, *Golden Age of Cinema*, 30.
18. Jewell, *Golden Age of Cinema*, 7.
19. "Jazz vs. the Classics," *Baltimore Afro-American*, September 7, 1925, 8. Though it is difficult to find exact figures, by 1939, of the ten million black residents living in the South at the time, only 17 percent had radios, and 28 percent had phonographs; this figure is compared with the nearly five to six million blues and jazz records sold annually, which suggests that few blacks were contributing to these skyrocketing sales figures. Rather, it is likeliest that most jazz record collectors were white (Collier, *Jazz*, 204).
20. Warren Scholl, "Hot Jazz Is Dead in America, but Duke Ellington, a Creator, Carries On," *Baltimore Afro-American*, November 16, 1935, 9.
21. Calvin, "Cab Calloway's Rise to Fame."
22. "Not Normal after Jazz," *Baltimore Afro-American*, January 25, 1920, 1.
23. "Jazz Music Makes Dancers Drunk," *Baltimore Afro-American*, April 20, 1923, 6.
24. Betty Barclay, "This Jazz-Mad Modern Generation," *Baltimore Afro-American*, September 20, 1930, 11.
25. Henry T. McCrary, "Philadelphia Minister Decried Prevalence of Jazz Music in Our Religious Services," *Baltimore Afro-American*, April 21, 1934, A10; "Cab Calloway Goes to Church," *Baltimore Afro-American*, November 12, 1932, 10.
26. Collier, *Jazz*, 219.
27. Ralph Matthews, "Capital Thrills Again to Voice of Roland Hayes," *Baltimore Afro-American*, December 28, 1940, 17.
28. Collier, *Jazz*, 203.
29. "Harlem Asking Itself, Why Is Duke Ellington Leaving the Cotton Club?," *Baltimore Afro-American*, January 24, 1931, 9.
30. Scholl, "Hot Jazz Is Dead"; "Duke Ellington's Trip Abroad Answers Europe's Plea for Best in Jazz," *Philadelphia Tribune*, June 15, 1933, 11; "Paramount Shudders as Duke Rehearses," *Atlanta Daily World*, May 13, 1934, 7.

31. Frank Marshall Davis, "Duke Ellington, 'Just Plain Folks,' Likes Drinks, Cards, and Movies," *Baltimore Afro-American*, February 2, 1935, 9.

32. "High Tribute Paid to Duke Ellington," *Philadelphia Tribune*, November 15, 1931, 7.

33. Scholl, "Hot Jazz Is Dead."

34. Edgar Wiggins, "Louis Armstrong Breaks with Manager; Sails Home," *Chicago Defender*, February 9, 1935, 9; Chappy Gardner, "Louis Armstrong Arrested in Big Dope Scandal," *Pittsburgh Courier*, December 6, 1930, 1; "Louis Armstrong out of Jail," *Philadelphia Tribune*, March 26, 1931, 1.

35. Gardner, "Louis Armstrong Arrested"; "Louis Armstrong out of Jail."

36. "'Black Rascal' Sold 100,000 Records," *Baltimore Afro-American*, June 18, 1932, 16.

37. James Miller, "Says Jazz Has a Place in Music," *Pittsburgh Courier*, June 28, 1930, A6.

38. Marshall, "Intimately Intertwined," 323.

39. Sternheimer, *Celebrity Culture*, 35.

40. Gamson, "Assembly Line of Greatness," 6.

41. "Race Press Is Ignored by Big Film Interests," *Pittsburgh Courier*, December 15, 1934, A9.

42. Fay Jackson, "Louise Beavers, Overnight Star, Snubs Colored Reporters," *Baltimore Afro-American*, December 22, 1934, 8.

43. Sylvester Russell, "Bill Robinson Tells His Story," *New York Amsterdam New*, October 16, 1929, 9; Fay Jackson, "Hollywood Turns on the Heat for Bill Robinson," *Baltimore Afro-American*, June 8, 1935, 9; Walter Welch, "Can Bill Robinson Cut the Fool as Much as He Pleases?" [letter to the editor], *Baltimore Afro-American*, September 14, 1935, 9; Chappy Gardner, "'Born Buddies' Star Stops Lafayette Benefit," *Pittsburgh Courier*, December 6, 1930, 18.

44. "Bill Robinson Wed 15 Years; Dancer Still a Baby to His Wife," *Baltimore Afro-American*, April 6, 1935, 5; Jackson, "Hollywood Turns on the Heat for Bill Robinson."

45. Regarding Fetchit's behavior, see, for example, "Three Views of the Lazy Actor Who Suddenly Came to Life, Last Week When His Valet and Helper Came to Rehearsal Late," *Baltimore Afro-American*, November 23, 1935, 17.

46. Bernice Patton, "'Mayor of Harlem' Gets Key to Hollywood," *Pittsburgh Courier*, December 8, 1934, A8.

47. "Bill Robinson Puts Over Big Benefit," *Chicago Defender*, October 15, 1927, 9; "Bill Robinson's Show Nets Charities $3,084," *Chicago Defender*, January 11, 1930, 10; "Bill Robinson Plays Santa," *Chicago Defender*, May 6, 1933, 5; "'Bojangles' Robinson Made Honorary Member of Kiddies Club at Tribune Annual Party," *Philadelphia Tribune*, April 16, 1931, 1; "Benefit Rackets Costly, Says Bojangles," *Baltimore Afro-American*, September 15, 1934, 7.

48. "She Performed for Charity—for $400" [caption], *Philadelphia Tribune*, August 2, 1934, 1.

49. Ralph Matthews, "An Open Letter to Miss Ethel Waters," *Baltimore Afro-American*, April 14, 1934, 20.

50. "Paul Robeson Film Cut," *Baltimore Afro-American*, October 7, 1933, 1.

51. Ralph Matthews, "Roland Hayes: Still Bachelor after 40 Years," *Baltimore Afro-American*, April 15, 1933, 9.

52. Spohrer, "Becoming Extratextual," 156.

53. The Viennese countess's name is spelled "Colloredo" in some reports.

54. "Hayes' Engagement Reported Smashed," *Baltimore Afro-American*, December 22, 1928, 1.

55. "Hayes' Engagement Reported Smashed."

56. "Roland Hayes Denies Rumor of Engagement," *Pittsburgh Courier*, May 8, 1926, 1.

57. "Hayes' Engagement Reported Smashed."

58. "He Is a Negro, a Singer and a Hero of a Countess," *Philadelphia Tribune*, December 25, 1926, 1. From the look of this front page, it appears that the *Tribune* was going through some changes itself, perhaps trying to shake its former conservatism in favor of trendier reporting, in line with the *Afro-American*, the *Courier*, and the *Defender*. Next to the Hayes story, dancer "Dot" Bell is featured in a seductive pose with the caption "Nudity: The Other Side of It."

59. Matthews, "Roland Hayes."

60. Harry Levette, "Sift News of Marital Intent of Jesse Owens," *Chicago Defender*, June 29, 1935, 4.

61. "Put on Spot, Jesse Owens Declares He'll Marry Cleveland Love," *Atlanta Daily World*, July 3, 1935, 1.

62. Bill Crain, "Miss Nickerson Explains What Jesse Owens Meant in Her Young Life," *Atlanta Daily World*, July 29, 1935, 1. For further coverage of the Jesse Owens love triangle, see Florence M. Collins, "Louis and Owens Create Mild Riot in Washington," *Baltimore Afro-American*, August 31, 1935, 13; "Jesse Owens Straightens Out Tangled Love Affairs," *Baltimore Afro-American*, July 6, 1935, 1; Fay M. Jackson, "Los Angeles Likes Owens, and Jesse Likes City Too," *Baltimore Afro-American*, June 29, 1935, 21.

63. Collins, "Louis and Owens Create Mild Riot."

64. Sternheimer, *Celebrity Culture*, 28.

65. Shipton, *Hi-De-Ho*, 1–22; 34.

66. "Cab Calloway and Missourians," *Philadelphia Tribune*, December 30, 1930, 1.

67. "Reviewer Finds Cab Calloway at Best Displaying Wares for Broadway Folk," *New York Amsterdam News*, October 28, 1931, 10.

68. Ralph Matthews, "What Becomes of Talented Amateur Actors? Many Successful," *Baltimore Afro-American*, March 14, 1931, 8.

69. Ralph Matthews, "A Boy Who Built a House of Dreams and Lives In It," *Baltimore Afro-American*, July 30, 1932, 16.

70. Ralph Matthews, "Cab Calloway and the Memphis Mob," Watching the Big Parade, *Baltimore Afro-American*, September 29, 1934, 4.

71. Matthews, "What Becomes of Talented Amateur Actors?"

72. "Cab Calloway Spurned Law Degree for Career on Stage," *Baltimore Afro-American*, February 8, 1930, 8.

73. Gamson, "Assembly Line of Greatness," 8.

74. George B. Murphy, "Cab Calloway, Cotton Club Maestro, Likes Home, Wife," *Baltimore Afro-American*, July 4, 1931, 9.

75. Oliver Smith, "Cab Calloway's Own Story of His Trip Abroad," *Pittsburgh Courier*, May 12, 1934, A8; Murphy, "Cab Calloway, Cotton Club Maestro."

76. Murphy, "Cab Calloway, Cotton Club Maestro"; Rilious Reed, "Cab Calloway Is Tops with Noise," *Chicago Defender*, May 4, 1935, 13.

77. Reed, "Cab Calloway Is Tops."

78. Frank Marshall Davis, "Duke Ellington, Who Goes to the Movies between Shows, Wrote Hit Song 'Solitude' Three Years Ago," *Pittsburgh Courier*, January 26, 1935, A9.

79. Shipton, *Hi-De-Ho*, 139.

80. Ric Roberts, "Cab Calloway, the Pedestrian, Finds Atlanta Interesting; Admirer Kisses His Hand," *Atlanta Daily World*, September 14, 1934, 1.

81. Edgar T. Rouzeau, "Joe Louis Here to Knock 'Em Out! Theatre Fans First, Carnera Next," *New York Amsterdam News*, May 18, 1935, 1.

82. Roberts, "Joe Louis, Jessie Owens, Oze Simmons, J. Henry Lewis, and Willis Ward Startle the World," *Atlanta Daily World*, November 4, 1935, 5.

83. Orrin C. Evans, "Louis Cool, Silent," *Philadelphia Tribune*, September 26, 1935, 1.

84. "On Top of the World," *Chicago Defender*, August 5, 1935, 1.

85. Florence M. Collins, "Louis and Owens Create Mild Riot in Washington," *Baltimore Afro-American*, August 31, 1935, 13.

86. Bill Gibson, "Mail at Joe Louis's Camp Totals 75 Letters a Day," *Baltimore Afro-American*, June 15, 1935, 1.

87. Russell J. Cowans, "Joe Louis's Fan Mail Is Increasing Daily," *Baltimore Afro-American*, July 13, 1935, 1.

88. Russell J. Cowans, "Joe Louis Gets Oodles of Love Notes," *Baltimore Afro-American*, August 24, 1935, 1.

89. "Joe Louis to Honeymoon at Sea," *Baltimore Afro-American*, September 14, 1935, 1.

90. Floyd G. Snelson Jr., "Crowned King of Kings: Polls 50,000 to Cop First Place; Henderson Second," *Pittsburgh Courier*, December 12, 1931, 1.

91. Gamson, "Assembly Line of Greatness," 10.

5. Marginalizing Black Female Celebrities

1. George B. Murphy Jr., "Cab Calloway, Cotton Club Maestro, Likes Home, Wife," *Baltimore Afro-American*, July 4, 1931, 9.
2. The phrase "male gaze" is borrowed from Laura Mulvey's seminal essay "Visual Pleasure in Narrative Cinema."
3. Wintz, *Black Culture*, 205–6.
4. Hull and Smith, "Politics of Black Women's Studies," xvii.
5. The terms "trivialized" and "condemned" are borrowed from Gaye Tuchman's seminal work on the objectification of women in media, *Hearth and Home*.
6. McGovern, *Sold American*; L. Cohen, *Consumers' Republic*; Goldow, *Big Vote*.
7. McGovern, *Sold American*, 41–42.
8. L. Cohen, *Consumers' Republic*, 22, 56.
9. L. Cohen, *Consumers' Republic*, 41–56. See also Drake and Cayton, *Black Metropolis*.
10. L. Cohen, *Consumers' Republic*, 52.
11. Bogle, *Toms, Coons, Mulattos*, 4–10.
12. Gooden, "Visual Representations of Feminine Beauty," 90.
13. Walker, "If the Present Looks like the Past"; Morton, *Disfigured Images*.
14. Higginbotham, *Righteous Discontent*, 190.
15. Quoted in Gooden, "Visual Representations of Feminine Beauty," 87.
16. Higginbotham, *Righteous Discontent*, 211–12.
17. Louis W. George, "Beauty Culture and Colored People," *Messenger*, July 1918, 25–26.
18. Gooden, "Visual Representations of Feminine Beauty," 89.
19. Stempel, *Showtime*, 238.
20. Wintz, *Black Culture*, 91.
21. "Why Men Go Broke" [caption], *Philadelphia Tribune*, February 9, 1928, 1.
22. "Made Glorifying Brown Skin Girls a Business," *Baltimore Afro-American*, October 25, 1930, 9.
23. "At the Colonial Theatre: 'The Chocolate Dandies,'" *Messenger*, July 1924, 323. It is pertinent to note here that black studies scholar Theodore Kornweibel argues in his cultural history of the *Messenger* that despite Lewis's predilection for chorus girls, he was vigilant in avoiding colorist rhetoric, which he believed was rooted in slave psychology. For more on Theophilus Lewis, see Kornweibel, *No Crystal Stair*.
24. "Alice Coleman" [caption], *Philadelphia Tribune*, May 30, 1924, 1.
25. Kitch, *Girl on the Magazine Cover*, 99. The phrase "New Negro Woman" is borrowed from the same source.
26. Alfred Edgar Smith, letter to Dr. Metz Lochard, November 3, 1943, Metz T. P. Lochard Collection, Black Press Archives, Moorland Spingarn Research Center.

27. W. E. B. Du Bois, letter to Robert S. Vann, June 2, 1932, Percival L. Prattis Papers, Moorland Spingarn Research Center.

28. "'Tired of Each Other'—Robesons," *Atlanta Daily World,* June 28, 1932, 1.

29. Rob Roy, "'Emperor Jones' Has More than Paul Robeson's Acting," *Chicago Defender,* November 25, 1933, 5.

30. "Guided Hubby to Fame" [caption], *Pittsburgh Courier,* September 27, 1924, 1.

31. "Geneva Gossip Links Paul Robeson with British Policy," *Baltimore Afro-American,* October 19, 1925, 23.

32. J. A. Rogers, "'Paul Does Not Need Me Anymore' says Mrs. Robeson," *Philadelphia Tribune,* October 27, 1932, 1.

33. Ralph Matthews, "A Woman's Defense of Paul Robeson," Looking at the Stars, *Baltimore Afro-American,* November 4, 1933,18.

34. "Harlemites Quizzed on Robeson," *Atlanta Daily World,* June 30, 1932, 1.

35. "'Countess' Josephine and 'Flo' Mills Rival White Actors," *Pittsburgh Courier,* July 16, 1927, A3.

36. Egan, *Florence Mills,* 162.

37. Egan, *Florence Mills,* 62.

38. Noble Sissle's "Pioneer" quote in Egan, *Florence Mills,* 64.

39. "$500 per Week for Florence Mills," *Baltimore Afro-American,* April 7, 1922, 11.

40. Salem Tutt Whitney, "Florence Mills," Salem Sez, *Chicago Defender,* February 24, 1923, 6.

41. J. A. Jackson, "Florence Mills Gets Diamond Medal," *Baltimore Afro-American,* January 4, 1924, A11.

42. "False Rumors Can't Hurt Florence Mills as a Star," *Baltimore Afro-American,* November 15, 1924, 6.

43. Rose, *Jazz Cleopatra;* Jules-Rosette, *Josephine Baker.*

44. Jules-Rosette, *Josephine Baker,* 57.

45. "A Chorus Girl Who Really Stood Out and Won Acclaim," *New York Amsterdam News,* May 13, 1925, 6.

46. Batiste, *Darkening Mirrors,* 9.

47. "Josephine Baker Continues to Make Good in Europe," *New York Amsterdam News,* September 1, 1926, 11. Also reprinted in the *Baltimore Afro-American* the same week.

48. J. A. Rogers, "Is the Star of the Folies-Bergere Really Married?," *Philadelphia Tribune,* July 14, 1927, 1.

49. Jules-Rosette, *Josephine Baker,* 151.

50. "Josephine Baker, Stage Star, Becomes Countess," *Chicago Defender,* June 25, 1927, 1.

51. Beda Jeffers, "Is Europe Heaven for Sepia Theatrical Stars?," *Kansas City/Topeka Plaindealer,* November 15, 1930, 1.

52. "Prepared to Go Abroad to Stay Robeson Claims," *Philadelphia Tribune,* July 7, 1932, 1.

53. Wood, *Josephine Baker Story*, 121.
54. Sternheimer, *Celebrity Culture*, 65.
55. Ralph Matthews, "Forgotten Husbands: What Happens to the Mates of Famous Women?," *Baltimore Afro-American*, December 22, 1934, 9.
56. "Florence Mills," *Pittsburgh Courier*, November 12, 1927, A8.
57. Robert Campbell, "Florence Mills' Life Story," *Philadelphia Tribune*, December 8, 1927, 9; Robert Campbell, "Florence Mills' Life Story," *Philadelphia Tribune*, December 15, 1927, 9; "wicked nudity" and "in atonement for outrages on morality" from "Josephine Baker Replaces Mistinguette in Gay Paree," *Baltimore Afro-American*, September 13, 1930, A19.
58. Wintz, *Black Culture*, 45.
59. Ted Haviland, "Ten Years Made a Lot of Difference in Josephine Baker," *Baltimore Afro-American*, December 7, 1935, 9.
60. Hilda See, "Race Actors Steal 'Imitation of Life': Louise Beavers, Fredye [*sic*] Washington Star in Film," *Chicago Defender*, January 12, 1935, 9.
61. Wintz, *Black Culture*, 179–80.
62. Verney, *African Americans*, 33.
63. "Their Drama Poignant" [caption], *Pittsburgh Courier*, December 15, 1934, 1.
64. "Louise Beavers Important Figure in Imitation of Life," *Kansas City Plaindealer*, November 16, 1934, 2.
65. H. S. Murphy, "'Imitation of Life,'" Brass Tacks, *Atlanta Daily World*, February 3, 1935, 4.
66. Bogle, *Toms, Coons, Mulattos*, 127–30.
67. Transcript of radio interview with Ralph Matthews, Fredi Washington Papers, Schomburg Center for Research in Black Culture.
68. George Hall, "'The Inside'–Louise Beavers," *Philadelphia Tribune*, March 14 1935, 1.
69. Louis R. Lautier, "Louise Beavers Wouldn't Use Epithet in 'Imitation of Life,'" *Baltimore Afro-American*, March 3, 1925, 9.
70. "Louise Beavers Believes Talkie Roles Misunderstood," *Baltimore Afro-American*, February 23, 1935, 8.
71. Transcript of radio interview with Ralph Matthews.
72. "Fredi Washington and Film 'Imitation' Capture the City," *Chicago Defender*, February 16, 1935, 9; "She Is Star in 'Problem' Photoplay" [caption], *Pittsburgh Courier*, September 1, 1934, 1; "Talent plus Looks" [caption], *Atlanta Daily World*, May 2, 1932, 1.
73. "Talent plus Looks."
74. Hilda See, "You Can Thank Georgia for Fredi Washington," *Chicago Defender*, March 2, 1935, 8.
75. Transcript of radio interview with Ralph Matthews..
76. Fredi Washington, letter to Porter Roberts, August 27, 1937, Fredi Washington Papers, Schomburg Center for Research in Black Culture, New York Public Library.

77. "Black Patti at Blaney's," *Baltimore Afro-American*, May 9, 1908, 5; "Black Patti Troubadours," *Baltimore Afro-American*, May 7, 1904, 4; "Beacon Lights for Negroes," *Savannah Tribune*, October 25, 1902, 1; "Black Patti Musical Comedy Co.," *Chicago Defender*, March 29, 1913, 6.

78. William Smallwood, "Louise Beavers in D.C.; Tells of Movie Stars She Knows," *Baltimore Afro-American*, March 9, 1935, 9; Lula Jones Garrett, "Nothing Delilah-Like in Real Louise Beavers," *Baltimore Afro-American*, May 18, 1935, 9.

79. Jones Garrett, "Nothing Delilah-Like."

80. Jones Garrett, "Nothing Delilah-Like."

81. "Fredi Washington Hands Hollywood a Lemon," *Atlanta Daily World*, April 15, 1934, 7.

82. Roi Ottley, "Louis Beavers Strongly Defends 'Aunt Jemima' Roles Given to Her," *New York Amsterdam News*, February 20, 1937, 8.

83. "Louise Beavers Believes Talkie Roles Misunderstood."

84. Kitch, *Girl on the Magazine Cover*, 99.

85. Bogle, *Toms, Coons, Mulattos*, 120.

86. hooks, *Feminist Theory*, 15.

87. "The Academy Award of Hattie McDaniel," *Atlanta Daily World*, March 12, 1940, 6.

6. National Heroes and Unhyphenated Americans

1. William L. Patterson, "Joe Louis Killed Nazi Supremacy Theory," July 9, 1938, *Pittsburgh Courier*, 4.

2. Wiggins and Miller, *Sport and the Color Line*, ix.

3. Ric Roberts, "Joe Louis, Jesse Owens, Oze Simmons, J. Henry Lewis, and Willis Ward Startle the World," *Atlanta Daily World*, November 4, 1935, 5.

4. Washburn, *African-American Newspaper*, 134–35.

5. Stevens, "Black Press and the 1936 Olympics."

6. Demas, "Brown Bomber's Dark Day," 257.

7. Ralph Matthews, "What Does an Artist Owe to His Race?," *Baltimore Afro-American*, June 27, 1931, 14; "Josephine Baker Continues to Make Good in Europe," *New York Amsterdam News*, September 1, 1926, 11; "Josephine Baker, Stage Star, Becomes Countess," *Chicago Defender*, June 25, 1927, 1; Beda Jeffers, "Is Europe Heaven for Sepia Theatrical Stars?," *Kansas City/Topeka Plaindealer*, November 15, 1930, 1; Ralph Matthews, "Paul Robeson, Hero or Coward?," Watching the Big Parade, *Baltimore Afro-American*, January 26, 1935, 4; "Musical Idol of London," *Baltimore Afro-American*, June 6, 1903, 1.

8. Frank Marshall Davis, "Duke Ellington, 'Just Plain Folks,' Likes Drinks, Cards, and Movies," *Baltimore Afro-American*, February 2, 1935, 9.

9. Franklin and Moss, *From Slavery to Freedom*, 434.

10. "God Save Ethiopia," *Pittsburgh Courier*, August 3, 1935, A10; Martin Dwyer, "Italy Pushes War Plans on Ethiopia," *Chicago Defender*, August 10, 1935, 1.

11. Al Monroe, "Joe Louis in Secret Drill," *Chicago Defender*, September 21, 1935, 1. According to Monroe, Louis singled him out as the "short one" from the collection of journalists present at camp and allowed him to watch the session because Monroe had lost a game of pool the previous evening.

12. "Courier Writers with a 'Punch' to Cover Louis-Carnera Fight," *Pittsburgh Courier*, June 22, 1935, 1.

13. "And the Courier 'Marches Ahead' Again," *Pittsburgh Courier*, August 10, 1935, 1, all-caps text in the original.

14. Romeo L. Dougherty, "George Lattimer and Jesse Owens," Sports Whirl, *New York Amsterdam News*, June 8, 1935, 14; see also Roberts, "Joe Louis, Jesse Owens, Oze Simmons."

15. Wiggins and Miller, *Sport and the Color Line*, xi.

16. Boddy, *Boxing*, 209–13.

17. "Louis Firpo Robbed of the Heavyweight Crown," *Chicago Defender*, September 22, 1923, 10; "Fay says . . ." [surviving fragment of original title], *Chicago Defender*, January 17, 1925, 9.

18. Chester L. Washington, "Downfall of Gans, the Old Master, in Boxing's Halcyon Days Recalled," *Pittsburgh Courier*, March 10, 1934.

19. Hudson, *Boxing in America*, 27.

20. Gildea, *Longest Fight*, 4.

21. Roberts, *Jack Dempsey*, 141.

22. "Walk Miller Thinks We're Out," *New York Amsterdam News*, August 25, 1926, 13.

23. Juli Jones, "1929 Was Best Year Boxers Had of Past Ten," *Chicago Defender*, January 8, 1921, 6.

24. Ira F. Lewis, "The Passing Review," *Pittsburgh Courier*, July 21, 1928, B5.

25. Brian Carroll notes that "prior to the emergence of pitching great Satchel Paige in 1936, newspaper coverage of games consisted of straightforward accounts of play, with little on individual players and only the rarest of occasions a feature story on a player" ("Early Twentieth Century Heroes," 40). Even so, coverage of Paige in 1936 pales in comparison with the coverage of Owens and Louis, who dominated not only column space in the sports pages but also enjoyed front-page attention. The sample of black press newspapers considered in this analysis did not have any front-page coverage of Paige from 1936 to 1940.

26. "Jesse Owens: He Wouldn't Let a Sore Leg Stop Him," *Baltimore Afro-American*, August 3, 1935, 6.

27. Edwin B. Henderson, "Race Hatred Tends to Decrease in the Olympics," *Atlanta Daily World*, August 15, 1932, 5.

28. Juli Jones Jr., "Battling Siki," In the Squared Circle, *Chicago Defender*, March 17, 1923, 10.

29. For example, see "Afro Reporter Finds Soft-Voiced Battling Siki Not the 'Savage' Pictured by the Daily Press," *Baltimore Afro-American*, September 28, 1923, A1; "Battling Siki Wins Crowd at Gayety," *Baltimore Afro-American*, September 28, 1923, 14; Warren Brown, "Knocked Out, Battling Siki Is Borne from Ring of Life Forever," *New York Amsterdam News*, December 23, 1925; 6; "Battling Siki Loses," *Chicago Defender*, December 26, 1925, A8.

30. Demas, "Brown Bomber's Dark Day," 262.

31. "Jesse Owens Just Normal American Boy, Howard U. Scientist Reveals," *Baltimore Afro-American*, November 30, 1935, 1.

32. Henry V. Edwards, "The Olympics!," *New York Amsterdam News*, August 10, 1932, 9.

33. Vernon Williams, "Jesse Owens, Schoolboy Sprinter, Born in Decatur, Ala., Always Was 'Swift Boy,'" *Baltimore Afro-American*, August 26, 1933, 20.

34. Nannie Burroughs, "Stars of Olympics have Set Example for Youth to Follow," *Baltimore Afro-American*, August 13, 1932, 16.

35. Burroughs, "Stars of Olympics." However joyful, the games were marred by one incident in which female track-and-field competitors Louise Stokes and Tydie Pickett were replaced on the day of their races by two white competitors with little explanation offered. Though clearly disappointed, journalists stopped short of suggesting that racism had played a significant role in the replacement of Stokes and Pickett.

36. Edwards, "The Olympics!"; see also "'Olympic Victories Not All Joy,' Says Tolan," *Atlanta Daily World*, August 16, 1932, 5; Thomas J. Anderson, "Eddie Tolan Wins 100 meter Olympic Classic," *New York Amsterdam News*, August 3, 1932, 1.

37. "A likable young star" from "Jesse Owens Straightens Out Tangled Love Affairs," *Baltimore Afro-American*, July 6, 1935, 1; "a modest boy" from "Jesse Owens: Popularity Is Worrisome to Sprinter," *Baltimore Afro-American*, September 7, 1935, 21; "Jesse Owens Has the World's Greatest Jumping Legs," *Baltimore Afro-American*, August 24, 1935, 20.

38. "What! Jesse Owens Considering Ohio?," *Chicago Defender*, August 5, 1933, 8; Williams, "Jesse Owens, Schoolboy Sprinter"; "Captain Jesse Owens: An Editorial," *Chicago Defender*, June 15, 1935, 13.

39. "Our Own Jesse Owens!," *Atlanta Daily World*, May 31, 1935, 5. See also "Jesse Owens Hopes to Coach Team of a Negro College," *Philadelphia Tribune*, June 13, 1935, 11.

40. "Jesse Owens Has the World's Greatest Jumping Legs," *Baltimore Afro-American*, August 24, 1935, 20.

41. Williams, "Jesse Owens, Schoolboy Sprinter."

42. "A favorite of both races" from Fay M. Jackson, "Los Angeles Likes Owens, and Jesse Likes City Too," *Baltimore Afro-American*, June 29, 1935, 21; "as if" from "Life Story of Jesse Owens," *Baltimore Afro-American*, July

20, 1935, 21; "One of the finest examples" from Williams, "Jesse Owens, Schoolboy Sprinter." The one exception to this overwhelming sense of acceptance was a *New York Amsterdam News* article that charged that the southern press did not sufficiently cover Owens's Big Ten performance ("Dixie Solons Would Ignore Great Athlete," *New York Amsterdam News*, June 8, 1935, 14).

43. "Our Own Jesse Owens!"
44. "Our Own Jesse Owens!"
45. Reprinted in "A Great Negro Racer," *Pittsburgh Courier*, July 13, 1935, 10.
46. "Great Negro Racer."
47. Al Monroe, "Joe Can Whip Max, Leroy Same Night," *Chicago Defender*, May 30, 1936.
48. Ted Benson, "The Battle of the Century—Joe Louis vs. Jim Crow," *Pittsburgh Courier*, February 29, 1936, A4.
49. "Odds Favor Louis by Knockout," *Chicago Defender*, June 20, 1936, 1; "Hitler Still Frowns on Max Fighting Joe Louis in the U.S.," *Chicago Defender*, May 2, 1936, 14.
50. Chester Washington, "Joe and Max Await Bell," *Pittsburgh Courier*, June 20, 1936, 1.
51. Washington, "Joe and Max Await Bell."
52. "German Fight of Joe Louis Bout Started," *New York Amsterdam News*, April 11, 1936, 14.
53. "Louis, Punch Gone, Easy for Max," *Chicago Defender*, June 27, 1936, 13.
54. Enoc P. Waters Jr., "Haile Selassie 1st, Now Louis; Who Next?," *Chicago Defender*, June 27, 1936, 14. In an analysis of newspaper coverage of Louis-Schmeling I, Lane Demas notes that the bout yielded several casualties—both black and white—wrought from the emotional stress of listening to the fight's unexpected outcome. The *New York Amsterdam News* reported several suicide attempts after the bout.
55. Demas, "Brown Bomber's Dark Day," 265.
56. Stevens, "Black Press," 99.
57. "The 1936 Olympic Games: An Open Letter," *New York Amsterdam News*, August 24, 1935, 1.
58. "Stay Out of the Olympics: An Editorial," *Baltimore Afro-American*, December 14, 1935, 23.
59. See, for example, "Owens, Peacock, Metcalfe, Favor Running in Olympics," *Chicago Defender*, December 14, 1935, 14; "Olympic Body in a Fuss over Jesse Owens," *Chicago Defender*, November 16, 1935, 15.
60. Eustace Gay, "Facts and Fancies: The Olympics," *Philadelphia Tribune*, December 19, 1935, 4.
61. Laucella, "Jesse Owens," 75.
62. There is a large degree of uncertainty concerning Hitler's decision to greet some athletes but not others during the Olympic Games.

According to John D. Stevens ("Black Press"), Hitler had intended to greet only German winners but was repudiated by Olympic officials, who requested that Hitler publicly congratulate all the winners or none at all. Owens was not publicly congratulated, but it is unclear whether Hitler intended the snub or was following the directive of Olympic officials. In either case it is clear that Hitler had no intention of greeting American—especially *black* American—gold medalists. Owens (like Vann) claimed that Hitler waved to him, but he did not seem concerned about the exchange one way or another.

63. Joe Richards, "Jo Baker Could Give Jesse Owens a Few Pointers Boys," *Chicago Defender*, September 12, 1936, 20.

64. Raymond M. Jackson, "Jesse Owens," *Atlanta Daily World*, August 8, 1936, 5.

65. J. A. Rogers, "J. A. Rogers off the War Zone: Rogers' Stories to Be Exclusive for the Courier," *Pittsburgh Courier*, October 26, 1935, 1; J. A. Rogers, "J. A. Rogers Gets Exclusive Interview with Emperor," *Pittsburgh Courier*, March 7, 1936, 1; S. T. Holland, "J. A. Rogers Thrills Crowd in Detroit; Talks on 'What I Saw in Ethiopia," *Pittsburgh Courier*, June 13, 1936, 10.

66. Robert L. Vann, "Hitler Salutes Jesse Owens," *Pittsburgh Courier*, August 8, 1936, 1.

67. Vann, "Hitler Salutes Jesse Owens."

68. "Louis Vote in Contest Takes Drop," *Chicago Defender*, February 13, 1937, 12.

69. Sammons, *Beyond the Ring*, 109–11; "stressed particularly the point" from "Remove Last Obstacle in Path of Louis-Braddock Title Bout," *Chicago Defender*, May 22, 1937, 1.

70. William G. Nunn, "Did Max or Marva Beat Joe?," *Pittsburgh Courier*, July 4, 1936, 1; "to Courier readers" from William G. Nunn, "Louis Has Right Mental Attitude, Nunn Finds on Visit to Joe's Kenosha Camp," *Pittsburgh Courier*, May 29, 1937, 16.

71. Nunn, "Louis Has Right Mental Attitude."

72. "Fist That Won the Title," *Chicago Defender*, June 26, 1937, 1.

73. William G. Nunn, "Nunn Describes South Side As It Goes Mad after Joe Louis Victory," *Pittsburgh Courier*, June 26, 1937, 16.

74. Chester "Ches" Washington, "Joe's Mad at Maxie," *Pittsburgh Courier*, May 7, 1938, 17.

75. William L. Patterson, "Joe Louis Killed Nazi Supremacy Theory," *Pittsburgh Courier*, July 9, 1938, 4.

76. Lule, *Daily News, Eternal Stories*, 81–103.

77. Klapp, "Creation of Popular Heroes," 136.

7. Journalistic Commemoration

1. "Joe Gans dead," *Chicago Defender*, August 13, 1910, 1.

2. Ryan, "Memory, Power, and Resistance," 155.

3. Ryan, "Memory, Power, and Resistance," 155–56.

4. Kitch, *Pages from the Past*, 63–64.
5. "George Walker Passes Away," *Baltimore Afro-American*, January 14, 1911, 1.
6. "George Walker, Actor of the Famous Team of Stars, Dead," *Chicago Defender*, January 14, 1911, 1.
7. "George Walker, Actor."
8. "Aida Overton Walker as the Public Knew Her" [caption], *Chicago Defender*, October 24, 1914, 1.
9. Alfred Noyes, "Samuel Coleridge Taylor," *Crisis*, November 1912, 21.
10. Samuel Coleridge-Taylor," Men of the Month, *Crisis*, October 1912, 278.
11. "Prominent Englishmen Honor the Memory of the Race's Greatest Composer—an 'Appreciation,'" *Cleveland Gazette*, November 23, 1912, 2.
12. Cripps, *Slow Fade to Black*, 19.
13. Blight, *Race and Reunion*, 304.
14. D. Brooks, *Bodies in Dissent*, 5.
15. Stempel, *Showtime*, 42.
16. Bogle, *Toms, Coons, Mulattos*.
17. Fay Jackson, "Movies Want Only 'Uncle Tom' and 'Mammy' Types," *Baltimore Afro-American*, October 12, 1935, 8.
18. Woodward, *Strange Career of Jim Crow*, 114.
19. Sammons and Morrow, *Harlem's Rattlers*, 491–97.
20. "Black Soldiers, Remarkable Warriors," *Cleveland Gazette*, August 17, 1918, 1.
21. Sammons and Morrow, *Harlem's Rattlers*, 124–26.
22. Burns, *Jazz*.
23. "Perpetuate Europe Music in Victor Records," *Chicago Defender*, March 7, 1914, 6.
24. Banfield, *Cultural Codes*, 121.
25. "James Reese Europe," Men of the Month, *Crisis*, June 1912, 68.
26. "Lieutenant James Reese Europe Buried with Honors," *New York Age*, May 17, 1919, 6.
27. "Jazz Music Is Now All the Rage throughout the United States," *New York Age*, May 3, 1919, 6.
28. "Editor Entertains New Yorkers," *Chicago Defender*, May 10, 1919, 16.
29. Sammons and Morrow, *Harlem's Rattlers*, 476–77.
30. "Lieutenant James Reese Europe Buried with Honors."
31. "Thousands, White and Colored, Attend the Funeral of Lieut. James Reese Europe," *Philadelphia Tribune*, May 17, 1919, 1.
32. Nahum Daniel Brascher, "'Jim' Europe Lives," *Chicago Defender*, May 17, 1919, 15.
33. Brascher, "'Jim' Europe lives."
34. Blight, *Race and Reunion*, 311.
35. Brascher, "'Jim' Europe Lives."
36. Lule, *Daily News, Eternal Stories*, 200.
37. Ryan, "Memory, Power, and Resistance," 155–56.
38. Gildea, *Longest Fight*, 37.

39. Aycock and Scott, *Joe Gans*, 3.
40. "Joe Gans Real Master among Ring Supermen," *Pittsburgh Courier*, May 25, 1929, B6.
41. Quoted in Ashe, *Hard Road to Glory*, 15.
42. E. S. Taylor, "Joe Gans, the Man, as I Knew Him," *Baltimore Afro-American*, November 18, 1933, 17.
43. "Erne Says—Gans Won the Lightweight Championship with Five Blows in a Single Round," *Cleveland Gazette*, May 17, 1902, 3.
44. Gildea, *Longest Fight*, 122–23
45. Untitled article, *Cleveland Gazette*, October 6, 1906, 2.
46. Gildea, *Longest Fight*, 192.
47. "Joe Gans Dead," *Chicago Defender*, August 13, 1910, 1.
48. "Game Fighter Loses Out in His Final Bout," *Baltimore Afro-American*, August 13, 1910, 5.
49. R.L.D., "Joe Gans Downed White 25 Yrs. Ago," *New York Amsterdam News*, March 17, 1934, 13.
50. The *Baltimore Afro-American* would intermittently run articles such as this one: "Jack Johnson, Peter Jackson, World's Greatest Heavyweights," *Baltimore Afro-American*, November 15, 1927, 12. The *Defender* ran a series starting with this article in 1923: Tony Langston, "Ringside Recollections," *Chicago Defender*, January 20, 1923, 7.
51. Johnson, *My Life and Battles*; Jack Johnson, *In the Ring and Out* (Chicago: National Sports, 1927); for information on Jack Johnson's recording career, see T. Brooks, *Lost Sounds*.
52. Jack Johnson, "Godfrey Greater Fighter than Wills but Dixie Pugs Are Timid," *Pittsburgh Courier*, May 18, 1929, B4.
53. "Jack Johnson, Pete Jackson, World's Greatest Heavyweights," *Baltimore Afro-American*, November 5, 1927, 12.
54. Ralph Matthews, "Joe Gans: Master Boxer, Great Lover, Champion Stone Thrower," *Baltimore Afro-American*, January 21, 1927, 4.
55. Ralph Matthews, "The Baltimore That 'Joe' Knew," *Baltimore Afro-American*, January 21, 1927, 4.
56. For example, see Juli Jones Jr., "Joe Gans, World's Welter and Lightweight Champion," *Chicago Defender*, July 24, 1920, 9; Jones, "Joe Gans, Old Master"; "Joe Gans Real Master among Ring Supermen," *Pittsburgh Courier*, March 25, 1929, B6; "Joe Gans–McGovern Battle Recalled," *Pittsburgh Courier*, December 11, 1926, 15; Washington, "Downfall of Gans"; "Joe Gans, King of the Lightweights, Fought Best Bout in 1898," *Baltimore Afro-American*, December 31, 1927, 11; Nat Fleischer, "Supermen of the Ring-No. 10: Joe Gans," *Pittsburgh Courier*, January 29, 1927, A5; R.L.D., "Joe Gans Downed White."
57. For example, see, "Joe Louis Tells His Own Story: Admires Sam Langford and Joe Gans for Lessons They Left Him," *New York Amsterdam*

News, September 7, 1935, 2A; "'Joe Louis Is Another Joe Gans'–Sam Langford," *Chicago Defender*, July 20, 1935, 14.

58. Jones, "Joe Gans, World's Welter and Lightweight Champion"; Jones,, "Joe Gans, Old Master."

59. Jones, "Joe Gans, World's Welter and Lightweight Champion."

60. Thomas R. Smith, "A Worthy Object Indeed: Joe Gans Memorial," *New York Amsterdam News*, December 28, 1927; see also "Joe Gans Memorial Is Begun," *Baltimore Afro-American*, December 17, 1927, 12.

61. "Joe Gans Memorial Is Begun."

62. *Bert Williams: Son of Laughter*, a tribute piece compiled by close friends of the actor in the months after his death, recounts the story of a meeting between the actor and the athlete. Gans was reportedly "interested in a dusky belle attached to the Williams and Walker organization" and offered fight fan Williams private lessons in order to "curry favor" with him.

63. Tony Langston, "Bert Williams, Famous Comedian, Dead," *Chicago Defender*, March 11, 1922, 1.

64. "Bert Williams Dead," Associated Negro Press, March 5, 1922.

65. "'Bert' Williams," *Baltimore Afro-American*, March 10, 1922, 7.

66. Langston, "Bert Williams, Famous Comedian, Dead."

67. Jessie Fauset, "The Symbolism of Bert Williams," *Crisis*, May 1922, 12–14.

68. Fauset, "Symbolism of Bert Williams."

69. "Bert Williams the Leader of Them All," *Philadelphia Tribune*, February 28, 1925, 4.

70. Regarding the processual nature of collective memory, see Zelizer, "Reading the Past against the Grain," 219.

71. Blight, *Race and Reunion*, 311, 317.

72. Sylvester Russell, "'The Bert Williams Interview, Its Value and Importance," Musical and Dramatic, *Chicago Defender*, October 10, 1910, 2.

73. Dolan, "Black Press."

74. Ralph Matthews, "Cab Calloway and the Memphis Mob," Watching the Big Parade, *Baltimore Afro-American*, September 29, 1934, 4.

8. Politics of Black Celebrity Journalism

1. Schudson, *Sociology of News*, 72.

2. Washburn, *African-American Newspaper*, 73–112.

3. Fay Jackson, "Fredi Washington Hits New Note in Imitations [*sic*]," *New York Amsterdam News*, December 15, 1934, 10.

4. The term "entertainer-activist" has been borrowed from Roz Edward, "Let's Hope Hip-Hop Steps Up in 2014," *Atlanta Daily World*, January 2, 2014. Edward used the term "entertainer-activist" in the context of describing rapper Jay Z's response to charges that an employee of the high-end chain of department stores, Barney's, had discriminated against two black shoppers who had entered the store. Jay Z had at the

time a marketing deal in place with the department store chain, and several critics had demanded he vacate the deal as a result of the controversy. Edward called on the rapper to act as an "entertainer-activist," and her use of the term aligns with the concepts of representation, collective action, and exemplarity that are discussed in this book.

5. Jessie Fauset, "The Symbolism of Bert Williams," *Crisis*, May 1922, 12–14.
6. This point is made in reference to celebrity biographies that eschew Black press perspectives, which include but are not limited to Teachout, *Pops*; Bergreen, *Louis Armstrong*; H. Cohen, *Duke Ellington's America*; Nagler, *Brown Bomber*; and Mead, *Champion Joe Louis*.
7. See, for example, Roberts, *Jack Dempsey*; Evensen, *When Dempsey Fought Tunney*.
8. "Fay Says . . ." *Chicago Defender*, January 17, 1925, 9.
9. "The Week," *Chicago Defender*, May 26, 1923, 13.
10. R. H. Kain, "Boxing Our Championship," Sports of All Sorts, *Philadelphia Tribune*, November 27, 1915, 3.
11. "Cause célèbre" in Roberts, *Jack Dempsey*, 214; "size as impressive as his record" in Roberts, *Jack Dempsey*, 141
12. "Dempsey Finds Another Loophole," *Baltimore Afro-American*, March 28, 1925, 9.
13. Ed Hughes, "Godfrey and McVey Color Line Victims," *Baltimore Afro-American*, January 7, 1928, 12.
14. Rollo Wilson, "'Harry Wills Worse Than I Thought'—Wilson," *Pittsburgh Courier*, July 23, 1927, A4.
15. Wm. Pickens, "Harry Wills—a Success," *Baltimore Afro-American*, July 23, 1927, A14.
16. Calloway briefly made a resurgence in popular culture as a result of his turn in the 1980 comedy *The Blues Brothers*. Also, in 2017 the hard-rock band Queens of the Stone Age released a music video for a song called "The Way You Used to Do," which singer Joshua Homme described as an homage to the late jazz singer.
17. Jesse Owens, letter to Art Carter, February 17, 1941, Art Carter Collection, Black Press Archives, Moorland Spingarn Research Center, February 17, 1941.

Bibliography

Archival Sources

Black Press Archives. Moorland-Spingarn Research Center. Howard University. Washington DC.
  Carter, Art, Collection.
  Lochard, Metz T. P., Collection.
  Prattis, Percival L., Papers.
Charles L. Blockson Afro-American Collection. Temple University. Philadelphia PA.
  The Crisis: A Record of the Darker Races, January 1910–December 1935.
  The Messenger, January 1917–December 1928.
  The Opportunity, January 1923–December 1935.
Schomburg Center for Research in Black Culture. New York Public Library. New York NY.
  Europe, James Reese, Collection.
  Johnson, Jack, scrapbook.
  Washington, Fredi, Papers.
  Wills, Harry, Collection.

Published Works

Alexander, Shawn Leigh. *W. E. B. Du Bois: An American Intellectual and Activist.* New York: Rowman and Littlefield, 2015.
Ashe, Arthur R., Jr. *A Hard Road to Glory: A History of the African American Athlete, 1619–1918.* New York: Warner Books, 1988.
Aycock, Colleen, and Mark Scott. *Joe Gans: A Biography of the First African American Boxing Champion.* Jefferson NC: McFarland, 2008.
Baldwin, Davarian L. "Our Newcomers to the City: The Great Migration and Making of Modern Mass Culture." In *Beyond Blackface: African Americans and the Creation of American Popular Culture, 1890–1930,* edited by W. Fitzhugh Brundage, 159–89. Chapel Hill NC: University of North Carolina Press, 2011.

Balshaw, Maria. "'Black Was White': Urbanity, Passing and the Spectacle of Harlem." *Journal of American Studies* 33 (1999): 307–22.

Banfield, William C. *Cultural Codes: Makings of a Black Musical Philosophy.* Lanham MD: Scarecrow, 2010.

Batiste, Stephanie Leigh. *Darkening Mirrors: Imperial Representation in Depression-Era African American Performance.* Durham NC: Duke University Press, 2011.

Beard, Richard. "The Associated Negro Press: Its Founding, Ascendancy and Demise." *Journalism Quarterly* 46 (1969): 47–52.

Bergreen, Laurence. *Louis Armstrong: An Extravagant Life.* New York: Broadway Books, 1997.

Bernstein, Matthew H., and Dana F. White. "*Imitation of Life* in a Segregated Atlanta: Its Promotion, Distribution, and Reception." *Film History* 19 (2010): 152–78.

Blight, David W. *Race and Reunion: The Civil War in American Memory.* Cambridge MA: Belknap Harvard University Press, 2001.

Boddy, Kasia. *Boxing: A Cultural History.* London: Reaktion Books, 2008.

Bogle, Donald. *Bright Boulevards, Bold Dreams: The Story of Black Hollywood.* New York: One World Books, 2005.

———. *Toms, Coons, Mulattos, Mammies, and Bucks.* 4th ed. New York: Continuum, 2004.

Boorstin, Daniel J. "From Hero to Celebrity: The Human Pseudo-event." In *The Celebrity Culture Reader*, edited by P. David Marshall, 72–90. New York: Routledge, 2006.

Brooks, Christopher A., and Robert Sims. *Roland Hayes: The Legacy of an American Tenor.* Indianapolis: Indiana University Press, 2015.

Brooks, Daphne A. *Bodies in Dissent: Spectacular Performances of Race and Freedom, 1850–1910.* Durham NC: Duke University Press, 2006.

Brooks, Tim. *Lost Sounds: Blacks and the Birth of the Recording Industry, 1890–1919.* Urbana: University of Illinois Press, 2004.

Brundage, W. Fitzhugh. "Working in the 'Kingdom of Culture': African Americans and American Popular Culture, 1890–1930." In *Beyond Blackface: African Americans and the Creation of American Popular Culture, 1890–1930*, edited by W. Fitzhugh Brundage, 1–42. Chapel Hill NC: University of North Carolina Press, 2011.

Bunie, Andrew. *Robert L. Vann of the "Pittsburgh Courier": Politics and Black Journalism* Pittsburgh: University of Pittsburgh Press, 1974.

Burns, Ken, dir. *Jazz.* Episode 2. PBS Productions, 2001. DVD.

Carney, Court. *Cuttin' Up: How Early Jazz Got America's Ear.* Lawrence: University of Kansas, 2009.

Carroll, Brian. "Early Twentieth Century Heroes: Coverage of Negro League Baseball in the *Pittsburgh Courier* and the *Chicago Defender*." *Journalism History* 32, no. 1 (2006): 34–42.

———. "From Fraternity to Fracture: Black Press Coverage of and Involvement in Negro League Baseball in the 1920s." *American Journalism* 23, no. 2 (2006): 69–95.

———. "This Is IT!" *Journalism History* 37, no. 3 (Fall 2011): 151–62.

Cohen, Harvey. *Duke Ellington's America.* Chicago: University of Chicago Press, 2010.

Cohen, Lizbeth. *A Consumers' Republic: The Politics of Mass Consumption in Postwar America.* New York: Vintage Books, 2003.

Coit, Jonathan S. "Our Changed Attitude: Armed Defense and the New Negro in the 1919 Chicago Race Riot." *Journal of the Gilded Age and Progressive Era* 11 (2012): 225–56.

Collier, James Lincoln. *Jazz: The American Theme Song.* New York: Oxford University Press, 1993.

Crafton, Donald. *The Talkies: American Cinema's Transition to Sound, 1926–1931.* New York: Charles Scribner's Sons, 1997.

Cripps, Thomas. *Slow Fade to Black: The Negro in American Film, 1900–1942.* Oxford: Oxford University Press, 1977.

Dagbovie, Pero Gaglo. *African American History Reconsidered.* Chicago: University of Illinois Press, 2010.

Daniel, Walter C. *Black Journals of the United States.* Westport CT: Greenwood Press, 1982.

Demas, Lane. "The Brown Bomber's Dark Day: Louis-Schmeling I and America's Black Hero." *Journal of Sport History* (Fall 2004): 252–71.

Detweiler, Frederick G. *The Negro Press in the United States.* College Park MD: McGrath, 1968.

Digby-Junger, Richard. "*The Guardian, Crisis, Messenger,* and *Negro World*: The Early-20th-Century Black Radical Press." *Howard Journal of Communications* 9 (1998): 263–82.

Dolan, Mark. "The Black Press." Presentation at the American Journalism Historians Association Annual Conference, New Orleans, Louisiana, September 26–29, 2013.

Dorr, Gregory Michael. *Segregation's Science: Eugenics and Society in Virginia.* Charlottesville: University of Virginia Press, 2008.

Drake, St. Claire, and Horace R. Cayton. *Black Metropolis: A Study of Negro Life in a Northern City.* Chicago: University of Chicago Press, 1993.

Du Bois, W. E. B. "Criteria of Negro Art." In *The New Negro: Readings on Race, Representation, and African American Culture 1892–1938,* edited by Henry Louis Gates Jr. and Gene Andrew Jarrett, 257–59. Princeton NJ: Princeton University Press, 2007.

———. *Darkwater: Voices from within the Veil.* New York: Harcourt, Brace and Howe, 1920.

———. *The Souls of Black Folk.* Chicago: A. C. McClurg, 1903.

———. "The Talented Tenth." In *The Negro Problem: A Series of Articles by Representative Negroes of To-day*, edited by Booker T. Washington, 31–76. New York: James Pott, 1903.

Dyer, Richard. "Stars as Images." In *The Celebrity Culture Reader*, edited by P. David Marshall, 153–76. New York: Routledge, 2006.

Egan, Bill. *Florence Mills: Harlem Jazz Queen.* Lanham MD: Scarecrow, 2004.

Evensen, Bruce. *When Dempsey Fought Tunney: Heroes, Hokum, and Storytelling in the Jazz Age.* Knoxville: University of Tennessee Press, 1996.

Ewen, Stuart, and Elizabeth Ewen. *Typecasting: On the Arts and Sciences of Human Inequality.* New York: Seven Stories Press, 2006.

Farrar, Hayward. *The "Baltimore Afro-American," 1892–1950.* Westport CT: Greenwood Press, 1998.

———. "See What the Afro Says: The *Baltimore Afro-American,* 1892–1950." PhD diss., University of Chicago, 1983.

Finkle, Lee. *Forum for Protest: The Black Press during World War II.* Rutherford NJ: Fairleigh Dickenson University Press, 1975.

Forbes, Camille. *Introducing Bert Williams: Burnt Cork, Broadway, and the Story of America's First Black Star.* New York: Basic Books, 2008.

Franklin, John Hope, and Alfred A. Moss Jr. *From Slavery to Freedom: A History of African Americans.* 7th ed. New York: Alfred A. Knopf, 1994.

Gaines, Kevin K. *Uplifting the Race: Black Leadership, Politics, and Culture in the Twentieth Century.* Chapel Hill: University of North Carolina Press, 1996.

Gallon, Kim. "'How Much Can You Read about Interracial Love and Sex without Getting Sore?': Readers' Debate over Interracial Relationships in the *Baltimore Afro-American.*" *Journalism History* 39, no. 2 (Summer 2013): 104–14.

Gamson, Joshua. "The Assembly Line of Greatness: Celebrity in Twentieth-Century America." *Cultural Studies in Mass Communication* 9 (1992): 1–24.

———. *Claims to Fame: Celebrity in Contemporary America.* Berkeley: University of California Press, 1994.

Gates, Henry Louis, Jr., and Gene Andrew Jarrett, eds. *The New Negro: Readings on Race, Representation and African American Culture, 1892–1938.* Princeton NJ: Princeton University Press, 2007.

Gildea, William. *The Longest Fight: In the Ring with Joe Gans, Boxing's First African American Champion.* New York: Farrar, Straus and Giroux, 2012.

Gildow, Liette. *The Big Vote: Gender, Consumer Culture, and the Politics of Exclusion, 1890s-1920.* Baltimore: Johns Hopkins University Press, 2007.

Gonzalez, Juan, and Joseph Torres. *News for All the People: The Epic Story of Race and the American Media.* New York: Verso, 2011.

Gooden, Amoaba. "Visual Representations of Feminine Beauty in the Black Press: 1915–1950." *Journal of Pan African Studies* 4, no. 4 (2011): 81–96.

Green, Jeffrey. *Samuel Coleridge-Taylor: A Musical Life.* London: Pickering and Chatto, 2011.

Guerrero, Ed. *Framing Blackness: The African American Image in Film.* Philadelphia: Temple University Press, 1998.

Hall, Stuart, ed. *Representation: Cultural Representations and Signifying Practices.* London: Sage, 1997.

———. "The Spectacle of the 'Other.'" In Hall, *Representation,* 244.

Hark, Ina Rae. *American Cinema of the 1930s: Themes and Variations.* New Brunswick NJ: Rutgers University Press, 2007.

Higginbotham, Evelyn Brooks. *Righteous Discontent: The Women's Movement in the Black Baptist Church, 1880–1920.* Cambridge MA: Harvard University Press, 1993.

Hogan, Lawrence D. *A Black National News Service: The Associated Negro Press and Claude Barnett, 1919–1945.* Rutherford NJ: Fairleigh Dickinson University Press, 1983.

hooks, bell. *Feminist Theory: From Margin to Center.* New York: Routledge, 2015.

Hudson, David L., Jr. *Boxing in America: An Autopsy.* Santa Barbara CA: Praeger, 2012.

Hull, Gloria T., and Barbara Smith. "The Politics of Black Women's Studies." In *All the Women Are White, All the Blacks Are Men, but Some of Us Are Brave,* edited by Akasha (Gloria T.) Hull, Patricia Bell-Scott, and Barbara Smith, xvii–xxxii. New York: Feminist Press at the City University of New York, 2015.

Jackson, Robert. "The Secret Life of Oscar Mischeaux: Race Films, Contested Histories, and Modern American Culture." In *Beyond Blackface: African Americans and the Creation of American Popular Culture, 1890–1930,* edited by W. Fitzhugh Brundage, 215–38. Chapel Hill: University of North Carolina Press, 2011.

Jackson, Ronald L., II. *Scripting the Black Masculine Body: Identity, Discourse, and Racial Politics in Popular Media.* Albany: State University of New York Press, 2006.

Jackson, Sarah. "African American Celebrity Dissent and a Tale of Two Public Spheres: A Critical and Comparative Analysis of the Mainstream and Black Press, 1949–2005." PhD diss., University of Missouri, 2010.

Jewell, Richard B. *The Golden Age of Cinema: Hollywood, 1929–1945.* Malden MA: Blackwell 2007.

Johnson, Jack. *My Life and Battles.* Edited and translated by Christopher Rivers. London: Praeger, 2007.

Jones Ross, Felecia G. "Preserving the Community: Cleveland Black Papers' Response to the Great Migration." *Journalism Quarterly* 71 (1994): 531–39.

Jones-Ross, Felicia G., and Joseph P. McKerns. "Depression in the 'Promised Land'": The *Chicago Defender* Discourages Migration, 1929–1940." *American Journalism* 21, no. 4 (2004): 55–73.

Jules-Rosette, Bennetta. *Josephine Baker in Art and Life.* Urbana: University of Illinois Press, 2007.

Kern-Foxworth, Marilyn. *Aunt Jemima, Uncle Ben and Rastus: Blacks in Advertising, Yesterday, Today, and Tomorrow.* Westport CT: Praeger, 1994.

Kitch, Carolyn. *Girl on the Magazine Cover.* Chapel Hill: University of North Carolina Press, 2001.

———. *Pages from the Past: History and Memory in American Magazines.* Chapel Hill: University of North Carolina Press, 2005.

Klapp, Orrin E. "The Creation of Popular Heroes." *Journal of Sociology* 54, no. 2 (1948): 135–41.

Kornweibel, Theodore. *No Crystal Stair: Black Life and the "Messenger," 1917–1928.* Westport CT: Greenwood Press, 1975.

Lamb, Chris. *Conspiracy of Silence: Sportswriters and the Long Campaign to Desegregate Baseball.* Lincoln: University of Nebraska Press, 2012.

Laucella, Pamela C. "Jesse Owens, a Black Pearl amidst an Ocean of Fury: A Case Study of Press Coverage of the 1936 Olympic Games." In *From Jack Johnson to LeBron James: Sports, Media, and the Color Line*, edited by Chris Lamb, 52–85. Lincoln: University of Nebraska Press, 2016.

Lewis, David Levering. *W. E. B. Du Bois: A Biography.* New York: Henry Holt, 2009.

Locke, Alain. "Enter the New Negro." *Survey Graphic* (March 1925), 1–6.

Logan, Rayford W. *The Negro in American Life and Thought: The Nadir, 1877–1901.* New York: Dial Press, 1954.

Lule, Jack. *Daily News, Eternal Stories: The Mythological Role of Journalism.* New York: Guilford Press, 2001.

Marshall, P. David. "Intimately Intertwined in the Most Public Way." In the *Celebrity Culture Reader*, edited by P. David Marshall, 315–23. New York: Routledge, 2006.

McGovern, Charles F. *Sold American: Consumption and Citizenship, 1890–1945.* Chapel Hill: University of North Carolina Press, 2006.

Mead, Chris. *Champion Joe Louis: Black Hero in White America* New York: C. Scribner's and Sons, 1985.

Mendelson, Andrew. "On the Function of the United States Paparazzi: Mosquito Swarm or Watchdogs of Celebrity Image Control and Power." *Visual Studies* 22, no. 2 (2007): 169–83.

Michaeli, Ethan. *The Defender: How the Legendary Black Newspaper Changed America.* New York: Houghton Mifflin Harcourt, 2015.

Mindich, David T. Z. *Just the Facts: How Objectivity Came to Define American Journalism.* New York: New York University Press, 2000.

Morton, Patricia. *Disfigured Images: The Historical Assault on Afro-American Women.* New York: Greenwood Press, 1991.

Mulvey, Laura. "Visual Pleasure in Narrative Cinema." In *Film Theory and Criticism: Introductory Readings*, edited by Leo Brandy and Marshall Cohen, 833–54. New York: Oxford University Press, 1999.

Nagler, Barney. *Brown Bomber.* New York: World, 1972.

Nelson, Stanley, dir. *The Black Press: Soldiers without Swords*. PBS Productions, 1999. VHS.

Payne, Charles M., and Adam Green. *Time Longer than Rope: A Century of African American Activism, 1850–1950*. New York: New York University Press, 2003.

Peretti, Burton W. *The Creation of Jazz: Music, Race, and Culture in Urban America*. Urbana: University of Illinois Press, 1992.

Pride, Armistead S., and Clint C. Wilson II. *A History of the Black Press*. Washington DC: Howard University Press, 1997.

Regester, Charlene. "Stepin Fetchit: The Man, the Image, and the African American Press." *Film History* 6 (1994): 502–21.

Richardson, Alissa V. "The Platform." *Journalism Studies* 17, no. 4, 398–414.

Roberts, Randy. *Jack Dempsey: The Manassa Mauler*. Urbana: University of Illinois Press, 2003.

———. *Papa Jack: Jack Johnson and the Era of White Hopes*. New York: Free Press, 1983.

Rose, Phyllis. *Jazz Cleopatra: Josephine Baker in Her Time*. New York: Doubleday, 1989.

Ross, Steven J. *Working-Class Hollywood: Silent Film and the Shaping of Class in America*. Princeton NJ: Princeton University Press: 1998.

Runstedtler, Theresa. *Jack Johnson, Rebel Sojourner: Boxing in the Shadow of the Global Color Line*. Berkeley: University of California Press, 2012.

Ryan, Lorraine. "Memory, Power, and Resistance: The Anatomy of a Tripartite Relationship." *Memory Studies* 4, no. 2 (2011): 154–69.

Sammons, Jeffrey T. *Beyond the Ring: The Role of Boxing in American Society*. Chicago: University of Illinois Press, 1990.

Sammons, Jeffrey T., and John H. Morrow Jr. *Harlem's Rattlers and the Great War: The Undaunted 369th and the African American Quest for Equality*. Lawrence: University Press of Kansas, 2014.

Schenbeck, Lawrence. *Racial Uplift and American Music, 1878–1943*. Jackson: University Press of Mississippi, 2012.

Schudson, Michael. *The Sociology of News*. 2nd ed. New York: W. W. Norton, 2012.

Shipton, Alyn. *Hi-De-Ho: The Life of Cab Calloway*. Oxford: Oxford University Press, 2010.

Sitkoff, Harvard. *A New Deal for Blacks: The Emergence of Civil Rights as a National Issue; The Depression Decade*. New York: Oxford University Press, 2009.

Snorgrass, J. William. "The *Baltimore Afro-American* and the Election Campaigns of FDR." *American Journalism* 1, no. 2 (Winter 1984): 35–50.

Spohrer, Erika. "Becoming Extratextual: Celebrity Discourse and Paul Robeson's Political Transformation." *Critical Studies in Media Communication* 24, no. 2 (2007): 151–68.

Stacey, Jackie. "Feminine Fascinations." In *The Celebrity Culture Reader*, edited by P. David Marshall, 252–85. New York: Routledge, 2006.

Starr, Paul. *The Creation of the Media: Political Origins of Modern Communications.* New York: Basic Books, 2004.

Stempel, Larry. *Showtime: A History of the Broadway Musical Theater.* New York: W.W. Norton, 2010.

Sternheimer, Karen. *Celebrity Culture and the American Dream: Stardom and Social Mobility.* New York: Routledge, 2015.

Stevens, John D. "The Black Press and the 1936 Olympics." *American Journalism* 14, no.1 (1997): 97–102.

Stevens, Summer E., and Owen V. Johnson. "From Black Politics to Black Community: Harry C. Smith and the *Cleveland Gazette*." *Journalism Quarterly* 67 (1990): 1090–1102.

Suisman, David. "Co-workers in the Kingdom of Culture: Black Swan Records and the Political Economy of African American Music." *Journal of American History* (March 2004): 1295–1324

Taylor, Henry Louis, Jr., and Walter Hill. *Historical Roots of the Urban Crisis: African Americans in the Industrial City, 1900–1950.* New York: Garland, 2000.

Taylor, Yuval, and Jake Austen. *Darkest America: Black Minstrelsy from Slavery to Hip Hop.* New York: W.W. Norton, 2012.

Teachout, Terry. *Pops: A Life of Louis Armstrong.* Boston: Houghton Mifflin Harcourt, 2009.

Teel, Leonard Ray. "The African-American Press and the Campaign for a Federal Anti-lynching Law, 1933–34." *American Journalism* (Spring/Summer 1991): 84–107.

Tuchman, Gaye. *Hearth and Home: Images of Women in the Mass Media.* Oxford: Oxford University Press, 1978.

U.S. Department of Commerce, Bureau of the Census. *Negroes in the United States, 1920–1932.* Washington DC: Government Printing Office, 1935.

———. *Negro Population, 1790–1915.* Washington DC: Government Printing Office, 1918.

Verney, Kevern. *African Americans and U.S. Popular Culture.* New York: Routledge, 2003.

Walker, Alice. "If the Present Looks like the Past, What Does the Future Look Like?" In *In Search of Our Mothers' Gardens*, 290–91. San Diego: Harcourt Brace Jovanovich, 1983.

Ward, Geoffrey. *Unforgivable Blackness.* New York: Alfred A. Knopf, 2004.

Washburn, Patrick S. *The African-American Newspaper: Voice of Freedom.* Evanston IL: Northwestern University Press, 2006.

Washington, Booker T. "Biographical Notice of Samuel Coleridge-Taylor." In *The Heritage of Samuel Coleridge-Taylor*, edited by Avril Coleridge-Taylor, 138–39. London: Dennis Dobson, 1979.

Wiggins, David K., and Patrick B. Miller. *Sport and the Color Line: Black Athletes and Race Relations in Twentieth-Century America.* New York: Routledge, 2004.

Williams, Chad L. "Vanguards of the New Negro: African American Veterans and Post-World War I Racial Militancy." *Journal of African American History* 92, no. 3 (2007): 347–48.

Wilson, Clint C., II. *Black Journalists in Paradox: Historical Perspectives and Current Dilemmas.* New York: Greenwood Press, 1991.

Wintz, Cary D. *Black Culture and the Harlem Renaissance.* Houston: Rice University Press, 1988.

Wolseley, Roland E. *The Black Press, U.S.A.* Ames: Iowa State University Press, 1990.

Wood, Ean. *The Josephine Baker Story.* London: Sanctuary, 2000.

Woodward, C. Vann. *The Strange Career of Jim Crow.* New York: Oxford University Press, 1974.

Young, Harvey. *Embodying Black Experience: Stillness, Critical Memory, and the Black Body.* Ann Arbor: University of Michigan Press, 2010.

Zelizer, Barbie. "Reading the Past against the Grain: The Shape of Memory Studies." *Critical Studies in Mass Communication* 12, no. 2 (June 1995): 214–39.

Newspapers

Atlanta Daily World
    Source: ProQuest Historical Newspapers: Black Historical Newspapers [digital]
    Dates available: December 1931–December 1932; January 1934–December 1940

Baltimore Afro-American
    Source: ProQuest Historical Newspapers: Black Historical Newspapers [digital]
    Dates available: January 1895–December 1899; January 1901–December 1940

Chicago Defender (big weekend ed.)
    Source: ProQuest Historical Newspapers: Black Historical Newspapers [digital]
    Dates available: July 1909–December 1940

Cleveland Gazette
    Source: America's Historical Newspapers: African American Newspapers, 1827–1998 [digital]
    Dates available: January 1895–December 1925; January—December 1940

Kansas City/Topeka Plaindealer
    Source: America's Historical Newspapers: African American Newspapers, 1827–1998 [digital]
    Dates available: January 1889–December 1940

New York Age
    Source: Center for Research Libraries, Global Resources Network [digital]
    Dates available: January 1919–December 1926

New York Amsterdam News
   Source: ProQuest Historical Newspapers: Black Historical Newspapers
      [digital]
   Dates available: November 1922–December 1923; January
      1925–December 1940
Philadelphia Tribune
   Source: ProQuest Historical Newspapers: Black Historical Newspapers
      [digital]
   Dates available: January 1912–December 1921; January 1923–December 1940
Pittsburgh Courier
   Source: ProQuest Historical Newspapers: Black Historical Newspapers
      [digital]
   Dates available: March 1911–December 1912; January 1923–December 1940
Savannah Tribune
   Source: America's Historical Newspapers: African American Newspapers,
      1827–1998 [digital]
   Dates available: January 1889–December 1922

Index

Carroll, Brian, 25–26, 35, 201n45, 218n25
Carter, Art, 195
Castle, Vernon and Irene, 170
celebrity, background and overview of, 2–3, 4–5, 7–8
celebrity status of black journalists, 186–87
"cheese champions," 145
Chicago Defender, 17, 18–19; activism of, 20, 22; black celebrity mythologizing and, 102, 106, 108; boxing and, 144, 145, 150, 151–52, 155–56, 158, *159*, 193; collective representation and, 33, 40, 43–45, 46, *47*, 50, 51, 53; commemoration and, 163, 164–65, 172, 176, 178, 179, 180–81; on *Emperor Jones*, 75, 119–20; entertainment coverage and, 1, 44–45, 53, 95, 169, 183, 187; female marginalization and, 122, 125, 131; on *Imitation of Life*, 129; integrationist tendencies of, 82, 209n85; on Jessie Owens, 152, 154; lynchings and, 199n39; on music, 170; networked journalism model of, 200–201n45; on northern migration, 58, 71; racial uplift and, 58, 63, 73, 75, 76, 79, 80–82, *81*; stereotypes and, 147
Chocolate Dandies, 116, 117, 123, 197n15
chorus girls, 116–18
churches and black performers, 34–35
circulation of black newspapers, 16, 17, 18–19, 95, 139, 185–86
citizenship, 15, 62–63, 113, 115
"The City of Refuge" (Fisher), 88
Civil Conservation Corps, 148
Civil Rights Act of 1875, 198n23
Clark, Jeff, 193

Clef Club, 170–71
Cleveland Gazette: Booker T. Washington and, 63; commemoration and, 165, 176; entertainment coverage and, 53, 169; on Fifteenth New York Infantry, 169; on Joe Gans, 175, 176; northern migration and, 58
Cohen, Lizabeth, 114
Coit, Jonathan, 59, 71–72, 73
Coleman, Alice, 117
Coleridge-Taylor, Samuel, 20, 56, 57, 64–69, 165
collective action, 20–21, 34, 57, 97–99, 191
collective representation: background and overview of, 31–34, 188, 190, 191; Bert Williams and, 31, 33–34, 37–44, 48–49, 52, 182; Jack Johnson and, 31, 32–34, 36–39, 45, 46–48, *47*, 49–51; Jim Crow realities and, 52; of 1920s, 57; sports heroes and, 160–61
Collier, James Lincoln, 93
Collins, Florence, 102, 108
colorism, 114, 133
color line: commemoration and, 163, 177, 181; global, 62, 137–38, 140; in sports, 138, 142–43, 145, 177; trope of, 26–27; W. E. B. Du Bois and, 60, 62
commemoration: background and overview of, 163–66, 192; of Bert Williams, 180–82; exemplary models and, 173–80; felt history and, 182–84; of James Reese Europe, 171–73; nostalgia for Uncle Tom and, 166–68
Comstock, F. Ray, 42
Conacher, Wenonah "Betty," 111, 116
consumer activism, 113–14
consumer culture, 112–14
"coon" stereotypes, 12, 32, 99, 181

Starr, Paul, 48
Stauber, George, 72
Stempel, Larry, 116
stereotypes: of black women, 114, 129, 134; boxing and, 176; in film, 12–13, 19, 99; in mainstream press, 14; minstrelsy and, 12–13, 19, 32; overview of, 9–10; self-presentation and, 41. *See also specific types*
Stokes, Louise, 219n35
Stowe, Harriett Beecher, 12, 167
success myth, 7–8, 87, 186
Suisman, David, 35
Sullivan, John, 145
symbolism: celebrities and, 2, 3, 5, 7, 29, 190; in commemoration, 163–64, 173–74, 178–79, 180; in sport, 32, 137–38, 145, 148–49, 152, 160–61

"The Talented Tenth" (Du Bois), 60–63, 68, 190; ethos and rhetoric of, 61–62, 69, 70, 84, 87; members of, 56, 65, 69, 75, 190; women and, 118
Tate, Bill, 193
Taylor, Yuval, 40
technological innovation, 3, 9, 17, 95, 141–42, 189
Teel, Leonard, 90
Temple, Shirley, 97–98, 167–68
Thompson, Eloise Bib, 41, 44
Thompson, Ulysses "Kid," 123
369th Infantry, 169–70
Tolan, Eddie, 146, 147, 148
track and field, 137, 146, 148–49, 152–55, 219n35
"tragic mulatto" stereotype, 12, 14, 114, 129–30, 134
Trevor, Claire, 132
Trotter, Marva, 107, 108
Trotter, William Monroe, 20, 63
tuberculosis, 58–59, 163, 179

Tunney, Gene, 194
Tuskegee Institute, 61, 63, 186
Twentieth-Century Fox, 98, 132
"Two Real Coons," 39

Uncle Tom's Cabin (Stowe), 12, 13, 78, 167–68
Under the Bamboo Tree, 50, 180
unhyphenated Americans, 150–60
UNIA, 113
Universal Pictures, 78, 96–97, 130
University of Michigan, 144
university sporting events, black, 35
uplift, racial. *See* racial uplift
urbanization in Northeast, 15–16, 85, 201n48
urban living, 58–59

Vann, Robert L., 18–19, 155, *156*
Van Vechten, Carl, 88, 89
Varesi, Gilda, 77, 78
Verdict: Not Guilty (Gist), 134–35
Verney, Kevern, 9–10
veterans, black, 72–73
Victoria Theatre, 11
villains, 19, 137, 138, 151, 157, 161
violence, racialized, 71–72, 73, 84
visual entertainment emergence, 9–10, 11–12
Vocalion Records, 69
Voice of the Negro, 63

Walker, Aida Overton, 122, 164–65
Walker, A'Leila, 88, 117
Walker, George, 12, 31, 36, 39–42, 49, 164–65, 183
Walls, William J., 20
The Walls of Jericho (Fisher), 89
Walmisley, Jessie, 65, 67
Walton, Lester, 42, 44, 49
Ward, Willis, 144, 152
Washburn, Patrick, 25, 139, 185–86, 200n39

CPSIA information can be obtained
at www.ICGtesting.com
Printed in the USA
LVHW091252260320
651281LV00005B/20/J